Feet of Clay

Ffyona Campbell was born in Totnes, south
Devon, in 1967, into a family with a strong
Royal Naval tradition. Before leaving home
at sixteen, she moved house twenty-four
times and was educated at fifteen schools.
She has worked in a variety of jobs from
migrant fruitpicker to commodity broker,
from cleaner to screen-writer's assistant in
Hollywood. At the age of sixteen she walked
from John O'Groats to Land's End. Two
years later she walked from New York to
Los Angeles. At twenty-one she broke the
men's world speed record by walking 3,200
miles from Sydney to Perth in only 95 days
and in March 1991 she began the walk the
length of the African continent from Cape
Town to Tangier, a distance of some 10,055
miles.

Also by Ffyona Campbell

On Foot Through Africa

FFYONA CAMPBELL

Feet of Clay

Her epic walk across Australia

Mandarin

A Mandarin Paperback
FEET OF CLAY

First published in Great Britain 1991
by William Heinemann Ltd
Mandarin edition first published 1992
Reissued 1994
by Mandarin Paperbacks
an imprint of Reed International Books Ltd
Michelin House, 81 Fulham Road, London SW3 6RB
and Auckland, Melbourne, Singapore and Toronto

Reprinted 1994 (twice), 1995 (four times)

Copyright © Ffyona Campbell 1991
The author has asserted her moral rights

A CIP catalogue record for this title
is available from the British Library
ISBN 0 7493 0807 9

Printed and bound in Great Britain by
BPC Paperbacks Ltd
A member of
The British Printing Company Ltd

For my mother,
the woman of substance

Acknowledgements

Sincerest thanks go to my sponsors and their employees, without whose support the walk would not have taken place. Listed in order of their participation: James Ferguson and Graham Wallace of James Capel & Co, London; David Sheridan and Nicole Swan of James Capel Australia Ltd, Sydney; Neil Franchino of Scholl International, Bracknell, Berkshire; Jan Patchell, Melbourne; Renske Mann of Holland Galleries, London; John Cracknell and Kerry Williams of Adidas, Melbourne; Hyatt Hotels and Resorts Asia/Pacific; Jeremy King of Good View Travels, Hong Kong; John Hammond of Newmans Campervans, Sydney; Jim Taveira of Yamaha Motor Australia, Sydney; The Australian Chiropractic Association; The Boots Company, Nottingham; Campbell's Soups, Australia; H. J. Heinz Company Australia Ltd; Marian Spencer of National Mutual, NSW; Robert Goldman of Phillips Consumer Products, Australia; Ever Ready Ltd, Whetstone; Zane Yates of Classic Trailers Manufacturing Ltd, Sydney; Qantas, Hong Kong; The Mentholatum Company, Berkshire; Victoria Caravan Parks Association.

I am utterly indebted to the following people for their constant encouragement and advice during the planning of the walk; my sister Shuna; my godfather, Colonel R. A. Hooper RM; my former colleagues of The Consulting Group especially Martin Armstrong, Elizabeth Sprague and Roger Leader; Daniel Rustymeyer who introduced me to David; Anthony Willoughby of 'I Will Not Complain', Tokyo; and Nigel de N. Winser of The Royal Geographical Society for being the first person to embrace me with the news that I would succeed.

I would also like to thank all the Australians, especially the truckies, who helped me to get across their country. Congratulations and thanks go to Roger Scott and Bon Sato for completing their journeys and spurring me on with mine. Bob MacDonald of the *Daily News* in Perth, Trudy Bennett of the Hyatt Regency and John Cattalini, Mayor of Fremantle, who worked many long hours to make my last day a memory I shall treasure for ever.

In the gestation of *Feet of Clay* my sincerest thanks go to the following people: the instigator, Michele Field for her invaluable correspondence and for editing the first draft; Australians Yvonne Gluyas and Jamie Kable; the owners of my bamboo hut in Bali who bought me a generator so that I could write through the daily powercuts; John Hillaby who corrected the second draft on the eve of his Mount Olympus ascent; Mark Lucas of Peters, Fraser and Dunlop for being the very best literary agent; Amanda Conquy and Lisa Glass of William Heinemann for their last-minute dash to get the book out before I went to Africa; and Max Arthur, my editor, who waded through the weed patch of waffle to pull the story together.

But my deepest thanks go to David Richard, who, despite my daily provocations, retained an unprecedented commitment to me and my dream.

Preface

England 3 October 1983

I forced the coin down the slot of the telephone with my thumb. For forty-nine days I had imagined this action, clung to it as my goal, mulled over the words which would follow; the pride in his voice; the rejoicing. My finger trembled as I dialled the number, in a few seconds my walk the length of Britain would be completed but only if I overcame this final challenge. I caught the end of our familiar number.

'. . . -nine-two-one?'

'Daddy? Daddy? It's Ffyona! I made it! And . . . I love you, Daddy.'

There was an embarrassed pause followed by a little laughter.

'When are you going to stop swanning around and get a job?'

I replaced the receiver which had been pressed hard against my ear and stared at it. Beneath it the red coin box had been slashed by a knife down to the bare metal. I turned away, pushed open the door and walked out into the biting autumnal wind, feeling very alone.

Part One Moulding

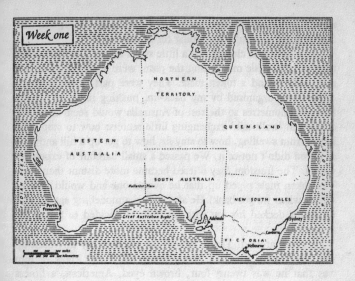

Australia 11 September 1988

Day 1

Bondi beach – cloudy sky and grey sea and a handful of people chatting with folded arms, kicking sand, waiting for me.

'Hullo, everybody! Let's get on with it.' I took off my shoes and walked into the sea for the television crews. Striding through the waves, I held my arms high, posing in exaggerated gestures.

Light shafted through the breakers at their peak as they were suspended for a split second, a freeze frame in the charade. I stared hard at the fading curtain of sea. Somewhere far across that ocean lay the shore of America where I had stood two years earlier, looking out to Australia and committing myself to this walk.

With my shorts still wet and my fake tan streaked in orange lines I tore in half a paper banner which marked the START. I turned my back on Bondi and as I set off I whispered gently to

5

myself as I have always done before a continent, 'Hey, don't be frightened Fee, you're just going for a walk.'

The clouds had cleared and a little sweat began. I walked faster than usual; beside me, setting the pace, were a wobble of female race walkers and a token male. They were part of the send-off celebrations organised by my back-up, pushing me hard for the first ten kilometres so the rest of Australia would seem easy. We chatted in 'walk-talk' exchanging little secrets: how to stop your hands from swelling, how to stay fit, how to get up a hill and look as if you didn't notice it. We passed a small harbour of expensive yachts. The freedom they offered became more distant than ever. The token male piped up that he owned one and would take us sailing when we got back. He also owned a modelling agency and no doubt decked his toy with his dolls. I decided to forget the invitation.

I glanced around. There, behind the wheel of my tiny back-up van, sat David, a man I barely knew. All I did know of him was that he was twenty-four, brown eyed, American, a fitness instructor and model. After two other men had reneged on their commitment to me only six weeks before the walk start date, I had retrawled through a dog-eared notebook of international business contacts to find a replacement. The job specification was brief: 'Three months sitting in a van driving at 6.5 kph, responsible for all domestic duties and on-the-road public relations co-ordination. Board and lodging thrown in, no fee but payment in adventure satisfaction.' On the strength of our brief social encounter eight months before in Hong Kong and a highly enthusiastic faxed recommendation from a contact there, I called David. He said yes, and so did I.

We were hot and the tiny lick of water from a small canteen a few dozen blocks back had heightened our thirst. So I was pleased to see the Hyatt Hotel. In the reception area a noticeboard announced the press conference and at the top appeared my name, mis-spelled, in gold letters. Herding the others, I led the way with drink on my mind to the press conference room, but it was locked.

When it was eventually opened I called the reception desk and asked for food and drinks. We waited, but nothing arrived except a woman with photographic equipment. Coupled with all the anxieties I suffered about my physical ability to complete this walk, the lack of media attention knocked my confidence to a level of 'complete insignificance'.

David staggered in, almost hidden beneath armfuls of yellow banner material, gaffer tape and marker pens. By now the race walkers had draped themselves over a row of chairs and looked embarrassed. I walked to the front of them, placed one of the chairs in the aisle and attempted to straddle it. As I did so I caught the edge of the chair and fell over. There was stunned silence. I picked myself up, righted the chair, sat down and looked up at the gathering. There were two new faces, both reporters: a woman from the *Sydney Morning Herald* and the other from somewhere in China. I began.

'When I was thirteen I had a dream to walk around the world and, like the dreams of most thirteen-year-olds, mine was laughed at. I finished my education two years early at sixteen and walked the length of Britain. At eighteen I walked across America. I'm now twenty-one and I'm going to walk across Australia. After this will be Africa and then Europe. I'll then be the first woman to have walked around the world. The first official world walk was by the American David Kunst between 1970 and 1974. He set the standard for distance; a walk must incorporate four continents and total at least 23,300 kilometres.'

'How many pairs of runners d'you think you'll get through?' from the *Sydney Morning Herald*.

'I don't know. Adidas are one of my sponsors and I've never walked in their shoes before. I'm also sponsored by James Capel, the stockbrokers, and Scholl the footcare people. They pay for my overhead costs and through the media . . .'

'What do you like most about walking?' From her again.

'Being alone. And through the media I hope to raise money for Sport Aid '88. In fact tonight, in over 120 countries they're staging a simultaneous ten kilometre run, the largest mass participation event in history.'

'What do your family and friends think of all this?'

'Mixed opinion. I am also attempting to break the ninety-six day speed record by three weeks. I'll be walking eighty kilometres a day, that's double my average on past walks, six days a week – must have a day off to do the laundry.' Silence. 'My route takes me from here through Canberra, Melbourne, Adelaide, across the Nullarbor Plain, to Perth.'

'What experience have you had in walking these distances?' from the Chinese chap.

'Oh, I'm sorry, don't you have a press release?' He looked down and shuffled some papers. This would be a long one. I glanced at my watch. I still had forty kilometres to walk and it was hot outside. 'I walked 1,600 kilometres the length of Britain and 5,600 kilometres across America.'

The *Sydney Morning Herald* woman leant forward in her chair, arms flopped across each other over her knee. She's going to ask me her most searching question, I thought.

'Why? Why do you walk?'

'I'll tell you in Perth.'

The people had gone, shouts of 'Break a leg' from the race walkers, (I thought 'Good luck' would be more appropriate) then out on to William Street and down a hill with the breeze and the afternoon traffic.

I hit the button of my Walkman and squealed 'Yeee Ha!' I was moving. I can't remember what I had chosen. The music was purely functional, the song irrelevant; it was the speed of the beat which set my pace.

Centrepoint Sydney Tower loomed to my right. I looked up at it for the TV camera and for myself. 'Goodbye, Sydney, I hope I don't see you for a while.'

It wasn't my first time in Australia. I'd been here at sixteen for three months immediately after my UK walk, fruit-picking in Victoria, New South Wales and Queensland. I'd loved it then, partly because it was such a dramatic change from the increasingly claustrophobic life I'd become used to, even though there was a period when I was so broke I had to throw myself on the mercy of the Salvation Army. I'd cut my finger so badly that I couldn't work, and since I was sure this journey too came under the heading

8

of 'swanning around' in my father's book, I'd had nowhere else to go.

The TV crew who had joined us outside the hotel turned off at George Street. As they did so a cameraman called out, 'Beware of the Nullarbor!'

'It gets hot, right?'

'Yeah, there's some strange shit out there. UFOs 'n' shit.'

Out of sight, David and I stopped to tidy up, like newly weds. We hadn't had time to stock up with food or drink; last minute pressures, like sealing financial deals, had taken precedence. The Adidas shoes I had worn for the benefit of the press were pinching and gave little support. I put on a pair of Reeboks and felt a tingle of excitement; with these 'pink fluffy clouds' on my feet I could walk for ever. I grabbed a piece of cheese, much to David's disgust at my ignorance of endurance nutrition, and stepped out again on to the road. David returned to the Hyatt to pay our food and telephone bill. The extent of Hyatt's sponsorship involved two nights accommodation in the five cities *en route* and the organisation of the major press conferences.

The Hume Highway runs from Sydney to Melbourne and serves as the busiest traffic route in Australia. Long haul trucks in convoy, burning gas and tyre rubber, race the smart business cars trying to get somewhere fast only to turn around and do it all over again.

Noise and thick fumes thundered around, brightly coloured flags adorned second hand car yards, harassed mothers struggled with burdens of shopping and babies in prams, old men with fat bellies muttered in gardens and one turned on his sprinkler to edge me off the pavement. I stepped away from their monotony, walked on past their lives and giggled to myself.

'Well done, Fee, you clever old bugger, you pulled it off.'

My thighs stretched backwards and pushed the road away buoyantly, the Walkman jiggled at my waist, and I breathed deeply in between bursts of inward smiles, head up, eyes towards the horizon as though I knew what I was doing.

David pulled up. 'Hi, Fee!'

'Hullo, David!'

'You're going the wrong way.'

Back on the right road, warehouses and disused petrol stations took over. High wire fences, electrical plants and walls of hardboard covered in pop music posters, litter in the gutter, cracked pavements with weeds and suburbs concertinaed by the roadside. The noise of trucks and the city dissolved my music. I didn't care, I'd soon be out of it.

Over a hill and there, stretching out like a great green rug was the continent of Australia over which I was about to tread. The sun began to set, its golden lights merging into a red and smoky fire. David drew up beside me.

'How do you feel?' he asked.

I gulped back a sob of glee. 'I feel as if I could walk around the world.'

He looked away. 'I almost envy you.'

He drove beside me for a while with the windows down, playing music and watching the sun's last rays bouncing off the blackening cars.

I was hungry. We hadn't had time for lunch and the piece of cheese David had so rightly derided had not been very satisfying. We spied a seafood restaurant and sat down to eat.

'Let's be quick, there's still four hours of walking to do.' I urged. But the menu quoted extortionate prices and even though we had something to celebrate, we were both conscious of the limited money supply that had to last us for another seventy days.

Opposite the fish restaurant was a line of fast food outlets; we sat in one and counted out our change. Just enough to buy half a roast chicken and a Greek salad. It was 9 p.m. and we were tired. I didn't relish walking another four hours in the dark on the main highway because David would be a traffic hazard if he drove behind me and I had no torch or reflective light to walk alone. Besides, I have never had the self-discipline to leave a party in full swing.

'You know what?'

'Wha'?' with his mouth full of chicken.

'I think we should call it a day. I don't think it's a good idea for me to walk at night in this traffic and I'd rather get to bed early and catch up over the next few days. What d'you think?'

'Whatever you say; you've done this before.'

Good. Relief. I could enjoy the meal. We'd have time to fall into the rhythm of the Schedule tomorrow and I was looking forward to the first night in the van, with David.

We parked by a lake and popped up the roof. David was worried the neighbours would complain, but I brushed it aside. He'd soon get used to camping where we could.

The van, a Toyota pop-top had been half supplied by Newmans Campervans, and half by money from Scholl. I had been used to near luxury having spent five and a half months walking across America followed by a thirty-foot monster equipped with micro-wave, shower, lavatory and eight beds of one shape or another. This van was far smaller, although it was equipped with everything we needed, apart from a lavatory. A curtain screened off the living area behind the front seats which was equipped with a two ring gas stove, a fridge, a sink with pump action tap, built in cupboards and a sofa which pulled out into a bed.

David pulled and pushed the sofa and cursed, but it wouldn't budge. Quite determined to have my bed, I fiddled around with the hinges, lowered the seat section and the bed stretched out a little larger than a single bed.

I had brought my duvet, a pillow and a couple of sheets. David had brought nothing. We scrambled under the duvet, David on the right by the window and I by the cupboards. I lay for a while thinking about the hilarious week we had spent together putting the final touches to the walk. Our outrageous flirtations had brought some badly needed comic relief, but I wondered how we would get along now that we were together for twenty-four hours a day.

Day 2

The Hume (Fume) Highway turned into a freeway. Warnings marked the entrance: no animals, no pedestrians, no cycles, no farm machinery. Looking down from a bridge, it was a beautifully flat road with two lanes in each direction divided by a section of grass, seven metres across, with two hard shoulders on each side.

Before I reached the freeway, my pace had been set by a small steady man up ahead. His movement looked slow but he was efficient and his bottom was a rounded shelf that didn't move. His arms hung forward and his hair was grey and white and very long I moved to his rhythm and imagined he might be an Aborigine walking his songline. I had just read Bruce Chatwin's *The Songlines* and I missed the mystery of it. I wanted some contact with the Aborigines. How do they move? What do they think of? Do they kick stones in the night? Do they look at the apex of their songline or do they hold their heads to the heavens and 'feel' their way across the land?

I didn't want to stop for fear of leaving his pace, but David drew up with what I thought had been a trip to McDonalds for Egg McMuffins. Instead he had apples, oranges and bananas. All very good for me, but not really what I wanted.

Children stood waiting to go to school. The grass was bright in the morning sun and the children looked fresh, ignorant of the things I had seen and known when I was a child. At twenty-one I felt old in the presence of youth.

'Hey, David?'

'Mmm?' peeling an orange for me.

'We don't have to go to school.'

He looked up and smiled. 'God, I've never thought of that. You're right, we don't have to go to school!'

'We're free! We can do what we like!'

But secretly I knew that we were more trapped than they.

An hour or so of suburban walking and we stopped for a pee at a petrol station. The map was a little unclear about where the road split from the freeway, so we asked the cashier. She gave us directions, but didn't know her right from her left, which made it all very complicated. It reminded me of a woman I had stopped on the British walk. When I asked her directions to the main road she said, 'I don't know really. You'd better ask a man.'

David bought me some milk, after much protest on his part; humans, he maintained, are the only animal which reaches maturity without being weaned. As an aerobics instructor and model, he was religious about nutrition and, after years of monitoring his own diet, he favoured the Hay system of eating. The plan establishes which food groups should be eaten together since acidic and alkaline digestive juices break down different groups and will cancel each other out. This results in poor digestion and an inefficient release of energy. According to the theory, the two primary food groups – proteins and carbohydrates – should be eaten separately leaving at least four hours between the two.

In order for my body to be provided with quick energy release, David designed a diet of simple carbohydrates for breakfast – fruit; complex carbohydrates for lunch – pasta, vegetables and avocados which act as a steady source of energy; more complex carbohydrates for afternoon tea – toast; and, if we had time, a small amount of protein for supper which would help to repair muscle breakdown overnight. Somewhat reluctantly I gave up my idea of chocolate bars for energy since these processed sugars disrupt the body's energy level giving it an immediate high followed by a low which, for lengthy endurance exercise, is destructive.

I had never considered my diet on previous walks, preferring to eat whatever I wanted as a boost to morale. I was extremely keen to experiment with David's suggestions and excited about the levels of fitness I would be able to achieve.

The old road out of town was bordered by tall gums with thin white mottled trunks and odd tufts of leaves as though applied by a sponge. It wasn't autumn, yet the dusty verge was littered with their thin oval leaves. Red and yellow American-style trucks with roo bars barged along the centre of the road and hooted at me in greeting. It didn't occur to me that they could have been telling me to get off the road.

When I reached David I found he had prepared a feast of avocados on toast and laid them out on the mobile table. I perched on the sofa and he lay outside in the sunshine. His silence was beginning to infuriate me.

'Hey, David,' I laughed over at him, 'you have to talk to me! If you don't I'll end up not being able to put two words together.'

David looked up with a slight smile. 'There were these two swagmen, right? Been mates for years. Tramping out west in the wheatfields, good young crops on either side. Harry takes his pipe from his mouth and points to one of the paddocks. "Nice crop of wheat there, Bru," he grunted. Five hours later when they were seated by the campfire, Bill broke the silence. "Wasn't wheat – it was oats." Then he rolled up in his blanket and went to sleep. When he woke next morning, Harry and his swag were gone. Under a stone at the foot of the nearest tree was a note from him. "Too much argument in this here camp," it said.'

I roared with laughter. It was a great way to break the silence and filled me with hope. This might just work. We might become friends. We might survive the trip.

David lay back in the sun.

'I must be off. Thank you for my lunch.'

'You're welcome.'

I had decided to take a chance with walking on the freeway, the old road really was too long and we hadn't seen any police. I scrambled down the embankment and took up my place on the right hard shoulder with the traffic moving in my direction. The sun was warming, the road was smooth and I danced with it, feeling the music in my feet, wind from the traffic in my hair, shutting out the noise and the world of Them, people who don't walk. Free energy. I grinned and all the warmth flowed up and out of my smiles and I squeezed inside with excitement.

I walked with the sun setting in front of me; the sky was fiercely blue and black and the gum trees cast shadows slashed with gold, like tattooed tigers on the road. The headlights of speeding cars projected my shadow on the reflective road signs in shades of black and grey.

I looked back at David. Time to stop. I pointed to a row of lamp posts and walked to the last one. Touching it, I waited for the van. Warm light inside, comfortable seat, throbbing feet, stiffening muscles, beauty at day's end. Another night in which to rest and gather strength, and spend some time with David.

I could hardly move. The muscles had locked. Although I had spent the previous four months walking twenty miles a day, I had allowed myself the luxury of relaxing in the last week. I regretted it now.

'Did you stretch today?'

'You know I didn't. What shall I do?'

'Stretch.'

'Show me.'

In Hong Kong David had taught aerobics to a group of Asian women he fondly referred to as his 'ladies'. Some would take him out to lunch and he would drive their cars and sometimes he would stay, after lunch.

Using the roo bar for support, he took me through the motions of calf stretches, front and back thigh stretches and some complicated arrangements for the bottom. I could imagine his 5'10" taut brown body strutting around the classroom in tight cycling shorts correcting the postures of his 'ladies' with a gentle touch and a clasp of firm flesh, flirting with their bodies. I looked across at him: youth beside my premature rigormortis. I thought of the things he had seen that I had not and the women who had stretched beside him because he wanted them there.

Day 3

It was 6.30 a.m. and too early for the road workers to be out on a closed off section of road. The hard shoulder and a whole lane were mine and I needed them; I couldn't trust my muscles to walk in straight lines; my back was bent forward and my legs bowed to accommodate their stiffness. But after a time they eased and the small blisters in my heels nestled into their places in the 'pink fluffy clouds'.'

Cows turned their expressionless faces towards me, until I crossed the road to them and they stopped, some turning away ready to run, others staring straight at me. When I walked on, they organised themselves into a line and followed me.

White gums stood on the grassy hills, naked in the spring, their distorted branches held to the sky, but they would bear no leaves for they were quite dead. Some had fallen, yet were still firm and solid. I wondered whether the bird that bleeped like an alarm clock was calling the gums to rise again from their sleep. And when they stood, would they ache like me?

Ahead I saw a sign to send my muscles into contortions, 'Welcome to the Southern Highlands'. Catherine Hill was the first of many. An extra lane was given for the trucks but there was no extra air space for their fumes. I knew when the top of a hill was near as the sign would read, 'Left lane ends 200m, merge right'. I used to laugh at the thought that the 'm' stood for miles. As I got to the bottom of the hill a band of roadworkers in reflective vests and old muscles stood looking at me.

'Where ya garwin'?'

'Perth.'

'Path?'

'Perth.'

It was a very hard word to say with conviction.

'Ya hitchin'?'

'Walking.' The workmen laughed to each other and shook their heads. I laughed to myself, they would soon be proven wrong.

The van was waiting by a sandwich bar at the end of a collection of houses. I checked my watch; I had walked for two hours and thirty-five minutes. Five minutes late. I had planned on having a break every two and a half hours which should be sixteen kilometres. I felt confident about sixteen kilometres because that was the distance from my home in London to my office in the City and I had walked it every morning and every night for four months. I felt I 'knew' the distance. But David was conscious of my varying walking speeds and even though he furiously denied it (until months later) he added an extra half a kilometre to each block. These blocks we called quarters. For the first week I would walk three quarters each day; the second week four quarters and for the rest of the trip five quarters. Quarters are easier to say and look forward to than fifths. In compliance with strict authenticity rules demanded by the Guinness Book of Records, a log book must be kept showing dates, place names and daily distance. Each daily entry had to be verified by an independent witness – not always an easy thing to find. The speed record I was trying to break was set by Sarah Fulcher who in 1985 ran 4,363.2 kilometres across Australia in ninety-six days.

We ate muesli in the van. The road ahead divided in two again: freeway and the old road which wound around the towns. Again we decided on the freeway as it was probably less hilly and certain to be shorter. In fact, a look at the map indicated I had made up all the lost distance from the first day because of the last stretch of freeway. Now we would gain time on the Schedule.

Up and over the small hills, like those of Derbyshire, on roads where gums grew thick and tall, my breath lying in puffs on the crisp spring air. England had been bathed in the first few weeks of autumnal gold as I left it, happy to miss the coming winter. My decision to begin the walk in spring was taken with hindsight after the American walk and very much with logistical restrictions in mind. I had crossed the Texan desert in winter to avoid the heat but I soon found myself walking away from a frozen back-up vehicle and without enough warm clothing in temperatures of $-15°C$. The original start for the Australian walk had been July, late winter early spring, but I hadn't secured enough sponsorship to begin by then. I also needed to link up with Sport Aid '88's Race Against Time to raise public awareness of my charity endeavour. I knew I was taking a risk with the seasons but the alternative of postponing the walk for a year was just not viable.

David pulled up and I told him to meet me at the sign for Berrima, at the end of the town. Berrima was very quaint, with lots of olde worlde shoppes and a row of very distinguished names such as Pringles of Scotland, Libertys of London, Crabtree and Evelyn and good old Fortnum and Mason. Dried flowers, woven baskets and little antiques were laid out on the pavement and from the tiny tea rooms came the smell of English tea with hot buttered scones. And there, at the end of the village with avocados and tomatoes on toast and a long stiff drink of Campbell's V8 juice, was my van and David. He was very amusing, lifting my spirits with jokes. After the meal I patched up my feet, stretched a little, and sent him ahead because I wanted to walk alone.

I continued up and over the hills, lulling my muscles back into rhythm and willing my arches to rest on their supports.

'G'day!' I jumped, startled. There was no one to be seen. The road tore a vast concrete slice through a valley of gum. No houses, no people, only trucks, concrete and me. 'G'day!' Spinning around again I caught sight of a man sitting on the high verge on the left.

'You frightened me. What are you doing?'

'Aw, just hanging out.'

'Funny place to hang out.' And I turned away and crossed the road to the other side. A good distance up the valley I crossed back again only to have to do it again when two bothersome beer-bellied leches slowed to my pace to stare at me.

Day 4

The swathe of grey-white concrete thundered over the hills of gum and far into the distance. Beyond the horizon the hills were steep and persistent; plateau after plateau for hour after hour. And the trucks, stinking of hot rubber, passing every twenty seconds, would stand on their horns, making me jump, thinking they were pulling on to the hard shoulder. If I looked back to check, they pulled up ahead and stopped for me. If I waved at them they stopped. Cars stopped too, but I wasn't going to talk to Them, to hear them puncture my thoughts with questions of 'why?'

Ahead of me the white line ran straight into the distance. I forced my mind into a desert blank: mouth open, eyes on the brow of the road, forcing a beat, lengthening the stride, conscious of the sun; no water, covering ground to get water. With burning skin, freezing muscles and pain in the tibia I kept my eyes on the brow, walking like a zombie on purpose, on purpose to get control, to see the distance and conquer it.

Day 5

I walked through Goulburn, looking at my reflection in windows and listening to myself on the local radio station, avoiding that question 'why?' with talk of solitude and the motion of walking.

I saw the van coming towards me but David didn't see me. I thought he'd turn around soon enough, but he didn't. Had I made a wrong turn? Was he searching the highways?

The road was narrow, with only one lane in each direction. The trucks were close and the hard shoulder of tiny stones slithered underfoot and sucked my pace from me. The sound of a siren startled me and a voice crackled over the speaker, 'Good on ya, Ffyona, keep going!' The policeman patrolling that stretch of road to Canberra called words of encouragement each time he passed. I wanted to flag him down to ask where David was, but I knew I would only have to talk to him about walking and he was bound to ask why I was doing it.

I was hungry, my balance was uneven and the road moved up and down like a ship in heavy seas. Where was David? Oh Lord, why was I so dependant? Couldn't I walk without back-up? No, I knew I couldn't. I wanted the movement, not a weight on my back. I needed someone else to take the strain, but where was he? My arches throbbed, I needed to change shoes, my lower tibia burned a little, my shorts pinched, the sea got rougher, my head swam. And there he was, come to rescue me.

'Hullo. Where were you? Am I going the wrong way?'

'No. The trailer had a flat and I had to stop to get it fixed.'

'How much was it?'

'You're on the front page of the *Goulburn Gazette* so they gave it to me for nothing.'

'That was kind of them but you could have left it and come for me.'

'I was only an hour.'

'I'm out of energy. You can't leave me like that.'

I ate and grew furious with myself for being so dependant. David took the butt of it, not because it was his fault, but because he was there and because he was late. I wanted to be alone to walk but I wanted him there whenever I needed him. He didn't understand that minutes count, every minute is sixty steps and every step took me further into thinking about 'why?'

I stepped out on to the road, waving him away from me, trying to show him what independence I had left. This wasn't a jolly hike, I was covering distances and I couldn't fend for myself. I got lost without him, grew hungry and thirsty without him, stiff and awkward without him.

On my journey through America I had discovered my Road Gods and Road Devils – and I was to meet them again in Australia. I could never see them, but I knew they were there because they left me their signs. I would come across a warning for users of the road to be aware that kangaroos might cross. This would be a sign from the Road God of Living Creatures. Quite often he would be waging war on the Road Devil of Dead Ones who would place a squashed roo beside the sign.

The Road Gods were a fairly sombre lot, but they were reliable and they were able to beckon me gently to walk west – especially the Road God of Daydreams, who was my favourite. The Road God of Daydreams had a house which was full of light and quietude. When I found my way inside, he let me free and closed the doors on all my anxieties. The Road Gods lived in the sunset which was over the next horizon and since somewhere over that horizon was Perth, my destination, I always thought the city would be permanently engulfed by the setting sun. The Road Devils were often out for kicks; they were always around getting up to mischief. Australia didn't like being walked across in a hurry, so they battled constantly with the Road Gods who beckoned me to the setting sun.

The Big Brothers (truckies) also knew one of the Road Devils – the Devil of Distance. They had a weapon against his temptations to make them think of how far away the destination was – the truckies ate amphetamines. My answer to him when he was in full swing in my head or when he placed a signpost for the kilometres to Perth, was to take the piss out of him. I would ask him why he didn't have a calculator because his sums were completely wrong and that nobody needed him anyway.

I had never met the Road Devil of Pain before – that is, I had never met him in quite such a battle as that which began that day near the town of Collector. I had felt a sharp burning sensation in my tibia the day before, I remembered the same pain from the British walk, somewhere near the Scottish-English border, where a doctor had diagnosed it as haemorrhaging. He told me to wear shoes with high tops, a piece of advice I had stuck to ever since. But my Reeboks were high-topped and the pain was beginning again. David passed and suggested that I tap my shoes up and down while sitting. I did and for a while the pain was relieved.

The hard shoulder had become whiter with scuffs of chalk and on the chalk there were butterflies of yellow and black. They fluttered from the ground in the rush of air from passing trucks, dancing on the unnatural breezes, but all were quite dead. The land eased up on the right into small hills and beyond them were mountains of gum, green and vibrant in the evening gold. But when the pain began again, the road grew louder and the smell of trucks more pungent. Those that carried sheep would splash me with urine and even though I walked forward, I seemed to get no closer to the horizon.

I stopped, sat on a metal barrier and tapped my toes, then walked again, but a searing pain shot up my leg forcing me to gasp. Again I stopped, tapped, and carried on, dragging that damned leg, hands clasping, fingernails cutting into my palms. David stopped and told me he would meet me two kilometres further on. I hobbled, dragged, ground out the steps, and spat obscenities at the cars that hooted. I threw back my head and screamed David's name. I tried to distract myself with the sunset, the colours and the shadows in the hills. But I hated them, I hated walking, I hated myself for being there. I finally crawled into the van and collapsed on the seat.

'That's Lake George.'

'I don't give a shit.'

'What's wrong?'

'My leg hurts.'

I wanted to scream at David for being so merry, blast him with all the hatred I felt for the road and the things that had brought me there. I never discussed my motives with him, brushing off his early inquiry, as I had done with all the reporters, with claims that I did it for the love of walking. But with every snort of pain, the smoke screen was wearing a little thin for David as well as myself.

We marked the road so that we could come back to the same spot and drove to the town. There we sat, ice on my leg blue-white with cold, and listened to talk of the lake. The Road Devils had had a good day.

Day 6

Grey puffs of mist combed through the trees on the western hills. Thick cloud covered the sun and drizzle darkened the trunks of the gum trees and the splitting, soggy wood of the fence posts. The puddles reflected the sky and rain-laden branches. Windows in the gloom afforded me glimpses of the flat green alluvial plain where high white cotton-tails darted, wild and free, among the rough rocky outcrops and the wet fresh grasses where Daddy Longlegs tangled and hummed.

For all the beauty of Lake George in the dawn of that early spring morning, I saw nothing but my orange reflection in the yawning puddles. My left leg took the strain while the right hip swung wide as though the leg were dumb and the knee's movement was exaggerated to push the tibia forward. The slightest nudge of my right foot on the wet tarmac sent pain spearheading up to the knee. The left foot thudded hard to compensate. Steps were short and I cursed each downward slope.

I reached the van and groped in the trailer for the feeble stick I had used yesterday as a crutch, but it was not there. 'The stupid bastard,' I cursed, 'he's thrown it away.' But no, under the tarpaulin was a new one; a strong sturdy branch, cut and shaped with my knife. I hobbled to the window.

'You're fabulous,' I whispered.

'Hang in there, Champ.' David pulled away and stopped a half hour ahead.

I tried to listen to music but frustration took over. A few days ago I had walked in time to the beat, but now it bounced ahead of me like the rabbits on the hillside who seemed to mock me with their play. I was forced to accept a gait which tortured the delicate balance of muscle function. It was not a walking movement. Although the van was there every half hour in case I fell, there was nothing David could do but rub Deep Heat into my leg, tighten the support bandages and worry at what the condition might be. I knew that walking further might worsen the injury, but I had a record to beat – I had to go on.

I struck out again, this time without the Walkman, reciting Kipling's 'If' and singing a lot of Simon and Garfunkel songs, working my mind away from the thousands of steps still ahead to walk. To lessen the jarring, I walked on grass but the water seeped through the holes cut for my toes.

I was chanting, 'Damn, damn, double damn, two bloody hells

and a bugger!' with such venom that when I got to the van it sounded so comical that we collapsed in hysterics. When we finally got ourselves together I asked David if he'd like to walk with me. When he leapt at the chance I thought he could see that I was struggling and wanted to help. I didn't realise he was just bored with sitting in the van and needed the exercise.

David drove the van ahead and hitched a lift back to me. Strong and clean, bouncing and joyful, he set a graceful pace which I tried to match. He fed me songs like an intravenous drip: Australian ditties, 'A Home Among the Gum Trees', 'Road to Gundagai', and the theme song from *The Man from Snowy River*. And he sang my request, 'The House of the Rising Sun'. Once I had overcome my shyness, I joined in, mumbling the words of the chorus. I tripped along, almost happily, thinking these were the experiences which would bond a lasting friendship. But I had absolutely no idea that David hadn't forgiven me for lashing out at him earlier in the day because of my pain. This misinterpretation of David was the beginning of a very necessary rift between reality and fantasy, a fantasy which enabled me to push on through the pain of the walk, but which also led to an inner confusion over my feelings towards David and his reaction to me.

David kept me distracted until in the distance I saw the sign 'Welcome to Canberra', and behind that was the van. He had really worked out the maximum satisfaction for that day. Climbing up on the seat, I sank down and grinned a hefty smile. I peeled off the shoes and socks and laid them on the dashboard to dry by the vents.

The luxury of the Hyatt hotel at Canberra awaited us for the first day of rest. It was essential to stop for one day in seven to break up the journey into manageable sections and give me something to aim for. I have always stuck to this rule, planning my rest days in advance to coincide with press conferences. Now I could have done with more time to allow my injury to heal, but with a speed record to break I could not afford myself that luxury – and I hated myself for it.

I knew that other people had crossed Australia on foot but foolishly I hadn't spent time tracking them down. Their advice on the peculiarities of the continent would have been invaluable. All I knew was the general route since there is only one which goes from Sydney to Perth and since it is essential on this kind of walk to stick to main traffic routes and not walk straight across the bush I had no choice. I also knew that most of them had done the walk the other way round but I had decided to begin in Sydney because I was walking round the world from east to west.

Day 7

I felt the joy of having a long bath and washing my hair and sleeping till 10 a.m. Ultra-sound was administered hourly for chronic shin splints and between doses of liquid anaesthetic, the doctor told me the Reeboks didn't have the necessary shock absorption to cushion the blow of every step. If I were to continue wearing them, I needed Sorbothane insoles. I had only walked 250 kilometres. I still had 4,870 to go. When he left I went back to bed and thought about David.

'He is ill at ease with men,' I wrote in my diary. 'Lots of gush and embarrassing gestures but with women it's arms around their shoulders, little giggles and that long look. That's fine for him, but it puts a question mark on me in other people's eyes. I think he's confused about the journey. It probably sounded exciting when I faxed him, but now he's plagued with the imponderable questions . . . "What am I doing here? Where am *I* going? What am *I* getting out of this?" I think this trip may give him a kick up the backside and make him create his own goals.'

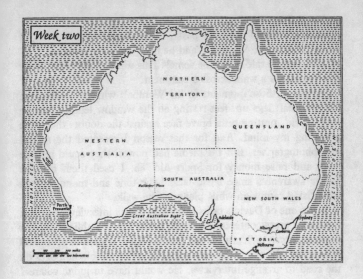

Day 8

No real strength, just getting by. Wind and rain buffeted against my covered head. The weather kicked off an automatic self-preservation mechanism; I became a self-contained capsule against the elements and felt no envy of the warm cars driving past.

At lunch David warmed me with pasta and Campbell's Bolognaise sauce. When we had finished I said, 'What are we going to call the van?'

'Pug? I mean, it's like, round, fat and sort of puggish looking.'

'I couldn't think fondly of anything called Pug.'

'The trailer should be called Tag; I keep seeing it in my wing mirror, just tagging along.'

'Tag it is, but think of something plumpish, homely.'

'Poppit? Pumpkin?'

A stream of hilarious animal, vegetable and mineral adjectives later, David came up with, 'Wombat!'

25

'Yeah! The Wombat!'

Taking a fistful of soggy pasta, David joyfully announced, 'I name this van the Wombat!' and he flung it on the window.

'Hang on,' I said, 'give me some!' This was a christening fit for any vehicle on a walk across a continent.

I clung to those moments in the Wombat; with my bottom on the sofa seat, legs up, feet resting on the window ledge, chatting with David, putting on a brave face against the doubts that were crowding my mind. And for that reason I resented the arrival of a photographer. But the media had power; they could tell the story and raise money for Sport Aid '88. I used them to raise public awareness since I had lacked the time and money for an advertising campaign while planning the walk.

It was one of David's tasks to arrange media interviews *en route*; the major press conferences we left to the Hyatt Public Relations departments in each city. It was a time-consuming job to post press releases in advance of my arrival and then to find 'phone boxes on the road to arrange interviews. He would have to judge where I would be and try to co-ordinate several papers, radio and television stations to interview me together during a break in the walk. The responsibility was enormous; the amount of money raised for Sport Aid '88 depended very much on him. But unlike the Trans-America Walk where I had one man to do that job and another to take care of me, David also had to buy supplies, cook the meals, wash up, do the laundry, get the witness book signed, find me every two and a half hours and give moral support. His reaction when I cursed the arrival of the media was understandable. It was to be a source of conflict between us; I knew what I had to do but found it almost impossible to talk to the media when I was chronically tired and vulnerable. If they were at all critical the interview was doomed.

When the photographer had gone I asked David to go ahead. I needed to be alone to struggle without being monitored. I felt excruciatingly alone when the Wombat drove away into the rainy horizon and with that feeling came the thoughts, 'What the hell am I doing here? I hate this. I'm cold, I'm lonely and I hurt. What am I trying to prove?'

We'd moved to America when I was two. I don't remember

much about it, except that I liked wearing dresses and beat up boys when they wouldn't let me play on their swings. When we got back to the UK my father's job, first as an officer in the Royal Marines and then as a pilot with British Airways, took us from pillar to post. We moved house twenty-four times in sixteen years, so loneliness and rootlessness were no strangers. It seemed like all our holidays were spent house hunting. Six months here, two years there. When we first moved to Shetland, we only stayed a week, then my older sister Shuna fell ill and we headed down to Aberdeen where she could be treated. For most of my childhood there was little time to say hullo, let alone goodbye.

I was sent off to boarding school when I was six. Though Shuna and I were just sixteen kilometres from home, our parents could have been a continent away. I still don't know whether my father felt that the odd strained and awkward visit would have made the pain of separation worse, or whether school, for him, was just another of life's assault courses. When I was still quite small we had gone on a rather gruelling camping holiday in Skye where ice clung to the inside of our tents. I had struggled to keep up, teeth gritted, refusing to let him see me cry, and he'd told me that I'd earned the right to wear the coveted Green Beret. But I never got to keep it. It was the closest he'd come to praising me, before or since.

I avoided further thought by playing a new compilation tape with a vibrating beat and the real walking suddenly took over. I felt it happening and I almost let go with relief for there it was again, the pure even rhythm of balanced walking, charging me up and down the hills, laughing again at the Road Devils, they who couldn't walk if they tried. A little shooting pain began but it only reminded me of how I had almost lost the battle back in Lake George. This was freedom, free energy and I thrived on it.

I arrived at the Wombat five minutes early and burst in to tell David, but my chin was frozen and I had to wait a while for it to thaw, almost crying with sheer relief. He videoed what I had to tell him and one day, far in the distance when we watched the whole tape of the walk, I did cry. I cried because three months and a lot of pain later I knew why I was walking and it was nothing to do with the joy of motion.

Day 9

I had a banana, ate half and was looking forward to the rest when a busload of children passed, whistling. It surprised me so much that I dropped the banana and furiously looked after them, feeling a lump gather in my throat. I thought about the loss of that nourishment for a full fifteen minutes wondering if this is how wars are started.

Fossilised carcasses of white gums, looking like the bony heads of dinosaurs, enchanted me as I walked beside them. Menacing black and white birds swooped low above me, sometimes so close I thought they would grab my hair. I wished, as I walked, that I could catch one and take it with me as a ferociously arrogant pet, to ride on my shoulder and leave me occasionally to sit on the dead gum and eat grubs.

I thought about driving my car. Weaning myself from thoughts of past luxuries especially those which concerned speed, was a battle I often fought against the Road Devil of Distance. 'Never, never, think of the end,' was a gem of advice given to me by a guru of walking. And even though it was my weapon to keep that Road Devil at bay, I never quite managed to wield it hard enough to smash the visions of the end. At those time I distracted myself with thoughts of what I would be doing if I wasn't walking: I would be in London, getting fat on coffee-flavoured Club biscuits, growing white-headed spots overnight and looking forward to endless weekends with no money and nothing to do. In a way it was a justification for what I was doing out here.

Day 10

After Jugiong a great hill stood at the end of a symmetrical tree-lined high street. The hill was a smooth steep climb with a twist to a resting place at one summit where David was poised with the video camera. I climbed past him and over the hill where the Road Devil of Pain had parked his favourite punishment: a sign which read 'STEEP DESCENT'.

But he wasn't going to win because I became enveloped in the beauty of it all. The clear skies were tufted with white summer clouds; cone-shaped hillocks dotted with gum trees provided resting places for white cockatoos and pink and grey galahs. The rocky outcrops, grey as Scottish granite, were shaped like large sheep droppings, segmented and square and smooth on the surface. Slow flying insects battled for lift in the heavy heat and the height of the hills. In a field by the side of the road a large nose-ringed bull took one look at me with my Walkman and limp and bolted with the herd in a stampede to the far side of the field.

A road repair truck droned behind me on the hard shoulder and wouldn't move on. I edged over. It slowed down. I held my response ready but when it drew up the men asked no questions. The driver took up most of the front seat with rolls of fat slopping over his trousers and big breasts hanging inside the folds of a sweat stained T-shirt. His face was heavy with a week-old beard and as he turned towards me his tongue hung out of his mouth. The one nearest to me didn't catch my eye, but looked me casually up and down and settled his gaze on my breasts. Despite their unpleasantness, I gave my standard response, 'I'm fine thank you.' And I slowed to walk behind them and prepared to cross if they didn't move on. They did. I let out my breath and screamed with the pain in my shin.

Another truck stopped ahead. I couldn't afford to suppress my short, pain-controlling breaths under the scrutiny of another lech so I screamed out, 'For God's sake FUCK OFF! I DON'T WANT A FUCKING LIFT!' He couldn't have heard me over the growling brakes because he got out of the cab. I knew I couldn't get away from him; I could hardly walk. As he approached me he reached behind his back, took out his wallet and handed me a $10 note. I felt utterly embarrassed. I thanked him and because I had no pocket, put it into my underpants. Somehow I lost it; it must be lying in a ditch somewhere between Jugiong and Gundagai. (I put $10 of my own into the fund for him.)

And then came a very steep decline. It was so steep that the trucks coming up drove no faster than a bush walk. My right leg began to scream, so I hobbled hard on my left and stopped at a railing, took off my shoe and rubbed the base of my tibia.

The rubbing turned to thumping, turned to smashing and when my knuckles hurt too much, I looked for a stone. 'Oh Christ, not this again.' I had once whirled myself into such a fury over some dispute at home that when three attempts at falling out of a tree failed to break a limb, I took a stone to my collarbone and smashed it. Pain could beat pain.

The hard shoulder was covered with loose, sharp gravel and broken glass. I walked barefoot on it, forcing the stones to dig into the tender parts of my feet. Breathing in time to alleviate the pain, almost snorting, I made my way further down the hill but as it got steeper and momentum accelerated my speed, the pain increased and I could do nothing but hop. I used my bent, outstretched elbow for balance and thought of how far short of my day's target I was. David would not have to drive far to find me.

The Wombat passed me and continued merrily down the hill. I put my arms straight up in the air, which was my signal for David to stop. He did, a painful distance down the hill. Forty minutes later, I reached it.

'Want some water?' he asked cheerfully.

'I want a new leg,' I said flatly. I reapplied the liquid fire cream from the chiropractor and hunted for a cigarette.

I walked no further that day. Instead we went to Gundagai and got very drunk.

Day 11

The shin splints had eased with a little relaxation and a lot of the amber nectar. I had my wish and ran down that hill, somewhat awkwardly perhaps, but the world looked good again and my spirits were high. Because of the late start, David made hot museli in the Wombat and ran out to give it to me on the road, I ate as I walked. He drove ahead and I was alone again.

The bell bird bleeped from a dead white branch, defending his territory. Beneath him the lerp insect multiplied and devoured the gum, safe in the knowledge that the birds that would feed on them were being kept at bay by the bleeping. Shell-pink-breasted galahs shrieked and dipped over the road; they have their mates for life and their movements are exactly in time with each other. I had learnt that the black and white birds of the aggressive swoop were magpies, but they had no interest in me or my shiny headset; they were staking their territory in the nesting season. There have been stories of over-excited magpies swooping away with a chunk of scalp from unsuspecting intruders. But I had little fear, for just throwing stones at them in flight seemed enough to call a truce.

David sat on the road by the Wombat writing poscards. Opposite sat 'The Dog on the Tuckerbox', a statue erected to the loyalty of man's best friend. The story goes that a cook in a camp of sheep shearers had trained his dog to guard the larder, a metal box of food. The cook was an ageing man and one day he left the camp and walked into the bush to die. The dog waited for his master and sat, in his place on top of the tucker box, unable to be moved by the shearers. He waited there for the rest of his life.

As I approached David, I was aware of the tension between us which had sprung from an incident that morning; we had left Gundagai to drive back to the starting place, but the Wombat was out of petrol. I suggested we use the motorbike which was there as an emergency back-up, but he refused, saying it wasn't yet 'run in' for two passengers over that distance. Fortunately we had found a petrol station that was open.

'Hullo!' I called to him. 'God I'm hungry! Have you got a cup of tea and a sandwich for an old lady?'

'There isn't any milk or bread. I haven't any money.' A pile of Dog on the Tuckerbox postcards lay beside him.

I was furious but kept my cool and carefully explained to him that I had not spent the previous eight months, and half my annual salary, planning the walk and raising sponsorship only to be confronted by these simple problems. I might as well be walking alone with a rucksack. He found a few coins and we ate in silence in the tourist café.

I had the 'runs' all day, probably as a result of our night on the town. It had been our first introduction to Australians in their 'natural environment' and we felt flattered by their friendliness and genuine interest in our project. Most of them had heard we were coming and the conversation was begun by a long-legged, khaki-clad Charles Atlas named James, who recognised me by my cycling shorts and asked, 'How ya feet, mate?'

He introduced us to his friends who filled the bar and soon the liquor was flowing with wild stories of the Australian creatures we should beware of on the Nullarbor. Later, we went back to his home for a feast of good Aussie tucker: lamb chops, shepherds pie, mashed pumpkins, potatoes and peas with thick, black mushroom sauce. He produced endless bottles of champagne from the fridge and we drank Bucks Fizz and listened to a few catch phrases of Strine which he thought would come in handy:

Gunnerspew	=	I'm going to be sick
Dry as a dead dingo's donger	=	I'm thirsty
Fair suck of the Savo	=	a good try

I attributed the piles of 'calling castles' I left along the roadside the next day to the beer and the food. Walking with the runs on a road that is undergoing massive roadworks poses quite a few problems. At one point I was desperate but on the other side of the road were earth moving machines in which sat a pair of workers who were looking at me. I squeezed my buttocks together but it was no good. Just in time I spied a drainage ditch. I leapt to the bottom, yanked off my shorts and knickers and produced a most impressive castle.

David had rather a frightening experience later on when he climbed a hill to have a pee (he was still embarrassed about doing it outside and naively sought safety in height). He aimed at a dead gum and out sprang a wolf spider, not at all pleased with an early morning shower! He jumped back in time to save himself any further embarrassment.

Day 12

The sound of my footfalls echoed thud, scuff, thud, scuff, thud, scuff – not just the result of the swollen calf but also because a blister had developed under the rim of my right heel. It was too deep to burst and would have to grow up to the surface.

There are two schools of thought concerning the prevention of blisters. John Hillaby, who has walked further than the circumference of the Earth four times over, and who trained me on my British walk, keeps his feet very soft. The idea is that once a blister forms, it is better to get rid of it as soon as possible rather than wait for many days for it to grow up through layers of hard skin. The opposite theory is to rub surgical spirits on the feet to toughen them; if they are tough they won't be so sensitive to the rubbing which is the primary cause of the blisters. My feet were soft except for a ridge of hard skin at the base of each heel which I found difficulty in removing. And beneath one of them sat the blister. It had developed as a result of inserting Sorbothane insoles to lessen the shock and help prevent shin splints. The section where the insoles met the back of the shoes had caused the rubbing.

Bitumen gets hot. I felt the hot, dry air rising in clods, and the sun baking my calves and elbows, squeezing the moisture from my neck and stabbing at the tender tips on my ears. I greeted the gush of air from high-sided trucks with my arms out like the wings of an aeroplane, to cool the wetness beneath. Tiny pricks of cold tickled my scalp from the breezes and hair was pasted to my neck with sweat.

The magpies were out in force again, swooping deeply with belching cries. A bird lay flattened on the road beneath them. The magpies seemed to be mourning the loss of one of their kin. But as I passed, I saw it to be only a duck with its middle picked clean. They had been eating it and guarding their territory. I threw a few stones and shouted, 'I'm not dead yet!'

Beyond Tarcutta, the halfway point between Sydney and Melbourne, a car lay in a ditch with the doors and windows smashed. It looked like a fairly recent accident. But I was wrapped in my own world, away from pain, going through the Kings and Queens of England – 'Willie, Willie, Harry, Stee, Harry, Dick, John, Harry Three . . .' so that when drivers slowed to ask if I had been in the accident, I would snap back at them, 'Yes, I'm all right, I'm fine.' Then on and on with 'One, two, three Neds, Richard Two, Henry Four, Five, Six then who?'

I had begun my twelfth day at 5.45 a.m., finished at 6.30 p.m., walked sixty-four kilometres, recorded a radio interview and hadn't raised a cent for Sport Aid '88.

Day 13

My bladder seemed to be getting weaker. As the bushes at the side of the road were not wide enough to block the view all round, I made do by squatting with my back to the road, taking my sweat shirt off and draping it behind me as a curtain.

I scuffled along in the dusty heat, reciting 'Albert and the Lion' in a mock Lancashire accent.

> So straight 'way the brave little fella
> Not showing a morsel of fear, took
> His stick with the horse's head handle
> And poked it in Wallace's ear.
>
> You could see the Lion didn't like it, and
> Giving a kind of a roll, he pulled
> Albert int' cage with him, and
> Swallered the little lad whole!

And when I had my fill of that, I sang 'She'll be coming round the mountain when she comes', making up the verses to fit my moods – 'She'll be popping big white blisters when she comes, she be humming Ozzie ditties . . .' This song was my favourite and I'd use up a lot of energy bellowing it out to the skies.

I must have appeased the Road Devil of Pain in some way for I didn't feel the discomfort in my feet which I should have felt when I took off my shoes that night. Half the right big toenail was black and dead, another nail was about to fall off and the blister under the ridge of my right heel had spread along its whole length.

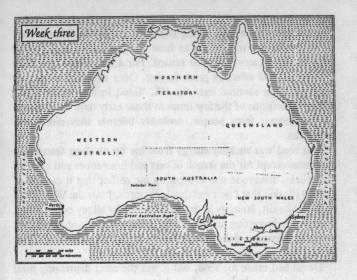

Day 15

I walked alone in the dawn listening to *Robinson Crusoe* and *Sinbad The Sailor* stories on my Walkman. Sinbad always got shipwrecked on islands, hitched rides on passing ships and made lots of money, whereas Robinson got shipwrecked once and was stuck.

The first break was in Albury. David cooked a pasta meal which was not supposed to be eaten until lunch, and I stayed an hour instead of half giving the excuse that I couldn't walk on a full stomach. I regretted allowing myself those extra minutes because I enjoyed them so much. Freedom had become the Wombat; freedom was not walking.

I walked over the Murray River and into Victoria, the first frontier. On the horizon I saw a fire engine, which had passed me earlier, parked on the hard shoulder. As I approached I could see the firemen unwinding the hose but there was no fire. They seemed to be engaged in a comedy routine, playing hide-and-seek

35

and spraying each other. I began to sweat, watching the water. The bitumen heated the spring day until it was hot. I knew they were waiting for my arrival to hose me down, but as I passed they lost their nerve and just smiled. For a long distance walker it had the same effect as prick teasing. Once they had caught up with me, they shouted over the PA, 'Good luck, Ffyona! Keep going!' It was one of the few times in those early days that I found encouragement from people, probably because they didn't ask questions.

The road was sucking energy from me by its sheer featureless hugeness except for the stench of cars and hot rubber and noise of the trucks. Everyone was overtaking me so fast that it caused an optical illusion that I was walking backwards. I saw the Wombat, a small white slit, far away in the distance but for all my even pacing, I seemed to be getting no nearer to it. All my suppressed frustration over the pressures of the schedule and the regimentation of the rest periods was about to be unleashed.

David had made me food, but it was the most depressing meal of the trip: mashed pumpkin, burnt toast and carrots which lay bending and raw on the counter. I pushed one experimentally with my finger. It wobbled. I just wanted a meal, but David was going on about the nutritional value of uncooked vegetables.

'You could at least have saved the toast.'

'This is really getting to me, Fee. I'm exhausted from inactivity.' Looking down at my lunch, I broke.

'I am not walking any more today.'

The noise had got to me and the day of rest yesterday had been spoiled by having to walk for two and a half hours to be back on schedule. I was overcrowded and needed some peace to rethink how I should tackle my head.

For days I had been stumbling along without reaching my daily goals, slipping backwards, settling for whatever motion I could get out of my body, counting the minutes, 'only two hours to go . . . only one hour and forty minutes . . . I've broken the hour . . . only forty minutes' until I reached the Wombat and then out to count again. One thing was certain – I couldn't continue like this; I was kicking against walking, fighting the very freedom I had spent so many months working for.

We marked the hard shoulder with a slash of white spray paint and drove up into the Mount Lady Franklin hills. I took my cigarettes and climbed over fences, past a ruined house and down into a field where I sat looking out across the valley. There were no people, no trucks, no foul smell, only green grass and an odd crow. I lay down and looked into the clouds.

From the time I had been met by David at Sydney Airport, our conversations were often interrupted by his visions of what he would do after the walk. There were constant references to sailing in Queensland and living in a bamboo hut on the beach where I would write my book. Because of his dreamings it became impossible to concentrate when the walk seemed tiresome in view of what would happen when it was done. I asked David over and over not to talk of it but he wouldn't stop, encouraging thoughts of a life on the golden sands, where I could sit and be still for a while with a wheelchair at my side if ever I wanted to venture far. Secretly, then, I knew it would never happen. But the road changes one's perception of reality, flips the coin to fantasy and somehow the two sides merge as the coin spins so that one is no longer sure which side of life one treads. But on that hillside I was brought sharply into focus by the futility of all this stuff in my head: mind games to get me to the next horizon without beating my fists on my tibia in frustration; exasperation at my limp and absolute despair at just being there and knowing I had covered only 684 km with another 4,436 km to go.

I couldn't accept reality so I misread comments that beckoned to a fantasy more palatable than pain. When David suggested he walk with me for distraction and company, I accepted the offer gladly and forgot his earlier words of lethargy.

When I got back to the Wombat, David had made the decision for us. He would walk with me.

We talked of films. David could retell the story of a film, reciting the words and each camera shot. Our favourite was *The Breakfast Club* and small catch phrases would recur. Our chatter was endless. He told me stories of his wild days in Hong Kong;

stories which began with, 'I was getting real dirty with these two girls on the dance floor . . .' He boasted of taking women home through the dark woods as a test of their substance, partying on junks, backflipping into the sea and swimming to other boats and climbing up to surprise the party.

The moon rose, almost full and we talked of ghostly stories to scare each other. Tired after the distance and the earlier tension, we reached the Wombat, stretched and collapsed into bed.

Day 16

> Humpty Dumpty sat on a wall,
> Humpty Dumpty had a great fall.
> All the Kings horses
> And all the Kings men said:
> Fuck him, he's only an egg.

We walked together in the first quarter. He was in my territory now, and I told him about what I look at and recited a few rhymes such as a version of Humpty Dumpty. He in turn told me the names of birds and plants and we played lateral-thinking games. But I always lost; I couldn't think, my mind had stopped its desire to learn. It only concentrated on my body and laughter to get me over the horizons.

As the sun set on the day, another section of new road branched to the left and I walked on it, wide and flat, empty except for me and my footfalls placed delicately on the surface as if my feet were eggs. David took up his position beside me, leaning his weight on the door with his elbow over the window ledge. I unlocked it and opened it suddenly. Out he fell, held only by his hand on the ledge and his shoe string caught on the accelerator pedal. His balance was lost, the Wombat was accelerating slightly. I broke into a trot, both of us laughing ourselves into a state of weakness. I pushed up on his lower back, he struggled with his foot, pushing the door out with his hand for balance. As the Wombat got faster, our laughter grew more uncontrollable. A final shove, up and into the Wombat. Slam went the door.

'I saved your life!'

The moon cut the dark gum forests into slices of black shadow and sharp leaf. It was our first full moon and I limped with my shadow when David left, promising to find me later. I had no torch – I didn't need one, since the moon was so bright – but I avoided the shadows for fear of tripping on something. The forest grew thick and wild to my left and whispered things which faded to nothingness as I stepped closer to look.

I walked an hour of the fifth quarter and I was tired. The eggs lay broken in my shoes.

Day 17

I was less frantic and under pressure as I stepped out. I had decided to follow Plan B, a take-it-as-it-comes schedule with rest periods taken at any length I wanted, usually an hour. I was learning to enjoy myself. Even though I was seventy kilometres behind the Schedule, I knew that I could make up thirty by taking a bypass over the top of Melbourne rather than walking through the centre. The remainder could be left to the Nullarbor, or simply allowed to eat into the three week leeway to break the record.

I praised the wonder of it all. The land was flat, the traffic less heavy, fields of flowers nodding in the cooling breezes, the soft purr of seeds popping in the spring warmth, and legs that worked well enough. The blisters eased into their places and I sang and chatted to myself. But just as I was thanking the Road Gods in turn, I must have left one out for I walked straight into a spring thunder storm, a change in the weather as dramatic as an average day in England. Within an hour the highway was under a two-inch river of water. My rainproof jacket, snatched from the Wombat before David left, proved only showerproof and stuck to my T-shirt in miserable cold patches, breaking my self-contained capsule of independence, but instead of grizzling with self-pity I roared with laughter, singing 'She'll be sloshing through the puddles till she's soaked.'

I had expected David to return from having the brake lights fixed, to give me shelter until the worst was over. But he came only when the rain stopped. When I raised the matter he burst out furiously, 'I can't be expected to come back for you every time it rains.' It was the first time I had ever suggested it.

I plodded on merrily through the last dribbles of the storm. David agreed to walk and returned after nightfall to scramble with me on the hard shoulder that had been reduced to slithering puddles of rubbly clay. Our voices filled the night singing 'Day-O', followed by the few verses we had learned of a sad Australian song, 'And the Band Played Waltzing Matilda'. Onwards under the beam of the torch, sheltering our eyes from the blasting headlights of the trucks and turning our backs to the needle sharp curtains of spray, David would gently pull me back when I strayed too close to the convoys of fairground juggernauts. Slowly, perhaps shyly, more of my back-up driver began to expose itself; the glossy veneer seemed to be cracking, at least around the edges. I liked what I saw but perhaps he saw nothing in me but dependence. And there was the Wombat, all wet in a ditch with the gum bearing down on the roof. We cooked up a feast of chilli con carne and warmed our hands around the gas fire of the stove. I changed my clothes again and David drove away.

I continued on in the black cloudy night, slithering and stumbling, ducking into the bush when the convoys stampeded past, humming gently to keep my spirits high. I had learned many times as a small child on family camping holidays that to be cold and wet was acceptable, but to be miserable as well was potentially fatal. It would also mean the loss of the highly praised Royal Marine Green Beret, which my father occasionally bestowed upon me.

Day 18

The day was disrupted at the first break when we marked the road and drove ahead to Melbourne to do a live television interview which could not be slotted into the next day's press conference. I resented seeing the distance I had yet to walk, but David was trying so hard with the media and we had raised so little money – perhaps $50 – that I agreed to it. The production assistant was very excited at the amount of money we could raise by being on the *Midday Show*. David got very excited as well. But I remained unconvinced.

A make-up artist painted character onto my face. We sat in the 'green room' watching the show. A doctor/writer entered with his book promoter, who was all a public relations female should be: great wads of padded shoulders, long glossy fingernails, chunky gold jewelry at her ears, heavily moussed hair, powerful scent, bulging Filofax and a strut that put me to shame. She barged in asking where she should take her client. Since none of us were station crew, we were silent.

'Does anyone here speak English?'

Eventually the doctor/writer was led on to the set and while we watched his interview, she insisted on laughing hysterically at his jokes.

A commercial break interrupted his interview. The door of the 'green room' burst open and a red-faced runner bellowed my name, fifteen minutes before my interview was scheduled. We ran back to the set, just in time to go on. My interview was good enough. I returned to the 'green room' and discovered why I had been rushed on so early. The doctor had not finished his interview because a woman in the audience had suffered a heart attack. He had probably saved her life. But the public relations female was strutting around with hands on hips. 'Oh for goodness sake, they could have called an ambulance,' she screeched. 'He's not going to have time to do his second half.'

We drove back to the reality of the bush where the she-oaks bend, where the daisies nod their heads in splashes of sunlight, where the bell bird calls and cockatoos fly in skies of azure and white and where there are no commercial breaks.

I had nothing with which to remove the make-up so I left it there until it was sweated out or washed away by the shower that night. The day was old and hot as I stepped out. The tempo of the road seemed to have changed since my departure. Above the thunder of the Road Hymn I sang a defiant 'Waltzing Matilda'. I felt polluted by the shock of civilisation and in retaliation I peed my pants.

There was nothing either side of the road to hold my interest, so I lilted myself into thoughts of swashbuckling warriors, tanned and muscular in white shirts ripped open at the chest, riding black horses with manes of gold, splashing through crystal brooks, leaping great canyons and castle moats with the war cry 'Cruachan!' ringing out from walls of stone, slaying pompous PR females and interfering reporters, defying death to reach the iron barred turret where I lay captured in a sweep of peach silk . . .

A hand was on my shoulder. I jumped and gasped. It was David.

'Hi!'

I resented his arrival now that I had found the Road God of Daydreams. The thump back into reality reminded me again of the stiff left knee and each footfall rubbing my heel against the back of my shoe, pumping the pus. But I listened to his chatter and thought of tomorrow, and the day of rest, and two nights at the Hyatt.

All too soon the Wombat appeared. We marked the road with slashes of white spray paint and drove through another thunderstorm towards Melbourne. I shut my eyes to the journey, I did not want to see again what I had not yet walked.

Day 19

A Day of Rest.

Back in civilisation for a day, a realisation of the vastness of the continent I was walking across took hold. It had taken me this long to not quite get to the bottom of the 'curved bit', I still had to go up it, over the top, through the bit which looks like India, across the Nullarbor, up to Coolgardie and then into Perth. A thousand kilometres down, 4,120 to go.

After a day packed with questions and media interviews, we made a trip to a blister doctor. He was very down-to-earth and announced straight away that I was suffering from blisters under calluses.

The blisters were trying to pad the area of pressure with liquid but the callus was so thick that it pushed down on the liquid, spreading it sideways under the skin. More liquid was produced and the process would continue until the blister eventually pushed up through the many layers of hard skin to burst naturally.

He suggested that instead of making a hole with a needle and then forcing out the liquid by rolling a finger over the surface towards the hole, we should drain them with a syringe.

However, it wasn't as 'painless' as the first method. He stuck the syringe through the outer layers of skin, past the well of fluid, embedded the needle deep in the inflamed skin below and tried to pull back the plunger. I thrashed, screaming loudly. When he had repositioned the needle and removed the liquid, he injected an iodine solution into the blister which made me scream even louder. It didn't just sting for a few minutes and then ease off, it thudded for over two hours.

When it was over, David put a soothing hand on my shoulder. It couldn't have been very pleasant to witness. I hobbled outside, forcing back the tears by consoling myself that I'd had all my pain at once. I wonder, if someone had told me then that syringing blisters would soon be a twice-daily occurrence, whether I would have given up. Thinking back, I think I would have done.

Later that day a question was raised at the press conference which caught me off guard, for all my careful rehearsals.

'How do you feel about the alleged bankruptcy of Sport Aid '88?'

When deciding which charity to support, Sport Aid '88 had seemed ideal: it was a continuation of Live Aid for which I had raised funds by walking across America and was raising money for underprivileged children around the world to be distributed through existing charities. I assumed that 100 per cent of the funds raised would be directed to the relief effort, and since I needed the credibility of an international organisation, I agreed to raise money for them.

My answer at the press conference was slick. 'I know nothing of these allegations, I have no comment.' But I was severely shaken. I sent a fax to the charity headquarters in London requesting information but there was no reply. I had no time to research the matter; I was walking across a continent and did not have a telephone. But it was disturbing to be associated with an organisation which had gone bankrupt. Months later I learnt that Sport for Sport Aid Ltd, which was the company set up to organise the overhead fundraising for the umbrella charity Sport Aid '88, had been liquidated. I decided to donate all the money I raised directly to their associated charity for underprivileged children, Care Australia.

During the informal part of the press conference, I pulled aside the PR girl from Adidas.

'You've got to do something about my shoes,' I whispered. 'I can't walk in them. I need some very light high-tops with as much shock absorption as possible.' She said she'd try.

We returned from the visit to the blister doctor to find a box of shoes from Adidas. David had been given the pair he had requested but neither of the two for me were high-topped. My feet were far too painful to try them.

However, there was nothing from my other sponsors, James Capel – they could hardly send me their latest stock market research product to mull over in my break. James Capel are a British international investment house. The company for which I had worked in London acted as Capel's 'headhunters' and because of the good relationship between the two firms, my managing director approached them on my behalf for sponsorship. They agreed to put up a quarter of the required amount once I had secured the remainder. Many months of letter-writing and heated sales talk came to an end when another colleague at work mentioned my walk to the owner of European Home Products who had recently acquired Scholl. I secured a deal with them. Scholl also supplied me with many of their products: a large box of Superfelt was waiting for me in my hotel room that night.

We had used up the intitial supply of this half inch thick padding foam by trying to mould my shoes so that they wouldn't slip at the heel. Admittedly my feet are a very strange shape – very wide at the front from walking a lot and very narrow at the heel. Consequently, shoes which fit across the width will slip at the back. My heels suffered because of this.

The PR lady from Scholl was primarily responsible for organising the media that day, and drove us around Melbourne from studio to studio after the main press conference. She was very beautiful but it was her natural laughter and almost 'airheaded' approach which took her further than those with padded shoulders and demanding struts.

Of all the questions at the press conferences and from all the people we met on the road, it was she who asked the most intuitive question. 'What d'you think about when you're walking?' Everyone asked that, but when I paused she added, in a very high pitched Australian accent which rose up at the end, 'D'you think about David?' Her hint at a closer relationship, coupled with my misinterpretation of his earlier warmth, lent fuel and reality to my fantasies of him. I sang her phrase many times in moments of jubilation through the journey.

That night David and I relaxed for a few moments alone and had dinner brought up to my room. White linen tablecloth, silver knives and forks, porcelain plates of delicately arranged, melt-in-the-mouth morsels and a simple white lily in a long thin vase. It was to turn anyone off mashed pumpkin and wobbly carrots eaten off paper plates in the cold damp of a tiny van shuddering from the whiplash of passing buses. The room glowed with shades of peach, the carpet was soft and thick, my hair clean and fresh and my clothes sweet-smelling and dry. So that the room would be bathed in even greater beauty, I got up to dim the lights, walking on tiptoe against the blisters. Sighing again in my chair, I breathed in the warmth, enjoying the luxury of not being on the road. David put down his fork.

'Fee?'

'Mmm?'

'I can't see my food.'

Day 20

We were driving back from Melbourne and the atmosphere was unpleasant. The national papers had carried my story but had not mentioned where to send the donations. I felt David should have insisted on this.

'I'm not really having fun, Fee.'

'You're uptight because you're not organised.'

'I'm working as hard as I can.'

'But you don't even have an action list.'

'I know what needs to be done.'

'But you don't do it, and it niggles you.'

'Oh yeah? Like what?'

'I'll make a list, shall I? Of all the things I need you to do, then you'll be focused and you won't have that nagging feeling that things are slipping through the cracks.'

'Oh, give me a *break*.'

It infuriated me how unconcerned he seemed to be about his responsibilities with the media. Easy as it was for me to criticise him, having designed and implemented every aspect of the walk myself, I did feel he was not pulling his weight.

My list incorporated everything and I read it to him.

'I know all that. You don't need to write it down. I've got it in my head.'

'But David you haven't done it.' What began as a reasoned discussion turned into a personal slagging match which subsided into an accusing silence.

For most of that walking day, I concentrated on how to improve my business relationship with David.

I concluded that the only way I could make his job easier was to accept that he might be late coming back from making phone calls or arranging interviews and would not be where he was supposed to meet me. I had to come to terms with the irritation I would feel and not make accusations about him dawdling because this would damage our relationship. I cursed the sponsor who had promised me a mobile telephone and then didn't deliver it. But cursing was not the answer.

Through all this it dawned on me that what I admired most in people was reliability. And reliable people had been few and far between. I was trying to make David more reliable because I was becoming more dependent upon him. Maybe the seven-year-old in me was trying to find some comfort. I have never been able to believe fully in anyone nor trust enough in myself. I have always set myself high goals, believing that if I reach them I will be able to live with myself, but somehow they are always over the horizon along with self acceptance.

I joyfully left the Hume Highway for a narrow country road which would bypass Melbourne. The night sky was streaked with the Milky Way and in front of me, for the very first time, I saw the Leo constellation of stars I came to know as the Half Heart. It also resembled a reversed question-mark and shone brightly, directly to the west; a constellation that would always guide my steps and become one of the most reliable friends I would make on the journey.

Day 21

It was cold and blustery, the hills gave way to undulations and pale green paddocks filled the horizons. The sky moved in low clouds of soft grey and the road was narrow and empty except for the occasional car, never a truck.

David drove beside me, listening to the radio. The Olympics punctuated our tedious endurance with the sudden victories of winning. It disturbed the equilibrium of my journey and I was glad of the air rushing past my ears, drowning out the noise of other athletes arriving at their Perth. But my head was high despite the soles of my shoes which had worn thin. Each town we got to I prayed for a shoe shop to buy some Reeboks but none were larger than a general store and a petrol station. My only wish, other than the sight of Perth over the next horizon, was for comfortable feet.

A bull stood with his women in a field, observing us as we covered our distance. His women looked like the caricature they call 'Daisy' with soft drooping ears, a thin face which broadened at the nose, big brown eyes with long eyelashes and prominent hip bones.

'Bet he'll run away in a minute, especially when he catches sight off me,' I said.

'I don't think so; he's protecting his women.'

I climbed through the long wet grass up to the fence and shouted suddenly, clapping my hands and waving my arms. But the bull stood his ground, watching me with some amusement. David climbed out of the Wombat and stood beside me.

'He'd run if he was being chased,' I said. It had turned into a matter of pride to get the animal to move.

'Bet you he wouldn't.'

'Prove it.'

'Watch this!' He tried to climb the fence but couldn't. It was barbed and high and the posts wobbled wildly with the weight of only one leg. The bull stood unperturbed in the field.

After Lancefield I turned left with the road and at a junction, decided on the route which would avoid most of the main highway to Ballaraat. Besides, this road seemed the 'natural' route as if I was meant to walk it. I walked alone for a while feeling the cold wind whipping my pony-tail and stoking my face to a rosy glow. My posture for the previous twenty days had been one of compromise; listing towards whichever part of my legs and feet hurt least. Therefore my lower back had curved inwards, pushing out my tummy to balance my gait. An observant ten-year-old girl, lacking social tact, had exclaimed that I walked like a 'duck with a backache'. The description was embarrassingly accurate.

The land reminded me of the Yorkshire moors, undulating and bleak. The tufty grass stood sturdy in the wind, and the evergreens grew tall in the sheltered hollows. My horizons were short. I felt high above the sea and to the regular beat of my footfalls the Road God of Daydreams filled my heart with visions. After a while I realised that all I wanted to do for the rest of my life, was to walk quietly around a chair and sit down on it.

I spied a curious hill almost completely covered with jagged boulders, black except where vegetation peeped between the crags. Hanging Rock. Mysteries surround it, not least the disappearance without trace of three Australian schoolgirls and a teacher in the early 1900s. Months later when we drove the Wombat back to Sydney, following my footsteps in reverse, David took a wrong turn and became confused at the junction of five farm roads near the Rock. I confidently directed him through the maze of country lanes until he recognised the way. I swore I had walked the route for I directed him from memory but a glance at the map showed that I had not been that way before.

In the fourth quarter David drove ahead to buy provisions and left me feeling confident and at ease in the drizzle and fading light. The grey cloud grew darker but I was merry in my rhythm, passing through Woodend, out over a railway bridge and into the country. Twilight was my time of day; it made me feel as if I was walking faster, walking taller, which was why I always wore dark glasses during the day. But in the evening I would take them off to feel the biting wind in my eyes. The horizons came and went and, as night set in, David pulled up beside me and grinned.

'Just look what I've got!' He picked up a brown paper bag and handed it to me.

'What is it?'

I lowered the bag to eye level but as I did so the bottom ripped and out plopped a dozen eggs and smashed on the road. We looked at each other helplessly, tears streaming down our faces. Any eye contact brought uncontrollable bouts of hysteria. Eventually he blurted out that a woman in the general store had heard I was coming and had put them aside. 'She must have her eggs,' she had warned, 'and mind she eats them and not you!' I hate eggs.

Darkness brought heavy rain. My rain jacket offered only psychological protection and when it got too much I told David to go ahead to the end of the quarter so that I could stamp through the misery without watching him, warm and dry in the Wombat.

The road was uneven and my torch very dim. The thick clouds obscured any light from the heavens and they felt heavy and claustrophobic about me. The rain fell in sheets which lit up like silver threads in the headlights of approaching cars, kicking up arcs of water as they passed. I saw only a semi-circle of the immediate road around me, and was blinded when the cars had gone, left to stumble and splash heavily in the puddles. Up hills and around corners searching the horizon for the tiny speck of light, a light so warm in the misery of the cold night.

I thought of the cold nights in Scotland when I was walking home the two miles from the school bus. Walking on that long road in the dark and the snow I would see the light of the kitchen window in the distance. I knew I was walking towards warmth and a kind of safety, but I also knew the anguish I would find there. I thought then about walking and felt that if the journey home was long enough, by the time I reached the kitchen light all the problems would be solved. I was still walking home, the longest journey in the world, staring at the light getting bigger and bigger. The Wombat would offer the same as my home – food and warmth but not affection – and I knew that in a short while I would be out again alone, facing the cold.

I sloshed inside, squinting in the light.

'Hullo.'

'Bit cold?'

'Bit bloody wet. Turn round.' I peeled off the layers of sodden clothing which stuck to my skin and tried to dry myself but I was tired and the rain seemed to have soaked into my body too deeply to dry with a towel. I cuddled myself in semi-dry clothes and shivered a little. I looked forlornly at the river of rain that streamed down the windows and ate hot soup. I was tired, but I had to go out again and endure the night for another two and a half hours. I just didn't want to go. It seemed so futile to walk just for the sake of covering distances, not going anywhere except some nebulous bit of road when the clock said it was time to stop. I was cold, wet, miserable and in pain but I wasn't doing anything useful with it like fighting a war for my country, or saving someone's life. Pathetic bloody journey. My eyelids drifted down, but my mother's voice mumbled in my head, 'Come on, Lovey, just one last ditch effort.'

Oh, but every time I get up from this damn sofa it's one last ditch effort. I sank the last of my soup, peering over the rim of the mug at the black storm outside and said to David, 'To go out again is what it's really about.'

'You're so full of shit.'

I pressed my hands on to my knees and pushed myself into a standing position, which because of the cold and damp was more like sitting in mid air, slid back the door and stepped out into a puddle. I stormed off, leaning hard against the thick tide of night.

David pulled up and sheltered me a little from the rain which came from the northwest. But as the road curved to the left the rain shot into his window and he had to roll it up. I moved to the front, away from the sound of music where it played in the warmth.

I was plodding, just covering ground. I longed for it to end but strangely enough I didn't want to call it a day. I didn't want to sip hot tea and eat biscuits – it would be like smoking half a cigarette and forgetting where you had put it down. But I didn't want to be out there either.

Car beams on the other side of the road slowed to a halt, windscreen wipers beating back the silver shafts of rain. I couldn't turn my head to tell them we hadn't broken down without the rain gushing in, so I continued and left it to David. He honked loudly. Then I saw the reason. Splashing across the black wet road without waterproof clothing, eyes squeezed shut and arm held high above the splashes, a little boy came towards me with pen and paper.

'Can I have your autograph?' I opened the passenger door of the Wombat and, using the seat as a table, I wrote with numb fingers the message I had looked for as a child; 'Have faith in yourself to follow your dreams.' I signed it. David was saying something about him being the son of the egg woman.

I turned back to the road. I hadn't spoken to either of them – I couldn't let myself. The splash from a passing car was just another drenching. Small stones lodged in my shoes and I flicked them out by bending back the sole but as I did so, mud flipped up and splattered my legs. Water bubbled out of the lace holes. My shorts rubbed between my buttocks and mucus dribbled from my nose. I constantly reached with my free hand to wipe it away, licking my lips spontaneously against the drips I missed. With head down I watched my feet and thighs pushing onwards. Every hour I glanced at my watch to find the hands had moved only a few minutes.

A car drew up beside me. I didn't look but just said, 'I'm fine, we haven't broken down.'

A voice sounded over the squeak-rub-squeak of unoiled wipers. 'You're that girl who's walking round the world, aren't you?'

'Yes.' I turned my head. Five boys were leaning across each other to look at me.

'You've got very big legs.'

I stumbled along, unsure of whether I was cross at the comment or glad of the distraction. I was breathing heavily against the hill.

'D'you want some beer?'

'Yes.'

They handed me a bottle and I drank a little. It only took a few moments for the anaesthetic to reach my knees so I handed it back.

''kyou, Can't speak prop'ly. Chin's numb.'

'We've got a chicken in the oven, you can come back to our place and get warmed up.'

'But I'm walking.'

'When d'you finish?' I looked at my watch – silly really, I already knew the time.

'Forty-five minutes.'

'You coming then? There's more beer.'

'Very kind. But I've been on the road for fifteen hours today, I just want to sleep.'

'Fifteen hours! You must be fit!'

'No, just British.'

They laughed and, somehow, so did I.

As their tail lights sped away, I felt my tiredness increasing. I wanted to get the day over with and I knew I could do it more easily if the Wombat were not groaning behind me. I slowed to the window.

'Can you go ahead to the end please?' I blurted out, almost delirious with fatigue.

'What did those boys say?' he said, laughing and eager.

'I'm cold and tired and very wet so just hand me the torch and let's get on with it.'

He passed it to me and, looking dead ahead, roared off, splashing me with mud.

I reached a junction and did not know which way to turn. The main road seemed to be to the left. David should have parked there to give me directions, but he hadn't. Following the main road I walked on into the night, cursing him for any reason I could think of, counting down the minutes, cursing him more when the time of ending was passed.

After an hour he pulled up.

'You're going the wrong way.'

'Where the bloody hell were you?'

'I didn't notice another road.'

We measured the distance back to the junction and drove in cold silence back up the right road where we marked the same distance with white spray-paint on the tarmac. The day, thank God, was over.

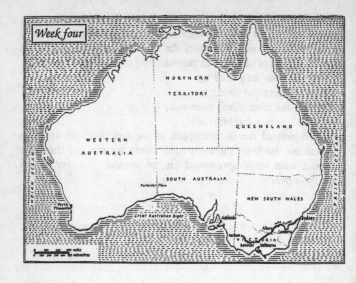

Day 22

The cold lino was muddy as David got out of bed to mix the muesli.
I sat up, fully clothed, bleary-eyed, hair matted and damp. I pulled
the duvet around me and pushed my feet through the covers to
inspect the damage: a new blister lay under my heel, too deep to
syringe; the skin was getting tougher there and it throbbed under
the pressure.

Few words were exchanged in the mornings. I had soon learnt
not to say the first thing that came to mind because David did
not like mornings either, somehow twisting what I said to take
offence. When days became almost unbearable out in the hot
screaming deserts, I would wake up and smile – not because I
was happy, but because it worked. A policeman in Venice had
taught me that as he kicked me awake from the pavement where
I slept.

I squeezed into an old pair of Reeboks. They were too small and my feet felt as if they were bound with bandages to stop them from growing. I put on three sweatshirts and rubbed my hands together. It was miserable and cold inside the Wombat and outside didn't look much better. But at least I might warm up as I walked.

'See you in a bit.'

'Bits are for horses.'

'Whenever you're ready, honey,' I said softly, trying to ease his tone.

'Don't call me honey. It's degrading.'

I left the Wombat feeling put down.

My clothes were so thick they pushed my arms out to the side like the small children one sees, dressed in oversized duffel coats, standing with the Lollypop Lady on cold winter mornings. Although I loathed the shock of another day, I thrived on the quiet of 5.30 a.m. before the people came out, when the birds and animals stretched themselves into life. There were few gums on the high plains and the bell bird did not bleep but kookaburras, taking the first deep breath of the day, laughed in the evergreens like jackasses, and galahs and crows fired their ricocheting squarks on the wing. Galahs cannot fly well, least of all in the morning, and they constitute 80 per cent of the dead birds on the road.

Though my feet had grown two sizes during the walk in shoes that were now too small, we often referred to that weekend, bypassing Melbourne, as the halcyon days of the walk. It was a time when we had thoughts to share. We also didn't know each other well enough to argue seriously. Debate became a favourite game. We'd pick a subject, usually sparked off by one of my 'sweeping statements' as David called them. I would make up things as I went along until I had totally contradicted myself.

David drove ahead to the second break to make lunch and I ambled on alone in the countryside, sometimes humming to myself, sometimes reciting poetry. By that time I had learnt exactly how far each piece would take me. If I recited all the Shakespeare I knew, I had covered 1.5 kilometres, but if I recited poetry as well I had covered 3.5. Odds and ends of prose might keep me going for up to six kilometres. Some I would repeat over and over again: 'The Jabberwocky', Kipling's 'If', 'Desiderata',

'The Whispering Waves of Mizzunoe' and 'The Suicide' by Louis MacNeice.

One of my favourites was from *Twelfth Night* in which Viola, using her own words, proclaims Orsino's love for Olivia.

> Make me a willow cabin at your gate,
> And call upon my soul within the house;
> Write loyal cantons of contemned love
> And sing them loud even in the dead of night;
> Halloo your name to the reverberate hills,
> And make the babbling gossip of the air
> Cry out, 'Olivia!' O, you should not rest
> Between the elements of air and earth
> But you should pity me!

Day 23

I walked through Ballaraat and noticed the inconsistency of the spelling. The new signs read 'Ballarat', but the one I always took my information from was the stone marker at the centre of town from which all distances to a town are measured. It was carved with the letters 'Ballaraat.'

No matter how people debated the spelling, nobody could dispute the beauty of Ballaraat: old stone buildings, azaleas and chrysanthemums in baskets, banks of spring flowers bordering grassy commons and a gargoyled stone archway carved with the words 'Memorial Boulevard'. The road beyond lay arrow straight and was lined on both sides with seventy-year-old trees standing to attention at regimented intervals. At the foot of each was a plaque for every soldier from the county lost in the First World War. I was moved by the trees, straight and strong, growing in memory of those who had fallen.

For five kilometres I walked in the shade of the graveyard, calling out the names of the men, until I noticed a plaque which had fallen upside-down. I read the name: Campbell. For a moment I stood not knowing whether to interfere. Gingerly, I took hold of a corner. It was wedged firmly between the tree and the stump on which it once stood. I tightened my grip and pulled harder. Suddenly it came free. From behind it a bulbous black spider the size of my hand leapt out and ran up my arm and I dropped the plaque in startled surprise. It seemed a bad omen. I stepped back to regain my composure and saluted the tree. 'Forgive me,' I whispered, 'I meant no harm.'

The trees ended and gave way to flat green paddocks that stretched out on both sides. The winds tore across the plains and pushed me over to the right. I was tricked into leaning against the winds until they dropped and I stumbled. When the trucks passed, they hauled me along in their tail wind. I was being manipulated, like a puppet in the air.

The Wombat appeared and I was grateful for it. The soles of my Reeboks had been compressed to the thickness of paper. David had tried to get me a pair in Ballaraat but the sales assistant in the sports shop had said, quite wrongly, that Reebok had discontinued the line. Anyone who denied me shoes I knew I could walk in was described in language only fit for scribbling on the wall of a gentlemen's lavatory in a whore house.

We discovered my feet were two sizes larger than they were at the beginning of the walk. This usually happened when wearing Reebok because the soft leather of their Freestyle High-Tops allows the feet to expand to their most comfortable width for efficient balance.

The choice of Reebok had evolved from thousands of kilometres of trial and error which began with a pair of Karimor KSB Asolo Sport boots. These had been donated by Karimor at the recommendation of John Hillaby who was instrumental in my training for the Trans-Britain Walk. Hillaby avoids walking on roads, he prefers the hills and country paths (a piece of advice I foolishly opted not to take in favour of the as-the-crow-flies speed of roads) and so his boots are designed for cross country terrain. For my fairly 'green' sixteen-year-old frame, the Karimor boots proved too heavy and I changed to a lightweight pair of cheap running shoes which I carried on the walk as a back-up.

After 400 kilometres I began suffering from what a local doctor diagnosed as 'haemorhaging on the tibia' caused by the shoe's tongue hitting against the lower part of the bone. High-tops, he advised, would prevent this. For the remainder of that first walk I used Lonsdale boxing boots which reach mid-tibia and are cut down at the back for calf movement. But these boots do not provide much shock absorption resulting in painful knees; and the crease they make at the heel when the foot bends backwards, cuts into the Achilles tendon.

During the first half of the Trans-America Walk I wore Nike 'court' boots simply because Nike were the only manufacturer willing to donate footwear. 'Courts', as the name suggests, are not designed for long distance walking but they were the only high-tops in the range at the time. The leather was thick and the space above my toes was shallow. Having lost a few toenails from the pressing down of the toe cap, I took the advice of a shoe salesman at a press conference in Tulsa, Oklahoma, to wear Reebok.

The Freestyle High-Tops seemed the answer to my problems: they were high-topped to prevent tibia haemorhaging; they were padded enough on the soles to give shock absorbtion; and the leather was lightweight and pliable – there was no need for 'breaking in'.

Even though the shin splints I suffered near Canberra were largely due to lack of comprehensive shock absorbtion for mountainous terrain, I was adamant that Reebok were more comfortable than any other shoe. And having reached that decision after five different makes of shoe (including a hundred kilometres of Puma in America), I wasn't going to give in to the second best very easily. Shoes are a very personal thing. I stubbornly *believed* in the Reeboks and nothing else. It was this attitude and the changing widths of my feet that sadly made it virtually impossible for me to walk in the shoes Adidas had provided. However, I do know of at least one other person who crossed Australia very comfortably in them. Unfortunately I had been unable to persuade Reebok to sponsor me.

We finished our soup and laughed a little as we tidied up, but the laughter soon subsided, at least from me, when a car pulled up and David said, 'It's a television crew.'

'Oh God.'

'Please be good.'

'I'll have to wear the Adidas.'

He stepped outside. 'Hi!'

I grimaced in the Wombat.

'This is Ffyona.' They looked around the door.

'Hullo.'

'Hi! How are your feet?'

'Fine,' I said through gritted teeth. 'Thank you.'

Looking back, I know I should have been a bit more accommodating to these guys, who were after all trying to make sure that David and the Wombat were not my only audience.

'We heard you'd got some blisters!'

'It's OK. They only hurt when I walk.' I didn't echo their laugher. 'Where are you from?'

'Wide World of Sports.'

It was Channel 7's top rated network sports show.

'Oh?' I looked blank. 'What's that?'

David shot me a withering look, and I knew he was right to, but I also knew that I wasn't going to be able to maintain a cocktail party atmosphere whilst my feet were on fire. I scowled into my cup of tea as they arranged their equipment outside and chatted to David. I thought about my father. On this occasion the coveted Green Beret would definitely not have been on offer.

David's head appeared round the door of the Wombat. 'They want to stay with us until tomorrow morning.'

My sharp intake of breath was not the reaction he wanted.

'Look, Ffyona, I've worked my butt off to set this up . . .'

I felt as ridiculous as one of those old Hollywood stars who refuse to come out of their trailer for the next scene, but I couldn't shake myself out of it.

David turned his back on me and did his interview. The wind was too strong for me to hear it, except for one question whose answer finally brought a smile to my face.

'Are you proud of her?'

'Of course I am!'

It was so unforced and spontaneous. Perhaps this man did have what it took to keep me going in the weeks ahead. Perhaps he understood how his mere presence acted as a focus for my insecurities and aspirations. I went out to talk to them while David prepared the Wombat and as soon as my interview was finished I laced up the Adidas shoes. We just weren't suited to each other. They might be fine for others but on my feet they were like thumb-screws.

I set off, pressing each sole firmly down on the asphalt to disguise my limp. The shoes rubbed my blisters raw. Twice a second they sliced into my heels like a cheese grater. With the cameras running, I tried not to wince, and when David finally drew up alongside I tried to distract myself from the pain by telling him about my interview, how I had explained his role, how the walk was definitely not a one woman show any more. I grinned at him, though every nerve-end was screaming; it was a team effort.

'You make it sound like we're having an affair.'

'You should be so lucky,' I returned smartly, but it hurt. He drove ahead with the TV crew before I could say anything. I yelled at the night, ripped off the shoes and smashed them to the ground. I tried to walk barefoot, but my shins jarred with each step. I clamped them back on, wondering how long I could keep this up. As I started to walk once more a car pulled alongside. A greasy, tattooed hippy leaned out of the window, leering at my bottom.

'You want a ride, lady?'

'Fuck off . . .'

I hated David then. Hated everybody that might see me and think she's not going to make it. Hated knowing that the more they thought it, the more I was afraid of it myself. Never again. Never again, never again, never again. The words became a chant, in time with the squelching of the blisters. I only kept going by losing myself in a world of self-pity.

When I got to the Wombat, I couldn't release my emotions because the crew were there, jovial, asking questions. I couldn't even smoke a cigarette.

I couldn't stand all of them around me, hammering into me, big faces coming closer, camera zooming into my shoes, throbbing, bleeding, burning feet. I wanted to scream, rip the skin from my face. What more did they want of me? I tore off my shoes. 'There!'

They drew back.

I hobbled out into the safety of the night where my face could not be monitored. I sucked my lower lip into my mouth and bit hard, against the new blisters. David drove behind me. The crew went ahead to set up somewhere in the distance. I stumbled on into the night, kicking at stones.

The light behind me shone on a kookaburra sitting on the hard shoulder, its eyes were closed. I was about to take a good kick at it when I realised it was alive. I stopped. The bird was stunned and in shock. Its left eyelid lifted a little. David got out and gently picked it up. It made no objection. He tried to put it on a tree stump off the road, out of the way of other animals. But it couldn't stand. He wrapped it tenderly in a sweatshirt and cuddled it on to his lap. He could do that for a bird – why not me? But his tenderness with this frightened creature caused my anger to abate.

The crew were waiting at Beaufort. We must have looked strange to the local people: a car with rear door raised and a cameraman perched in the back, a limping walker and a van trailing a motorbike with a kookaburra sitting on the dashboard.

I walked up a hill. The camera was directly in front of me and I breathed hard against the steep incline, inhaling their exhaust fumes. When I slowed, they slowed, and when I moved to the side of the Wombat, they objected and David pushed me away with biting words.

Eventually they left and I danced inside with relief. But the strain had taken its toll. I walked on for as far as I could until a campground sloped down to the right.

'We'll stop here.'

'Let's push on, Fee.'

He obviously had no idea what was going on.

'No.'

I climbed into the Wombat when it stopped under the trees and fell on to the sofa, breathing heavily. I lay down and my feet throbbed. The kookaburra tried to move – David was at its side.

Day 24

Long road, sharp spinifex, blue bush and ghost gum, dead lizards, ants in my pants where I squatted, ants in my shoes where I trod, wind in everything. As I approached the Wombat for the first break, the anterial tibial muscles began to split away from my left shin bone. David greeted me with news of our kookaburra's first flight.

'It wasn't very successful. He flew up to a tree where he sat quite happily until two other kookaburras swooped down and knocked him to the ground.' He was now sleeping on a shit stained sweatshirt.

I tapped my toes in silence and reached for the painkillers. As a rule I steer clear of drugs for two reasons: if the pain is numbed I will be oblivious to additional damage and because I might become immune to the drugs' effect if I take them too often. This time, though, I was sick of being in pain.

The town of Ararat passed, nodding heads of palm. Life slid by beside me, out of focus on the verge. I was aware only of throbbing the same beat, touching the same sky, being drawn to the same horizons as the white line and the sun. My senses slept as I covered distances I knew I mustn't acknowledge.

At the second break I dozed a troubled, thirty-minute sleep and was awoken by a swallow lying unconscious on my pillow. I laid him in the grass where the wind nudged and breathed life into him and the sun warmed him on the wing as he flew away.

A van pulled up. 'We've got company,' said David. Shoo them away, thought I.

'Hi! You the girl that's walking around Australia?'

I peered out at the intruder, he needed an answer. I thought for a while. 'Something like that, yes.'

'I read about you in *The Sun*. How ya feet?'

Moments passed. The question whirred a little. 'Getting better. Thank you.'

'I suppose you must be raising money for a charity?'

A person eager to give. Another answer needed. 'Care Australia under the banner of Sport Aid '88.'

'Never heard of it, but I'll believe you, millions wouldn't.' I shot him a filthy look. How dare anyone doubt it? In that vulnerable state I saw everything as accusing; I couldn't see he was joking.

'I've seen you a couple of times back there on the road. I drive a van along this stretch and I thought you might want some food. Save me giving a donation anyway.'

It never ceased to amaze me how people could believe my overheads were paid for out of the money for charity. Gifts to me did no good. But I wrestled with his kindness at stopping and knew that no matter how I explained it, offence would be taken. It was ridiculous that I had to succumb to accepting his gifts, but that's how it was.

I struggled to my feet and limped to his van. He gave us three packets of wholemeal pitta bread, two kinds of cheese in wholesale packets, frankfurters, bacon, ham, pate and two tubs of yoghurt which I devoured straight away. We never ate meat unless we ate out, but this man didn't know that. We could hardly turn down what he so willingly gave. He tried to get us to stay the night with him after the day's walk, but I hurriedly explained that we liked to camp near the road to set off as early as possible in the morning. I couldn't face making small talk after a long day.

This incident took me back to America, to another time when a van pulled up to offer food – walks repeat themselves.

I had been walking on through a straight, flat, cornfield-lined road with little of interest except a dark blob on the horizon. It didn't seem to be coming towards me, just sitting on my side of the road. As I walked closer I saw it to be a man. He had no legs.

Bob Wieland had fought in Vietnam and had lost his legs in a booby trap. He was sickened by the poverty he saw there and swore that one day he would return to help. After considerable training on his upper body, he set off on an incredible journey. Bob Wieland 'walked' across America. He began from California in 1982 and reached Washington DC in mid 1986. With thick leather pads on bottom and knuckles, he swung his body forward with arms the size of small tree trunks that substituted for legs. He was so low on the ground that all he breathed was exhaust fumes. As we talked, a van pulled up, carrying cakes and biscuits. Bob didn't eat sugar, but my back-up driver and I loaded up from the back of the van with food which carried a shelf-life of seventy-five years.

Before shaking his hand goodbye, I had to ask Bob where his courage came from.

'From God,' he said.

Day 25

Tucked away in the bush on a small mound of higher land was a group of smooth sandstone monoliths twice the height of a double-decker bus. I stopped. Sisters Rocks must have been an Aboriginal religious site but the invisible words of their songs, sacred for 40,000 years, were now replaced. The holy giants stood, raped of their beauty, adorned with words of infatuation in streaks of fluorescent green, purple and orange.

The wet wind spun the dead leaves on invisible waves. I stepped between them, avoiding their touch. It was harvest and the trucks carried more sheep, splattering me with urine as they passed. I would have to carry the stench with me for the rest of the week; showering took precious time away from sleeping and walking, so we generally washed once a week on the day of rest.

At least I knew I smelt bad; there had been a time when I was oblivious to it. When I was six I had never had a bath alone. My father had usually been there at some point during the proceedings and my sister and I would hide our tiny nipples behind wet flannels, shyly answering the arithmetical questions which he wrote with soap on the steamed up mirror. Mother would be there to wash our hair and hug us in towels as we stepped out. But all that was gone when I went to boarding school. For seven weeks I didn't have a bath, because I didn't know how to do it and because the nuns didn't mention it. I thought the reason my sister wouldn't play with me was because I'd done something to upset her so I begged sweets from the day girls and solemnly carried them in sweaty palms to offer her as reconciliation. She took the sweets but she wouldn't answer my tugs at her sleeve and I wandered away to my playmates who didn't seem to notice the smell, perhaps because they hadn't washed either.

A police car pulled up. It was going in the opposite direction. The man in the passenger seat rolled down the window. I had to stop.

'Where ya goin'?'

'Perth.'

'Path?'

'Perth.'

Looking at my lips while I repeated the word, his mouth struggled to mirror the movement.

'P . . . p . . . path?'

'No, *Perth*. Oh for God's sake! It's on the Indian Ocean.'

'Aw, Purrth. You on a Bicentennial project?'

'No. I'm walking around the world.'

The policemen looked at each other, a look of 'we've got a right one here Bru' on their faces.

'Where's your luggage?'

'I don't carry any.' Trying to stir them into taking me down to the depot as a runaway.

'Aw yeah.' The driver nudged his colleague, leaning forward to look at me. 'I heard about that, something in the paper. You're walking around Australia.'

'Across Australia. Around the world.'

'You're two days late.'

I glared and walked on.

I saw the Wombat parked in a layby, next to a twelve-metre koala. Its head was sitting on the ground and a sculptor was busy with a pot of foul smelling glue, daubing on tufts of fibre glass for ears. We ate at the café and headed off.

Bursts of rain sent David scrambling over the seat into the back to retrieve my coat while I leant inside and steered. Under the grey opaque clouds the drizzle whipped around in the wind. Often when David and I were miserable or bored we would take the advice of Maria von Trapp and talk of our favourite things.

'What d'you like?' I ventured shyly.

'I like waking up when it's cold outside and snuggling deeper into the covers, pulling them around me and knowing I'm warm and it's snowing outside.'

'But then you've got to haul yourself out to go to school.'

'To work,' he corrected.

Why did I say that? A memory was trying to push through, triggered by something dark and cold. I wrestled with it, concentrating, looking down at the road, at my feet. But it had gone and I felt strangely vulnerable.

'How many kilometres have I done?' He peered down at the mileometer and his lips moved silently in calculation.

'Eight.'

'Oh hell. Go ahead will you, I want to be by myself.'

When he went, the invisible wall of wind grew stronger. I forced myself into a trance by focusing my eyes on the horizon with my head held high and steady and left my body to walk. The feeling was total forward motion – pure confidence. To look directly ahead and feel my hips sway from side to side, my feet pass each other very close and my legs straighten when the foot was on the ground, shoulders down, arms swinging evenly, felt sensual and self-assured. It amused me that walking in a trance aroused me as nothing else ever had. I laughed at myself, brimming with want. I ached for relief as I had ached for the trance.

Day 26

A Day of Rest.

I got into bed, wrote my diary and turned out the light. All through the night my sleep was broken by the sound of David sleeping. I would doze and wake again to find the bedclothes were soaked with sweat around my neck. Sweating had become an exhaustingly uncomfortable means of expelling toxins and there was nothing I could do to prevent it.

We had decided that I could not reach the daily target of eighty kilometres because my feet would be deprived of air for an extra two and a half hours and already they were rotting. I would walk seventy kilometres a day. This meant that I would break the record only by a few days. But this didn't trouble me. I was not going to risk permanent damage for a record.

All the adventurers I have met have had some source of drive outside themselves: some had the drive for money, some for fame. I seemed to be walking to find out whether my drive was internal and if so, what on earth it was that drove me. But pain was refusing me that journey, rendering the walk futile.

We rode into Horsham on the motorbike for a complimentary appointment with a member of the Australian Chiropractic Association, my favourite sponsor. He massaged my neck, shoulders and lower back and placed pads underneath me to increase my magnetic field. My buttocks were kneaded to relax and stretch them while my shins rested on an ultrasound machine to repair the damage of muscle ripping from the tibia bone.

Again a doctor tried to syringe my blisters. This time it was worse. The needle missed the well completely and sank deep into the inflamed tissue. An hour later I apologised to the doctor's ten-year-old son who was waiting in the surgery office with his hands clamped firmly over his ears.

Back at the campground with a bottle of apple juice and a handful of chicken wings, we began a serious attempt to make each other laugh while eating. David came up with a new noise to make me spit out my food.

'When really cheap comedians make some dumb joke on stage the band emphasises it on the drums and cymbals by going "brrrrum, tish!"' He made the movements with his hands and I collapsed, shrieking.

I was longing to drink, and settled myself on the bed with a plastic cup of apple juice. I looked at him over the rim.

'Don't make me laugh, please don't make me laugh. I'm thirsty.' It was an invitation. I took a gulp.

'Brrrrum, tish!' I blurted out a laugh but hadn't quite swallowed and choked, gagging with apple juice and spitting saliva. I gasped for air, heaving.

'Relax, Fee, just relax. It's OK.' No air was coming. I tried to relax, but apple juice was blocking my lungs. At last I breathed in, and juice and saliva dribbled down my face with tears. He was laughing.

'You fucking idiot, I told you not to make me laugh.'

'What d'you call a man with no arms and legs in the sea?'

'What?'

'Bob. Brrrrum, tish!'

'What do you call a . . .' and on and on until, with aching stomach muscles and tear-stained faces, we collapsed into bed.

Day 27

Droplets of dew traced the traps of spiders from fence posts to grasses. The white line detached itself from the fog wall to hug the bitumen, glistening with frost. Mallee thickets melted into the yellow sand where gum leaves stirred and grew in the grey of the dawn.

I stretched as I stepped out into the cloud with eyelids squeezed tightly shut, the whirring noise of a yawn in my ears and a pulse of energy in my thighs from the day of rest. I felt fit.

I broke our morning silence.

'Why don't you grow a beard?'

'You've asked me that before. Why d'you bother to ask questions if you don't listen to the answers?' Oops. Too early for conversation.

Despite twenty-seven days of living together, I still didn't know David. I found his silence intimidating and this contributed to the power struggle we were oh so subtly conducting. And nor did he know who I was since I was forever borrowing pieces of myself from former personalities to deal with boredom, relief, tenderness and stubbornness, emotions which, due to pain or the weather or a passing car, would erupt suddenly and then fall away to make room for another. My dependence on him made me feel frighteningly vulnerable so I bitched at him even harder to convince him that I was invincible. It probably had the opposite effect and encouraged him to lose respect for me. But despite all the circumstances, I was often guilty of baiting him simply because I felt downright bloody-minded.

I began to stretch my stride in the dawn, savouring the first few hours of the new week before blisters and shins and hips began to complain. I had gone barefoot around the campground yesterday so now my feet felt comfortable and thickly cushioned against the old bitumen. Heavy trucks had split the edges into pot holes where small stones had broken from the highway and crumbled into the earth from which they had once come. I glided over the land, the scars of the road kissing my own.

The sun burned away the fog and a wind crept up from the north. Iceberg clouds rose from the west and sailed eastwards. The four corners of the world above were in motion and made me feel dizzy.

I removed the last measure of progress – my watch – so that the Road God of Daydreams was in his element. Together, we flew past fields of sugar cane and pineapple, the sun strong and yellow in the bright blue sky. We were clean, tanned and fit, dressed in white, my hair caught in a Hermes scarf at the nape of my neck. We laughed and sang. I was relaxed in the white leather driving seat. The hood was down, the wind was fresh, light bounced off the white bonnet of the Mercedes Sports: the world was ours.

The Road Devil of Thirst drove me back to the road. My mouth was dry and my skin sticky with sweat. I licked my lips but when no saliva came, I picked up a small pebble and sucked on it until the juices returned. My eyelids felt like sandpaper, forced open just enough to catch a glimpse of bitumen running on over horizons I could not see. I bent my head to shelter my eyes just in time to sidestep a geriatric snake dozing on the hard shoulder.

The Wombat pulled up and parked in the open land; there were no trees for shade and temperatures were higher than an English heatwave.

'I bought some eye drops.' David took the bottle from its wrapper and handed it to me. I put my head back and tried lamely to administer a few drops but my eyes closed and they rolled down my face.

'Let me do it,' he said gently and squeezed the bottle. The drops hit their mark and bit. I drank water, a little at a time, and was silent, staring at nothing.

'What's wrong?'

'It's hard out there,' I whispered.

'I know what it's like, you know.' He always thought I was provoking him, but if he *had* ever known what it was like, I suspected he had forgotten, for he rarely offered a word of praise.

I rubbed my left shin with Deflam cream to keep the inflammation down and 'liquid fire' cream to increase the blood supply. Only a tiny amount of the latter was applied because it burned the skin bright red within minutes and beads of sweat would puncture the surface.

'How is it?'

'Bearable.'

'And the blisters?'

'I'd rather not look. But the Second Skin seems to be helping.' It was a product recommended by the chiropractor in Horsham to reduce rubbing by acting like a layer of new skin which breathes and heals the wound.

If I had ever stopped to think of all the places where my body hurt, damage which made the return of perfect walking impossible, it is doubtful that I would have remained confident about finishing. But out there, away from the monitors, I kept going. There *had to be* something internal driving me, but I was too wrapped up in dealing with each step to look for it; perhaps if I had I would have doubted it too much to continue.

Then there was that moment of knowing I had to stand up, bend to reach for the door and take the first awkward step out on to the ground. It was enough to stall me – I'd ask for another cup of tea, light another cigarette, point out another blister. But always the road was waiting for me.

Day 28

A garish green Kombi van slowed and stopped up ahead. My face was screwed up as I turned my head against the downpour to say I was fine. But two obese women in tracksuits clambered out. Oh God, I thought, they want to walk with me. They crossed the road unsure of where to look as I fixed my stare on them defensively.

'Have you come from a foreign country to walk around Australia?' I wondered if obesity effects the brain.

'I'm from England and I'm walking across Australia, around the world.'

'D'you mind if we walk with you for a couple of kilometres?'

'It's extremely hard work and if you don't mind I'd rather endure it alone.'

'D'you want a banana?'

'Yes.'

They returned to the Kombi and drove off.

A microclimate of thought surrounds a solitary endurer, a cocoon like an isolation chamber woven from many hours of concentration. But it is easily shattered by pain from a dislodged blister, or a yelled enquiry from a concerned motorist. I often repaid their kindess for stopping with a blunt retort. They would drive away feeling insulted and I would stumble on in self-conflict. On one hand feeling extremely guilty and on the other thinking they had no right to treat me as public property to be probed at with questions. Australians bore the brunt of this treatment because that walk was by far the most painful and because more people stopped in Australia than in America and Britain.

In Britain motorists tended to stare, perhaps because we are reserved by nature and don't like to get involved. The Americans asked me so often if I'd broken down that I had some leaflets printed which explained the walk and the charity. I recall handing one to a woman in her car who promptly screamed at her husband that it was a bomb and wound up her window. I didn't know what to expect from anyone who stopped and similarly they didn't know what to expect from me.

David returned with a dictionary and handed me my rain jacket. We were both becoming aware that our vocabulary was shrinking from solitude and our most common adjective, 'fucking', was losing its punch. Boredom and the greyness of the day encouraged us to play a game while I trotted beside the Wombat.

'I'll read out a word and you've got to give me the meaning.

OK? We'll start from A.' He settled himself deeper into the woollen driver's seat, resting one foot on the dashboard with elbow on his knee. He cleared his throat.

'Aardvark.'

Each time I gave the wrong meaning, I would take the dictionary and ask him the next word. He once caught me cheating; I had read the meaning of the next word before passing the dictionary over to him.

'Ffyona, I could have done that too, but I didn't. We're trying to play a game here. If you don't want to improve your vocabulary, fine, but don't come complaining to me at the end of the walk when you can't talk. Right, new game. D'you know how to play "Dictionary"?' he asked.

'No.'

'D'you want to know?'

'Yes, please.'

'I'll read a word and then give you three different meanings. You've got to pick the right one. The word is BOHUNK. The meanings are . . .' thumbing through a few pages, 'an Aboriginal hunting spear. Or a native of East Central Europe. Or a starchy tuber.'

'An Aboriginal hunting spear.'

'Wrong. A native of East Central Europe.'

'Where the hell is East Central Europe when it's at home?'

We stopped for a break after another hour or so and the game continued as we slurped our pasta. Speaking through mouthfuls, we tried not to blast food when we laughed. David had been on a winning streak, I just couldn't catch him out. I leant forward again to flip through the pages and turned around unexpectedly to find him peering over my shoulder. He was caught! An embarrassed, yet amused expression on his face.

'I'm sorry! I can't get out of this, can I?'

'No, and you get the Plonker Award of the Day!'

A cyclist was coming towards us with a back-up van speeding behind. He had a good tailwind. The sign on the van told of a Scouts relay race from Adelaide to Melbourne so we cheered him on loudly over the rain. Startled, he wobbled violently and nearly fell off. Each cyclist that passed us received the same encouragement. They were far from evenly matched, passing us every twenty minutes to two hours.

David drove ahead for the next break, seven kilometres away. Time for flights of fantasy which drifted me in and out of a tumbledown jungle house on a Queensland beach. But it was too removed from the wet, drizzly day, so I changed the subject, preferring instead to sing 'Plodding Australia', my adaptation of 'Waltzing Matilda,'

Another cyclist broke the horizon, very close to the kerb. I watched him come. Lean and muscular, pedalling furiously, head down. Aerodynamic. I cheered, and he stretched out his arm.

'Touch my hand!' he shouted. I reached up and brushed his fingers for a split second. The energy transferred was incredible. The back-up van approached and over the PA the driver shouted, 'Come on, my darling! Don't stop walking!'

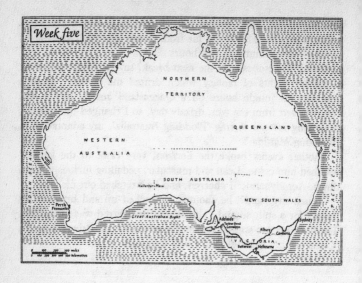

Day 29

I tired of the sight of gum. I tired of the road with its white line that led to Perth. It was unusual for cars to honk their encouragement when it rained; they were fair weather friends. But today, the majority of cars which passed us bellowed out their greetings over the swish of wipers and arcs of spray. We puzzled over this.

I walked into South Australia. The border was nineteen kilometres south of Bordertown where I had expected to be, so it came as rather a pleasant surprise. There would only be one more border to cross. It was a very damaging thought to dwell on, and I tried not to.

When I reached the Wombat, David was reading. There was no gas in the bottle and no water in the jug. I bit my tongue for a moment, giving him time to apologise. But he didn't.

'David.' I took an exaggeratedly deep breath. 'I think we've had

74

these talks once too often. You cannot allow the water, especially, to run low.'

'I'm not worried about the water supply.'

'I don't care; *I* worry about it and I should not be given cause for concern.'

He was looking out of the window, obviously trying not to explode.

'There are plenty of water taps on this road.'

'Then why haven't you used one David?

He turned back to me and spoke in a tone of pure condescension, slowly shaking his head at the melodrama he presumed I was creating. 'You are not going to die of thirst.'

'That's not the point. It'll be desert soon, and if you delay filling up on the presumption that the next truck stop will have water because the last one did, we could soon be in trouble. Use the first one always. The second might be dry.'

Still looking out of the window, he let out a breath. He wasn't dependant on anyone. He had a car – he could always get away. I couldn't. I decided to try to undermine his confidence.

We ate in a truck stop.

'You're not indispensable, David.'

'Oh?'

'I can replace you in Adelaide.'

I suffered complete self-conflict over David. On one hand his incredible good looks fuelled endless daydreams, they had inspired me to walk quickly to find him again and I knew no other man could replace him in fantasy. It is possible that I lashed out at him in case he ever suspected these thoughts, trying to disguise my attraction to him with bitching. On the other hand, he infuriated me with his irresponsibility over practical support. Perhaps, on the cosmic scale of things Ffyona's little tantrums at the lack of water were so insignificant that they just washed over him. The psychology of walking is far more powerful than the physical effort, of course I didn't want a replacement, I was simply trying to bully him into doing his duties, no other man could have got me to Perth on time.

I got back on to the road, feeling a little more in control. It dawned on me that it was I, and my will, which would halt or continue the walking each day.

Adelaide was to the north, three days' hard walk. It was a place to find the luxury which sometimes drove me on instead of my wish to conquer each step for its own sake. The press conference was to be held tomorrow. We did not want to delay it until I actually walked there in case the media lost interest or re-arrangements were confused. We needed them to raise money for the charity.

The temptation of luxury in the hand was greater than five more hours in the bush.

'Let's go to Adelaide now.'

'Let's push on.'

'No.'

We marked the road and drove ahead to Adelaide. My words stamped the end of that stage of the walk as unknowingly as a blind deaf mute steps into the path of a road-train.

Day 30

A Day of Rest.

Oh the pure, unashamed luxury of Hyatt.

I woke to the sound of knocking and, wrapping my sleepy body in a white towelling dressing-gown, I opened the door. Breakfast was brought in on a trolley spread with white linen; delicate fruit pastries warmed in a woven basket; a stand of jams, Blue Gum honey and lemon marmalade, a bone china bowl of summer berries and a silver jug of cream.

I left the curtains closed, unwrapped my dressing-gown and trailed it behind me on the floor, nibbling on a pastry as I moved into the bathroom. The marble was cool under my calloused feet. Draping the gown over a rail, I turned on the white taps to fill the bath, big enough for more than just me. The water gushed out to steam the full length mirrors and the three glass walls of the shower. Everything was pink. Wiping away the condensation with a sweep of my hand I stood naked in front of the mirror and looked at my body.

My thighs were leaner, waist more defined, ribs pushed through my skin, breasts firm and round, collarbones protruding, definitions in biceps were deeper. I breathed in and felt my body tighten.

The telephone rang.

'Good morning, Miss Campbell and how are you feeling today?'

'Fine, thank you.'

'There's a doctor and a public relations lady here in the lobby to see you.'

'They're not supposed to be here for another hour and a half. I'm in the bath. You'll have to tell them to wait.'

I replaced the receiver and hurriedly bathed, cursing that my precious morning alone had been disturbed. I would have to walk another 3,500 kilometres before I had another.

The telephone rang again, it was a radio station. I did the interview while applying my make-up and hung up. It rang again. I dressed during the second interview. Both were live. They asked after my feet, my motives, my expectations of the Nullarbor, my charity and what my family and friends thought of it all. Live telephoned radio interviews were my favourites. I could mention all my sponsors and disguise my nerves by pretending I was speaking to a friend from home. There were messages and letters for David at each hotel, especially from his mother, but there weren't any for me from my family. I took it as a rejection, allowed it to fuel the anger I often drew upon to walk but it wasn't until I returned to England that I discovered why there was no correspondence. The itinerary I had left for my parents had been lost by my future brother-in-law. There was a knock on the door. It was David.

'Hullo.'

'I've got a chiropractor and a neurotic PR woman in my room. The press are arriving.'

'I'll be ready when I'm finished.'

He walked towards the door and turned, 'Please be nice.'

David worked very hard on the organisation of the press conferences with the Hyatt PR departments. He felt embarrassed and disappointed with me if I wasn't co-operative with the reporters or if I was too harsh on the Australians for the miserable amount I had collected for the charity. We needed the exposure for the sponsors too, but I hated answering inane questions and so blamed David for lining up the interviews. Caught between a blister and a soft spot, he could never win.

I dried my hair and carried the Adidas shoes into David's room. It was full of people. The chiropractor sat me on the edge of the bed and turned on the ultrasound. Television and still cameras focused on my feet from every angle, and as the chiropractor rubbed my shin they zoomed in on my contorted face. The reporters asked questions. I tried to be 'nice'.

A five-kilometre walk on the banks of the River Torrence followed. A group of amateurs walked with me; children with skinny calves posed for the cameras and the adults, in all the latest gear, were eager to get a chance at the Hyatt raffle. The Hyatt PR girl was switched on. She had conceived the raffle to raise charity money from the walkers; the prize was a night for two at the Hyatt. But no one had given any money. The hotel would announce the winner in a few days once money had been collected.

I thanked them all for being there, then walked into the hotel.

'Hey Fee,' whispered David, 'let's be really degenerate and watch a film!'

We tumbled out of the lift and, without a moment's hesitation, went to David's room. It was natural to be together, but once we both stood there, alone in that beautiful room, the enormous bed seemed to question our friendship far more than the last thirty nights of sleeping together in one a third of its size. Trying to be casual in its presence, I flopped on to the bed while David found the remote control and the film information card. Elbowing his way beside me, he read out the choices.

'Hey, *Casual Sex* is showing!' He pressed the buttons and we lay with chin in hands and watched.

I could feel him near me, and sensed that he was aware of me too. He moved closer and we watched the film, turning to look at each other after an intense scene. I blushed and turned back to the film, but David moved so close that our faces were inches apart. Again we turned away from the film and looked at each other. I didn't trust myself; this was David in reality, not fantasy.

Even though we had gone through a lot together already and the atmosphere between us was so warm, we still hung back under the weight of another 3,556 kilometres. I left and went down to the pool where three tanned men were playing water polo. I laid myself in the sun on a poolside bed with a thick pink towel under my body. Three heads turned towards me.

'Are you the girl walking across Australia?' It broke what ice there might have been but it destroyed the possibility of light, much needed, flirtation. They were all attractive men and I enjoyed their attention.

I arched my lower back to the sun and drifted asleep.

Later I showered and returned to David's room. He took me to the chiropractor again for a full massage and manipulation. My big toe joints were displaced and when he manipulated them, my heels were pressed into the bed. The pain was excruciating but I held it. After an hour and much relief, he dropped me at the hotel where David was expecting a visitor. An old girlfriend from Hong Kong had seen us on Wide World of Sports which had aired the feature two days ago. She was meeting him for a drink.

'D'you want to join us?' he asked, but I hated the media with venom then. 'Us' no longer included me.

'I'll see you later. I'm going for a swim.'

I plunged into the floodlit pool and lay on my back watching the stars and the steam rising to meet them, the clean cut arrangement of pool furniture, the palm trees and the tall pink and pale grey windowed building of the Hyatt. I was alone. I lay above a jet of hot water and thought of how lucky I was, how lucky just to be alive.

My thoughts drifted back to my life in London, led by another person who loved to dress up for balls, drink champagne and flirt dangerously with deliciously pretentious men. I wandered among many groups of acquaintances, losing friends to my walking career because of the dedication it demanded for training and sponsorship raising, and perhaps because they didn't believe I would succeed. When I returned from a journey my friends' lives had progressed in different ways to mine; they had developed their careers in the financial world, or married or stayed relatively still. I didn't spend much time reacquainting myself with them for I had changed also and enjoyed the company of people in similar fields. But I was beginning to understand how small the world is, and how important it is to make and keep friends rather than dropping them and moving on to the next. This habit had been cultivated by my childhood. Moving schools fifteen times, I knew that if I didn't like someone it didn't matter, I would always make new friends when I moved on.

There were a handful of special friends, some of whom were lovers, who would always greet me back into their lives. I thought for a long time about my sister, Shuna. The petite, dark beauty who was the gentle one of us, feminine and loving. Although she was two years my senior, I had grown taller than her and after an illness she suffered at the age of twelve, I took care of her, becoming the stronger one. In recent years I had turned to her for encouragement, becoming addicted to her pep talks when sponsors weren't biting. She was the calming factor in my troubled relations with my parents, a diplomatic adviser who made such strides in pulling me back together.

But as I left London, I knew that when I returned Shuna would not be there for me again. She had fallen in love very quickly with a man I didn't know. A few days before I left, they became engaged and a few days after I returned from writing the book in Bali, they were married. Naturally I felt protective over her, I wanted to dissect her fiance, check him out, spend time with him, make sure she was doing the right thing. I couldn't bear to be away from her at this time, but worse, I couldn't even call her because she was travelling in South America. I knew that a very important part of my life with my sister was being dismantled and because of my absence, the distance between us grew. I felt utterly powerless, almost dismissed from her life and I miss her still.

I slipped out of the pool and a toenail fell off. Picking it up I dressed and returned to my room to shower. There was a knock at the door. David and his friend stood in the corridor.

'Hullo.'

'Fee, this is Sarah. Sarah, Ffyona.' She was tall, intelligent-looking and boyish.

'Hi! Coming out for a drink?' Her face was open and friendly; there was no cause for alarm. I could sense she was a friend.

We drank in the bar. Sarah was an insurance broker so we talked of the markets and investment banking. It was good to use the vocabulary again, good to exercise a mind which had been so consumed with which foot hurt least and when the Wombat would appear. But David was not familiar with this talk. I felt his awkwardness and changed the subject to more general chatter. Laughter dominated the conversation but it was the emotions inside which we could not articulate. They were our secret and as if sensing this, I looked over to David many times to find that he, too, was looking at me.

Part Two **Firing**

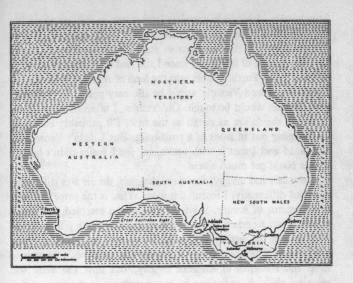

Day 31

We drove back to the smiling face which David had sprayed on the back of a signpost as the day's end. It was 11 a.m. We had bought an apple pie in a bakery and both of us stood on the verge cramming it into our mouths, sugar and pieces of apple sticking to our chins.

'Back on the road again.'

A cream-coloured barley silo formed the brow of the road. When I reached the silo, the road stretched far into the distance with the tip of another silo at the end. When I reached that, there was another in the distance and then another.

The land beyond was hidden from view by thick rows of dark gum which were so stunted that the trucks looked far larger and I felt far smaller. The road lay flat, cutting a swathe between the trees and the golden sand of the hard shoulders, where myriad small white shells clung to everything – the gravel, the signposts, beer bottles, disposable nappies. I tried not to step on them but they were too many and I was too clumsy.

I was now one third of the way across Australia. But I allowed myself no sense of fulfilment since I still had to walk twice as far in order to reach Perth. People said the land of rain and food in New South Wales and Victoria would be the easy part, the Nullarbor with its heat would be tough. Oh crumbs, I often thought, if the next two thirds are as tough as the first, I'll probably end it all by stepping out in front of a road-train. But I didn't know what lay ahead and I met it with optimism, for I really didn't believe things could get much worse.

It was hot and muggy, flies were sluggish, the air was still. I saw the road differently, I resented it more. That is the price one pays for moments of luxury. It wasn't simply the marbled bathrooms of the Hyatt Regency Hotel or the chocolate on the pillow before bed, it was the luxury of choosing my own movements that I longed for. The novelties of the walk had once been enough to keep the anxieties of distance at bay, but now the walk was growing old only variations in my movement could replace that novelty. But I was restricted to placing one foot in front of the other, 100,000 times a day. The Road Devil of Distance was having a field day.

I often filled my head with poetry to keep myself from asking 'Why?' Now I thought about David. I built him up in my mind until he was a fantasy figure to sustain me through the quarters, and daily he fell from the pedestal I had built for him when I got to the van and encountered the human reality. Stepping into the Wombat at the first break, I foolishly allowed him to remain perched up there by writing a line of romance in my diary: 'Woman cannot live on bitumen alone.'

I looked up at him to make him more real, while warm thoughts meandered in my head. Laughing happily, I poised my pen to write more.

'That's very rude.'

'What is?' I covered my diary, lest he should see what was written there.

'Looking at me and laughing and then writing in your diary.'

I felt myself blushing at my thoughts of him and my behaviour. He was tired. I was bored. It was hot and muggy.

I attacked him back, about stupid things of no meaning or relevance. I got out on to the verge, while he leapt into the driving seat. I crossed to the opposite side of the road. Between the passing cars we shouted personal abuse at each other. When we finally acknowledged the futility of arguing over nothing, we exchanged apologies. In an effort to give mine more meaning, I crossed the road and walked beside him then leant over and planted a small kiss on his shoulder. I was later to wonder if that gesture stopped him ever apologising to me again, for he hated me then, and, in fact, I couldn't stand him either.

A small roadside township emerged to the left. Standing beside a low, redbrick building signposted as the WC, a group of weary people stood and watched us. One of them was reading a paper. My face stared back at me fixed in a happy black and white grin.

'These people might be waiting for you.' There was a warning in his tone.

'I think they're waiting for a bus.' As we moved past, they read the banner with its description of my walk and were silent, looked at their feet and kicked the dust.

An old white ute, an open-backed van, rusty and dented, stopped on the other side of the road. A sleepy-eyed dog leant over the rail in the back and stared at me. The driver's window was down and a wizened brown face fixed a glare in my direction. I nodded.

'You want some money?'

I hurriedly crossed the road.

'Yes, we're not doing too well for the charity.'

He sucked his lower lip in and out of his mouth and scrunched up his nose. Reaching in the glove compartment, a long way on the other side of the cab, he pulled out a note.

'Saw yous back there a ways and come back to borrow a fiver for yous.'

He turned to me and I saw his eyes, watering and yellow at the edges – old eyes. What had they seen? He pushed back his slouch hat and wiped his forehead. Shaking, the hand pressed the note

87

into mine. In a soft country drawl, he said slowly, 'Good on ya, do samthen for the kids.'

He was so knowing, that anything I might have said would have sounded affected.

'Not many people have done this,' I said. 'God bless.'

And for a moment he held my hand with the bill between the two and looked into my eyes. Moving the gearstick into first, he clattered over the stones on to the road. The blue heeler stared back at me.

By lunchtime I could hardly walk. I breathed correctly against the pain, I limped correctly, I dipped into fantasy but none of it worked. I whined. I sang. David had stocked up on syringes and Second Skin. While I ate pasta, he lanced four enormous blisters, each filling two syringes, and squirted the contents into the bush. I gritted my teeth and watched a horse galloping in a field. Throughout our journey David never touched the sensitive skin beneath the blisters with the point of a needle.

That morning while driving back to our start line, David had fallen asleep for a split second at the wheel. We veered on to the hard shoulder, but he jolted awake just in time. I began to realise then that I was pushing him too hard, I needed to shoulder more of the responsibility; we were heading for the desert and the real walking. He was strong but I didn't know him, he might break.

'You're a hero,' I said, recoiling my feet to nurse them next to me. 'Bit hot out there,' I added, and looked down at the white and yellowing wounds. 'I don't think I can do more than three quarters today.'

'Yeah,' he agreed, 'it was a late start after all.'

'I think I'll sleep for an hour. It's so humid.' Trying to sound casual, as if we were just on a rambling holiday.

'Jolly good idea, what?' he mimicked playfully. 'If you're going to do that, I'll just move the Wombat further over on to the hard shoulder.'

No steps could be missed on a walk to break a record. We were religious over this. I stood up, unsteady on my feet, I slipped into his thongs and eased myself out on to the verge. He parked a few feet ahead and I lamely limped to it, clambering back inside and sinking down into the sofa as if I had just walked sixteen kilometres. David stretched out in front.

That night after walking David lanced my blisters again, and again each one filled two syringes. He was very tired.

'Why don't you pull out the bed, lie down and let me cook you a good meal?' I said gently. It was the first time I had cooked anything in the Wombat, and even though it only amounted to baked beans on toast, it was a start.

There was only one other entry in my diary for that day, in letters four centimetres high. It said:

MY FEET HURT

I knew then, with the certainly of a dying man, that I could not make it to Perth. I felt no fear, the question was just how long will I last? I kept those fears to myself. I didn't even write them in my diary. The time to quit always seemed to be just ahead of me – tomorrow perhaps. Things could always get worse. I wasn't crawling then.

Day 32

I strained to concentrate on the horizon, aware of my flagging speed, wiping sweat from upper lip, brushing away the flies. Are they territorial? I thought I had recognised the same ones since Sydney. Maybe my face was their territory.

I soft-focused my vision and let the loose muscle in my right eye (which looked like a squint when I relaxed it) wander to the side giving me double images. I moved into a trance punctuated by pain; each time a truck passed, I hobbled on to the hard shoulder, flinching from all the stones there. I stared at a silo in the distance and nothing else. The inside heel of my right foot was aching – not a rub, but a pain. I stopped a few times and slipped my index fingers between my shoe and my foot. I wiggled it and it felt good, a tickling of pain. I wanted to scratch it but it was too tender.

I puffed and grizzled and whined my way to the Wombat and slept for two hours. When I woke, the blister on the inside heel

89

of my right foot was infected. David syringed the others around it, a couple on my toes and then redressed them.

'You think you can walk?'

'I'll have a go.' The wrath of that infection shot up my leg as soon as I stood. I grimaced but fought against it and stepped out into the heat, only treading on my toes. The rubbing grew more harrowing; if I placed my foot on the ground I had to breathe deeply before lifting it up again. I turned again to the horizon. The gum looked sternly down at me, the trucks looked bigger, their noises louder, the sun hotter, the humidity higher. Sweating, grimacing, rubbing, straining, fighting, I stumbled on and on. I looked back at the parked van. It was only fifteen metres behind me.

I burst into tears and crumpled into a heap on the roadside.

The old Ffyona stepped in and grabbed me by the shoulders. 'You're so weak. Take off your shoes and walk on that road or you'll pay for this.' I took them off. 'Now walk!' I forced my feet on to the road, there was no padding. I thumped, unsure of the distance to the road surface. I looked to the horizon, tried to empty my head of thought, pushing against pain, rods of fire shooting up my right leg. Four steps breathe in, four steps breathe out. 'Walk! Walk! WALK! WALK! WALK!'

David pulled up. He saw that I had no shoes on, a sure sign that it was bad.

'I'm going to find you a doctor. Will you be all right on the road?'

The old Ffyona said, 'Yes.'

I watched him turn around and go. I wished I were inside the Wombat, I wished I had not said I was going to walk across this country, I wished I could end it, I wished I could walk into Perth. I was only a third of the way to Perth. Perth, bloody Perth, that's all I could think about.

The old Ffyona interjected, 'He had a good home and he left, right, left, it jolly well served him right, left, right, left . . . one, two buckle my shoe, three, four, knock at the door, five, six, pick up sticks, seven, eight, lay them straight, nine, ten, a big fat hen, eleven, twelve . . . eleven, twelve . . . oh, what was it? Eleven, twelve, dig and delve, thirteen, fourteen, maids-a-courting, fifteen, sixteen, dumpty, dumpty, seventeen, eighteen, maids in waiting, nineteen, twenty, my plate's empy. Move up and down and pass the gum and pass the bush and pass the ant and follow the line and pass the silo and up and down and on to the gravel and watch out 'cause this truck looks like it's going to smash into you and smear your guts all over the road and who will walk the highway then and sing to the birds that touch the sky that soar so high that eat the ants that make the holes that lie in the sand all soft and warm that drinks the rain from clouds above that sail in the sky all wild and blowy that pass the sun all hot and muggy that bakes my skin so brown and cracking that covers my body all tight and stiff that makes me walk with a limp like this!' I smiled. I could do it! I could walk! But the concentration was lost and I tripped over the pain. 'One, two buckle my shoe . . .'

'Oh Hell. What's the use? I've got thousands of kilometres to go.'

David came and I stumbled across the road.

'How does it feel?'

'Not good. Did you find a doctor?'

'I called Adidas – they're having some special insoles flown out from Germany for you. They're also trying to find out about a sports medicine doctor in Adelaide. And there's a GP in Tailem Bend.'

'Where's that?'

'About sixty kilometres up the road.'

'Let's mark the place and go now.'

As we drove there I looked back. 'Road Devils, you are not part of me.'

We arrived at the surgery just as it was closing. That is, David arrived; I was hobbling far behind in the carpark, worried about what the doctor might diagnose. Doctors before him had told me to stop over knee and back injuries. There was only a point up to which I would listen.

When the doctor got out the syringe, I cowered.

'You must have had a bad experience with this,' he said. 'It doesn't hurt.'

I told him about the two previous doctors.

'Well I can assure you that I am not going to allow you to scream in my surgery.'

And he didn't. After syringing the other blisters, he cut open the infected one with a scalpel, let the pus seep out and then sprayed it with antiseptic. 'It'll take a while to heal. When will you be walking on it?'

'Tonight, as soon as we get back to the place where I stopped.' He frowned and turned to David.

'Just keep it under control and watch out for any others that look like they might be going the same way.' He walked us to the reception area. 'I'll give you some antibiotics to speed that up. What are you wearing on your feet for walking?' He was looking down at a pair of old Reeboks which David had cut the heels out of so they wouldn't rub. 'Have you ever tried to walk in thongs?'

'They don't have the cushioning that I need for shock absorption.'

'You might need to try a pair if the blisters continue, you're not doing them any favours by keeping them in a sweating, rubbing environment for fifteen hours each day.' He glanced at his watch. 'The shops will be shut, but I've got a pair at home you can have.' And we went to his house where his wife gladly and very kindly parted with hers. I had forgotten that families existed beside the road, pockets of gentle life where people cultivate their gardens, chatter with their neighbours, and don't spend an hour dressing their feet before walking the dog. I was becoming so self-centred that I had forgotten people actually care about others and when I saw the doctor's wife giving me her only thongs I wanted to collapse into her maternal arms. As we said goodbye a horde of children ran up to give us a donation.

Back on the road David padded the gap between my toes where the thongs would rub. I tried to walk in them. I hungered to tread out those miles and feel my muscles stretch but the silly hell of those tiny skin wounds was a battle impossible to win by tenacity alone. I prayed to the Road Gods to heal my feet. Out there in the dark night with the traffic roaring past and the headlights blinding me, trying to walk to Perth with seventeen blisters, one of them infected in a pair of thongs . . .

I wished I had spoken to other long-distance walkers to gauge the point at which one gives up. Would it be acceptable now? Perhaps just a little bit longer.

It helped me to think of the men who had gone before me in the days when there was no road, no back-up, scarcity of water and no certainty of ever returning home alive. Edward John Eyre came to Australia from England in the mid-nineteenth century. He was the first man to cross the Nullarbor, hugging the coastline between Fowlers Bay in South Australia and Albany in Western Australia. His journey was marred by terrible hardship and the murder of his companion, John Baxter, by two of the party's Aborigines. And I thought of Sir John Forrest who crossed the Nullarbor with his brother in 1850 at the age of twenty-three, and Ernest Giles who had made an east-west crossing in 1875 including part of the Great Victorian Desert. For this and other explorations he received the Gold Medal of the Royal Geographical Society. But Giles died in poverty in Coolgardie. I saluted those men. It was not acceptable to give up at any point.

Day 33

As I was soaping myself in the shower that morning I felt a large round lump under the skin at the top of my right thigh. 'Oh God, what's the matter with me now? I won't tell David, he'll think I'm whingeing.'

But the dilemma that morning was whether to risk walking on the infected blister since if I didn't it might heal by itself, or whether to give it a complete break and go back to Adelaide to do the shopping for the Nullarbor. We decided to take the day off.

In Adelaide we stocked up on food and medical supplies. The Adidas representative there let me choose four new pairs of shoes in mens size 8–9. They were the only ones which would fit the width of my feet but all of them were too big at the heel. This, I explained to the agent, was the reason why I could not walk. He referred us to a sports doctor. I thought, Here we go again.

The lobby was covered with photographs of the Olympics, real athletes. He sat me down on the consultation bed and I unwrapped my feet. He looked at the infection.

'That's staphylococcus. Any swelling at the top of your leg, or maybe underarms?'

'Yes! Yes! At the top of my leg!'

'That's the lymph gland, it swells because it's filling up with poison from the wound.'

'I have some antibiotics.'

'That should be enough. Soak your feet in salt water for ten minutes at least once a day. How often are you syringing the blisters?'

'Twice, sometimes three times a day.'

'You must fill them with antiseptic. I know it's extremely uncomfortable but you can't afford to get infections like this on the Nullarbor.' He knew that I would not see a chemist for 1,662 kilometres and thirty-seven days. But he didn't know that I would suffer 640 blisters and pull a gallon of pus from my feet before I could restock my medical kit. 'I'll give you more antibiotics and a kind of Second Skin we use for our football team.' It was thicker than Second Skin and made of a grey rubbery plastic which could be cut and then taped over the areas that rubbed.

I explained to him that my feet got so sweaty that the tape wouldn't stick. Equally, the dressings rubbed horrifically. Miraculously he had some adhesive spray which I had never heard of and he showed me how to spray around the wounds before dressing them. He asked to see my shoes. It was such a relief to know that I was in safe hands at last. He took the new Adidas pairs and examined them. He said that by tomorrow, if I left them with him, he'd fix them and he promised I wouldn't get any more blisters. It was unbelievable. My insides danced with excitement – no more blisters. David and I celebrated over a croissant at lunch. If only I had seen him before. I had faith in him though David was sceptical.

We drove back to Coonalpyn and camped the second night in the campground. An arrogant redback spider (one of the most deadly in Australia) had claimed the power hook-up as his territory and David had to fight it off. He boiled water and mixed it with a quarter of a packet of salt in the waste-bin which was now part of the operating theatre.

'He didn't say anything about it being hot water.' Dipping a toe in and retracting it quickly.

'Better to be as hot as you can bear it.' And just to prove it was bearable, David put his foot in and tried to hide a wince. I soaked my feet and he began on my favourite book, *Wuthering Heights*. Though I wanted to discuss the book with him, for I had strongly identified with Heathcliff as a child, he guarded his escape jealously by ignoring my comments.

There we were, being gently rocked by the wind, under the bright summer stars of the Milky Way. Had I not been so happy for myself, I might have noticed the strain in David's eyes as he folded himself away, far from the dependance of a small girl stumbling blindly around the world.

Day 34

I plunged into the wind, back on that road, only one and a half day's walk from where I had begun, five days before. The road seemed to smile at me, as though it missed me.

'I miss you too,' I whispered and shuddered involuntarily. I tried to walk on a partially constructed road but too many small stones disturbed the blisters. They throbbed and rubbed. At the last count there were twenty-one.

When David came, after an hour and a half, I gave up. In the early days, to give up was not an option, now it was a daily occurrence. I had walked nine kilometres to Coonalpyn.

'This road,' said David, rather more forcefully than I'd heard before, 'is not going to beat us.'

'No, David, we'll eat it, somehow.'

Day 35

If I had kept to my schedule of eighty kilometres a day, I would have been halfway to Perth. David calculated that if I averaged seventy kilometres a day, we would get there in another forty-two days and break the record by a day. I had not been naive in setting myself such a schedule, but I had underestimated the injuries I would sustain by walking in what were for me unsuitable shoes.

It was beautifully warm and blustery. The colours of barley and gum and sand and sky were their real colours, not the grey of days before. Cars sped along like rockets, leaving arcs of red dust behind them. The sun burned through the zinc oxide cream leaving my nose raw and deeply pitted. I swapped the nylon, skin tight cycling shorts for the cotton ones I had brought from Hawaii, and cruised.

By the first break, the shoes, despite being adapted when I'd visited the doctor, had slashed a cut against my Achilles tendon. David padded the shoes with Superfelt covered with moleskin. The rubber had also cut through the underside of my ankle bones. He trimmed the rubber with a scalpel and applied two layers of the new Second Skin to the wounds, covering them with plasters.

My feet had made squelching noises at every step, a sure sign of rubbing. The rubber which had been glued to the inside of the heels was hot and my feet sweated more than usual. The sweating increased the rubbing, encouraging the blisters and unsticking the dressings. I dusted my feet with foot powder and sprayed adhesive gum around the wounds. By the end of the day, the foot powder had congealed in white doughy pockets between my toes and the adhesive spray had formed long grey strings like the glue I rolled between finger and thumb as a child. The dressings stuck to the socks.

By second break, the shoes were left in the sun to dry and the infected blister had healed to a thin yellow line of pus.

'Looking good!'

'Must have been that slit with the scalpel and the hydrogen peroxide you gave it last night. I think you're living up to your initials, DR!'

He farted. 'Thank you, madam.'

In the Wombat one farted to show thanks. We greeted each other in the morning with them and last thing at night. David made musical noises, sometimes whistles, sometimes long, low rumbles. I made no noise, only smells.

Out on the road, we picked over odd pieces of conversation which stuck in our minds from weeks before.

'Fee? Why did your father call you Squdge?'

'When did I tell you that?'

'Canberra.'

'You really want to know?' A raised eyebrow was the response. 'Because I was tubby and I didn't like sports.' Another raised eyebrow. 'And I still don't. Now you tell me something.' I picked a subject and he looked coy. We tiptoed carefully around tiny pieces of ourselves, monitoring the other's reaction, waiting for the signal to leap in and defend ourselves.

Even before the sun had fully set, dew began to form in cold pricks on my bare skin. The sky was flooded with tiny crystal stars as though they made the dew and sprinkled it to Earth. The air smelt of salt. Lights from the trucks below the horizon cut swathes through the night sky. When they fell on me they stayed there. I shaded my eyes and when they drew closer, cupped my hands over my ears and soft-focused my vision. Between the trucks, when the night was silent and still, I walked in peace with my body and the land. Then I heard:

'Grrrrrrrrr!'

I jumped out of my skin.

'Aaaaah! What was that?'

David was laughing his head off.

'You bastard!'

'God, you jumped! But there was a delay of about two seconds before you responded! It was really funny,' and he wiped away a few tears.

'I'll get you back.'

'Nobody, like *nobody*, makes me jump.' How could I resist such a challenge?

Some time later, the small lights of Tailem Bend appeared in the distance. I looked up to see David wrapped in thought.

'Boo!'

'Aaaaah!'

'Gotcha!'

'Bitch.' Large smile on my face.

We were a tired sight as we moved under the streetlamps through the main street of Tailem Bend, a small town with a water tower, a railway and a road, its existence justified only by the longhaul trucks and the odd lonely walker.

'Let's stuff ourselves silly,' I said.

It was one of those roadside cafés where the smell of grease was thick, goldfish swam among plastic coral, hamburgers came with the 'lot' or nothing at all and fat, aproned women, were forever wiping tomato sauce from cigarette-burned pale blue formica table tops.

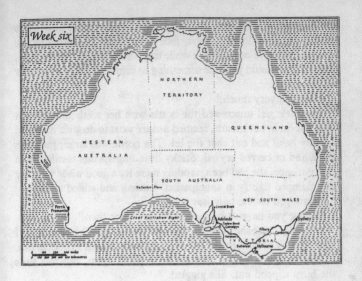

Day 36

The flat land stretched out to left and right. The air was salty and I walked over the plains to a lake encircled with salt crystal tidemarks. Small white snail shells lay in clusters. I wondered if they were a kind of parasite which fed off the barley. I crunched as many under foot as I could.

Tangles of weed and small yellow balls covered with shells littered the hard shoulder. I pulled one of the 'balls' from its netting and smashed it open on the ground. It was green inside and smelled of water melon. There was little fresh water available, so I tried a piece and spat it out, 'Pah!' Too young.

My hair had dried to straw in the wind and my face was caked in layers of salt; sand dusted the salt and sweat slithered through it in tiny creeks. I threw a stone to the Road God of Thirst.

A valley stretched ahead where I spied something red at the bottom. It moved and something glittered. A little girl. In one hand she held a bottle and with the other she wiped a large glass on her Mickey Mouse T-shirt, face screwed up, squinting in the sun. We held eye contact for a while and when I was within earshot, she called, 'Would you like something to drink?' Almost a whisper on the wind.

'I would, very much.'

The little girl unscrewed the bottle with her teeth and, caught with the lid in her mouth, seemed unsure what to do with it. I held out my hand and out shot the lid. The bottle was large, the glass thick and of carved crystal. Sticky little fingerprints testified to a rare patience, she had been standing there for a good while with her gift clamped tightly in anticipation. I drank and stifled a burp.

'I saw you on the telly last night.'

'I hope you haven't been waiting here since then!'

'No, silly,' and she blushed. 'My brother saw you this morning.' I spotted a bit of her brother peeping out from behind a rubbish bin.

'You're much braver than he is.' I drank again, but this time the burp slipped out. She giggled.

'What day is it?'

'Saturday.'

'Thank you, that was wonderful.'

It was getting hot. I had only just reached the top of the hill when the lemonade was ready to come out. I ducked behind a few sturdy evergreen bushes and wondered if they had been planted for that purpose. For there, under the branches were three pairs of running shoes in varying stages of decay. The oldest were thickly overgrown with cobwebs and the heat had bent the toes to a vertical position, cracking the leather on either side. Perhaps, if I looked closer, I might see a shrivelled up foot inside. It reminded me of an article I had kept from the *Independent* newspaper in London:

FOOT FOUND

A human foot was found on a beach at Heysham, Lancashire. The left foot, severed at the ankle, was complete with a training shoe identical to one found containing a right foot on 5 August.

David pulled up and welcomed me with light banter about how bad

I smelt and I returned the compliment. But when the conversation included an observation of nature –

'You know the golas?'

'Ffyona, they're not golas, they're galahs.'

– his snide lecturing made me scream obscenities and send him ahead. These outbursts were becoming more and more frequent; I could not express an opinion without David criticising it.

I walked on the old road which was rocky and dusty and the stones dislodged the blisters. I walked there on purpose. Then I heard footsteps on melting tarmac and the sound of regular breathing. It was Joshua, the man who appeared when things weren't going too well. He had no face, but he was tall and muscular and would walk just behind me on the left without a shirt on. He had wavy blond hair. Often, when I strayed too close to the road where there were trucks, I could feel him rush up behind me to protect me. He listened patiently to me singing to him and telling him the situation with David that day, but never commented on how awful my singing was, nor how terrible my treatment of David had become.

I was never completely happy when Joshua was there with me because he represented a listening ear, and when you know someone is listening it means you've got a problem to tell them. I had not calmed down by the time I reached the Wombat. The wind had been so drying and so hard that I fell asleep, sticky and confused.

David was driving beside me as we descended into Mannum. The mature Murray River nourished a valley of luscious trees and a cool breeze swayed the weeping willow over the banks and shallow waters. Islands thick with vegetation dotted the north shore and smells of hibiscus and pine replaced the dust of the road.

The wooden car ferry arrived and we rode alone across the Murray.

'You should be swimming this bit!' said the guard.

'A reporter once asked me what I did when I got to the ocean. I said, "I swim of course," and that's what he printed!'

Mannum was a green town of fruit and palms, the sun seemed more golden there and the drinkers at the bar spilled out into the streets to wish us well. Few people ever read my banner with its map and donations address. Perhaps my journey was so absurd one had to be drunk to understand it. David bought two cans of XXXX and when I had a swig my knees almost buckled. Up the steep hill out of Mannum we chatted over our beers.

I asked David if I could be alone and he drove ahead. It was the first time for days that I had walked in the dark by myself. Usually David was beside me for the first three hours after sunset. The trees whispered to me and the cars were dragons darting out of the night. I felt small in the darkness. But the wind was refreshing and I mumbled some poetry, learned as a child with a photographic memory. As my confidence with the unknown grew stronger so my repertoire grew more Shakespearean; the characters spat out their words or murmured them in moods of yearning, laughter cackled from the mouths of witches, soldiers mourned the loss of youth, and mothers searched their souls to understand.

I reached the Wombat all warm inside.

'Hullo!'

'Hullo!'

'A guy stopped and asked "that girl back there belong to you?" I said, "yes"' – I liked hearing him say that – 'and he was just about to drive off to get you when I stopped him. Australians are such good people you've almost got to fend off their generosity.'

He was right and I regret now being so wrapped up in my own discomfort that I did not notice this for myself.

Because of the solitary endurance of the walk, we found ourselves reverting to childhood pranks. The bread had gone mouldy so we tucked into a can of Heinz coleslaw which was mostly cabbage and mayonnaise. With half chewed food swilling around in our mouths, we looked at each other and simultaneously returned a verdict of 'unpalatable' by spewing it out. David took the can and chucked the contents outside. The wind was blowing in the opposite direction, so he came back with cabbage hanging from his T-shirt, beaming an enormous grin.

There were no clean plates or spoons so we ate, or tried to eat, tomato soup out of the pan with ladles. Huddled together on the sofa in the soft light, we delved into the pan, clanging our utensils together – 'Your health!' – and then slurping the soup with ghastly noises. David was doing well until . . .

'Brrrrum, tish!' Soup spurted out across the shelves, dribbled down his face, splattered his clothes in fits of giggles. He bravely tried for another – 'brrrrum, tish!' – and on and on until there was no soup in the pan and no soup in David. We didn't care; we were full of laughter and continued the hysterics through another quarter. Laughter in the face of adversity is a Commandment of the Road.

Day 37

The hill rose steep out of Palmer. Rabbits scurried and darted among the rocks. The land was too rugged for cattle, and only sporadic sheep grazed there. The hill continued up and over the first horizon where the road slashed deep into the base rock on either side. Climbing higher I looked back at the stretch of Australia I had walked through the previous night, oblivious then to its colours and contours.

Before Palmer, the plains were mildly undulating. Now rocky outcrops scattered the mountainsides like glacial screes, pockets of small hardy bushes clutched the soil in gullies, and creeks trickled over stone. Tufty grasses hugged the contours like old velvet where sheep had worn their pathways and left their pellets.

The road curved upwards and there, around a corner, the beauty was gone. Brian loves Sharon, Cindy for Kev, Happy 21st Mengee, AC/DC, The Stones. And a million more, layered one over the other with garish spray paint. No rock was left unbranded. And not just the rock, but the road – my road – was mutilated. They must make a pilgrimage from far away with spray cans in hand, to kill beauty.

The valley of Mount Pleasant was lush and in a perfect meadow stood perfect cows, their skins well groomed, glossy and pale peach, their udders pink and scrubbed, their noses soft and their eyes bright and brown, and free of flies. I wanted to run to them and hug them.

Small white flowers lifted their heads to the light and seemed to turn and stare at me. When I walked closer to stare back at them, my hair caught in a thick sticky cocoon which hung among the leaves of a young oak tree. With a twig, I twirled the flaxen strands into a candyfloss ball and tried to see what lay inside: a transparent wet wing, a slender soft abdomen, something not yet formed, so I let it alone and dropped the stick.

In the afternoon I passed the turning for Barossa Valley, wine growing country. Somehow the gums seemed more alive, surrounded by new trees, pines, willows and fields of flowers. Passing a burnt out cottage, overgrown with lavender, I picked some and threaded it through my hair. When David came, I let him smell it but he snuffled when it stuck in his nose.

Through Williamstown we moved past a school where a wooden lady on wheels stood in the middle of the road holding a board saying 'Thank You'. Someone had taken a saw to her leg and her knee was missing. Australians have a tendency to take the piss out of everything, especially American, and bring it down to earth. Which is where the wooden woman with one leg seemed to be percariously teetering towards.

There was a halo around the sun as I walked to the Wombat. The air had lost its freshness and the day was growing old. David had been given an enormous bag of roasted almonds by an old English couple who owned an avocado farm. Piles of avocados lay on the dashboard in the sun. How rich people were with their generosity where the rain fell.

I walked alone into Gawler where children played on the pavement. As they heard me walking up behind them, they increased their speed, I was whistling softly 'The ants go marching two by two'. They were afraid of me. I overtook them with ease and whistled merrily down the hill, stealing glances behind me as they had done.

A T-junction. I studied the signposts, but none of them registered the way to the day's end. David had driven past a couple of hours earlier and hadn't seen me. Looking very sheepish because he didn't know how I would react, David drove up. I was glad to see him, and didn't mind that he had lost me.

The road to Mallala had one of those distressing signs parked across it by the Road Devil of Fourth Quarter Irritations – 'Road to Mallala closed. Use detour.' David and I tried to talk to each other during the detour; conversations began, but stopped in mid sentence lest the other should take offence at an innocent observation or gesture. It was hard work to be together when we were tired. Tactfully, David went ahead after a few hours and made fodder. We were bored with food. Bored with breaks. Bored with gum trees. Bored with each other.

Day 38

A paper plate of fruit was shoved beside my head; while I dozed the morning chores had been done.

'Get up.'

I couldn't hang on to such comfort any longer. I flung off the covers and swung my legs over the edge of the bed, dizzy in the sudden movement.

'You've spilt the fruit.'

I looked down at the bed, apple, orange and pear had tumbled between the folds. 'Fucking stupid thing to do. You could have waited till I got up.' I picked up a piece at a time and put it in my mouth. I stared outside, breathing slowly, looking at nothing.

'Get off the bed.'

I stood up gingerly and my lower back ached as I tried to straighten it. There was not enough room for both of us to stand so I sat on the cooker lid while he rolled up the covers and pushed the bed into the sofa position. I sat down.

David pulled out the red plastic First Aid kit. How I hated the smell of antiseptic. How he must have hated facing my feet. I pulled my right foot under me and laid it sideways on the sofa. Plastic rustled as he tore open a new syringe. He stuck the needle under layers of skin, probing, watching for my reaction in case he hit the tender flesh. He found the well and pulled back the plunger. The skin deflated, sticking to the tenderness beneath.

'Don't flinch.'

I stared at my heel and the yellow liquid that filled the syringe as he moved from blister to blister turning to squirt a yellow projectile of pus out into the morning air. He filled another syringe with Betodine and moved the needle back under the skin. I could see it there. He pushed the plunger, a split second of fascination as the brown cloud separated the layers of skin before the shock of burning. I gasped.

'Don't flinch.'

It burned harder, fiercer, as he pushed it through the blister with his finger. I stifled a sob. Out came the needle, he refilled it with Betodine and pushed my foot sideways, plunging it in again until five blisters were brown and throbbing.

'Give me the other one.' I rested the toes on the floor and moved the left foot into place on the sofa. 'Fuck, look at that bastard!' A new blister had formed over night at the back of the heel. I felt proud that my pain was rewarded by something tangible. See! I thought, I'm not exaggerating.

He plunged the needle into the well. The blister yielded two full syringes and I giggled nervously at the proof. He slit the skin with the scalpel, lifted the cover of the blister with tweezers, then poured hydrogen peroxide inside.

'Aaaaaaaaah! Oh God, don't! Please stop!' It tore at the flesh inside and fizzed out of the cut. He wiped it away with lavatory paper and then poured more inside. Once he was satisfied that it was clean, he poured in Betodine. The burning thudded. He moved on to the next blister, leaving me gasping from the first, and then the next, drawing and squirting. David was so gentle; I had to stop myself throwing my arms around his neck and weeping for the considerable suffering he saved me with his care.

'How superhuman I must be to now go and walk seventy kilometres after such an operation!' I exclaimed, pumping myself up with confidence as fuel to step out on to the road again.

'How d'you expect me to respond to that?' I mistook an attempt to encourage me for a sneer.

'I don't expect anything.'

I limped alone. The road began to vibrate and I thudded, unsure of the distance to the surface. I was soon out of energy; the fruit had gone through my system. I felt like vomiting. David was at least an hour and a half ahead. I could think of nothing but food, and was groaning from visions of gooseberry fool when an old Falcon drove a little further ahead and stopped.

As I limped towards it, I could see a woman with lank grey hair sticking to her cheeks as she peered out and delved into her purse. A mangy labrador-cross salivated over her shoulder. I moved towards her and she turned and smiled at me, handing me a $20 bill. She was smiling too much to say anything, and I returned the gesture with a gasp of disbelief.

'Oh you sweetheart! Thank you, thank you very much!' She nodded, a little embarrassed and turned the car around. I waved. She beamed and drove away. Good old Australia, I thought, right there when I needed you!

My head swam. But there was a glimmer of white ahead, perhaps? It bobbed up over the horizon and broke into the shape of the roof. It was! I stumbled to it and trudged on the verge at the side.

'I'm so hungry, David, I am so fucking *hungry!*'

'It'll be ready soon.' He was cutting up the avocados. I would have to wait a while; he had been reading. Silence.

'A woman gave me $20, but I don't think she could afford it.' I put the note in the money box.

'I hope you said thank you.'

Stunned silence. I could hear my father's voice.

It had grown hot while I ate, and the wind blew dry and strong. I watched the horizon melting into the sky and limped a little easier with the concentration. Sweat framed my eyelids. I couldn't neutralise my mind for the discomfort in my feet. Everything bright, too bright, every hill followed by another, every thud followed by a scuff, every scuff followed by a sharp intake of breath.

I thought of nothing but the thought of no thought until far in the distance, where the bitumen melted and fused with the sky, the Wombat slowly detached itself from heaven.

I slept for forty-five minutes. Still it was too hot. Even 1,200 kilometres from the Nullarbor, the heat was unbearable. I drank water, but it was warm and tasted of hot plastic. The water jug sat in the trailer under the baking sun. For some reason

David refused to keep water in the fridge even though I begged him to.

To drive ahead, we knew, was bad luck but we needed to shower and find shade from the heat. Balaklava was the closest town ten kilometres away. We marked the road with spray paint and drove to a campground of few trees and many flies. I knew that the flies with brown markings on their abdomens were female. Sometimes, when I felt irritable, I would catch one and squeeze it until tiny white maggots squirmed in the light.

I locked myself in a cubicle and stood naked under the cold fresh water watching the drain fill up with brown streams from my body. Then I sank to the floor and scrubbed my feet while the water trickled over me. Six days of adhesive spray and foot powder had congealed between the toes. How lovely to see white at the end of my toenails.

I stepped out into the light and there was David. I had forgotten how beautiful he was; the white of his singlet and shorts gleamed against honey coloured muscles.

We drove back to the mark and now that my feet were clean, the dressings David applied felt cool and comfortable and my shoes much lighter under foot. The stars were bright above. I looked to them for energy and steadied myself with a hand on the side view mirror. David had fetched his razor and a cup of water, to distract me from the pain. I held the cup and he adjusted the rearview mirror. Squinting this way and that, stretching his skin, he shaved the 'cobwebs' as he called them, from his neck.

Under the blue starry sky we moved through the shadows, balancing the resentment that had grown between us with the acceptance that we were all each other had.

Day 39

The dawning sun was the first I had walked beside for many a morning. It was 5 a.m., and I usually began at 6.30 a.m. when the colours had already dispersed. Light poured red and yellow between the gums, but when the sun had peeled away from the horizon, the pageant moved on, leaving the world engulfed in grey. The road was flat enough for David to take his foot from the accelerator and, while the Wombat was still running, heave himself through the side window where he would sit on the ledge. There he sat, while I walked and we giggled.

David drove ahead and left me laughing to myself about nothing in particular until I reached the Wombat and began my stretching exercises. He turned away from me, peeing, but misjudged the wind and the pee splattered all over him. He turned, stretched out his arms and started running towards me. I shot off, with David close on my heels.

'Give me a hug, Fee!'

'Yikes!' I darted and dodged. He was quick, but he had no shoes and I ran on to the gravel shoulder where he slithered and hopped, clasping his feet in turn. Giggling and breathing hard, we marked the road, climbed in the Wombat and drove back to Balaklava to sleep through the midday heat.

Back at the campground I couldn't sleep in the filth of the van so I got up and began heaving out our equipment and dumping it on the grass. David took the layers of plates and pans, plastic utensils and mouldy cups to the water tap by the shower and squatted over the all purpose bucket. I scrubbed the floor, the windows, the fridge, the sink and that part of the sliding door which stood as testimony to every food fight since the walk began. Then I swept out the front and thrashed the seat covers against the Wombat. When I was done, David came back with gleaming plates and looked at what I had done.

'What a sweetheart,' he said gently, rubbing my back. It was the only time he ever did that.

The moon was bright that night, it was cool and I thrived on being alone. I was happy and warm, thinking of David. A faint light shone from a window in the silhouette of a house; the people were watching television oblivious of me slipping silently past. I wandered off the track and walked in the moonlight. Out of the silence a horse whinnied, making me jump. I suddenly realised I didn't know what lay beyond the shadows. Another house shone its warming light through the dark. A dog barked anxiously as it heard me, but the owners ignored it; they trusted the plains and the night.

But soon there were no lights and no horses or dogs. I came to a crossroads and turned left. Then another crossroads. I hesitated for a moment, and went straight on. Time had gone by, and David had not returned. I wondered if I was going the right way. I thought again of his directions. Yes, I had followed them. All was well.

My footfalls disturbed a family of crows and they squarked and thrashed the gum branches with their wings, flying away into the night. I just looked at them; my heartbeat hadn't risen, I accepted everything. But what if I was going the wrong way? The plains were crisscrossed with tracks which were all the same, David might get lost himself. I glanced around for the glimmer of any lights. There were none. No cars had passed me since I had left the main road and there were no more houses. Another crossroads.

'Oh Lord!' I went straight on, glancing around every few minutes. He must be coming soon, but another hour went by and there was nothing. Once I saw a light to the left, but it vanished. I must be going the wrong way. Perhaps he would search for hours and never find me. When would I give up? Maybe he was trying to find me but had given up and returned to Balaklava to fetch help.

I tried to concentrate on him, tell him where I was. I thought of his eyes and looked directly into them, 'David, David,' I called, 'turn right and left and keep going, David, David, David, listen to me.' I heard something and glanced around. A fox ran out in front.

Ah, but there, far across the plains, I saw two sets of red lights; they must be the trailer and the Wombat. The lights were moving parallel with me, moving slowly. Yes! It must be him, I *was* going the wrong way. I flashed my torch on and off and waved it over me in high arcs. But the lights were getting further away until they disappeared.

He would turn soon. Yes, there, on the left, were the headlights of the Wombat with the yellow hazards flashing. It was moving much more slowly now. He might have the window down, he might hear me. I frightened myself with the first scream, 'DAVID!' I called again and again but the Wombat didn't stop. Still waving my torch, I watched it disappear below the horizon behind me. I stumbled on.

I glanced around. Another light, and the low distant rumble of an engine. It might be him. I stopped and watched the lights grow stronger, the noise louder. But then I stepped off the road in case it was not him, in case it was someone who might rape me.

I knew those lights! The car hardly slowed. Perhaps I was mistaken. No, I could pick out the Sport Aid '88 patch on the front. David stopped beside me, the window was down. He looked ready to collapse. I rushed to him and hugged him in silence. He was trembling a little.

'Thank God I found you. I was just about to turn back and get the police.'

'Am I going the wrong way?'

'Yes. Oh God, Fee, I'm so glad I've found you. I've been searching for at least three hours.' He averted his eyes. 'I went along every road, every track I could find.'

'I watched you.'

'You could see me?'

'You had the hazards on.'

'Fuck, you could see me.'

'I was shouting and flashing my torch.'

'I didn't see you. I thought you might have been frightened by someone and I put the hazards on so you'd know it was me.' He covered his face with his hands. I glanced at the fluorescent clock by the rearview mirror. I had been walking for almost four hours.

We turned on to the main road and drove over twenty kilometres to where I should have been. There I sent David ahead to sleep, and walked on through the night, glowing with the knowledge that he cared for me.

Day 40

Thick-tailed 'stumpy lizards' lazed in the road on their fat little bellies – ten inches of highly putrid reptile if you stepped on one. One stayed in my path and turned to look at me, opening its mouth and flicking out a wide flat pinkish tongue in indignation. I wanted to pick it up for David but I didn't know whether they were dangerous.

We had been so tired that morning that we began an hour and a half late and paid the price for the lie-in. By the time we reached Snowtown it was 38°C. I felt lightheaded and my words were slurred.

'David, I think I'm going to stop soon. See that junction? I'll just walk to that.' The heat consumed me, there was no wind, and my slouch hat felt tight on my head. I drank some water but the breath came in tight knots as I tried to drink more.

We parked beneath a row of gum where the temperature was 35°C and I fell asleep until it cooled off. As I slept, I had visions of flies feeding off my wounds and awoke to find that David had decorated the Wombat with strips of sticky fly catchers. They were, as yet, bare of prisoners, but it was a step in the right direction. At about the same time I found myself sprinkling salt on the floor each night. Exasperated by the blisters, I had decided that since they appeared from nowhere, perhaps they were like slugs and crept inside at night to slip under my skin. Salt kills slugs . . . strange logic I know, but it made me believe that I actually had control over their growth.

David looked up from his book.

'A doctor in a really expensive airconditioned car stopped to talk to me.'

'Did he give a donation?'

'No, he asked if I was James Capel!' For some reason we found this hilariously funny and as we laughed David stood up, straight into the fly catcher. I was in tears. It was stuck to his hair and neck and after I peeled it away, it left a sticky, smelly residue. He flung the fly catcher at the windscreen and there it stayed, flyless, throughout the journey.

As I stepped out again on to Route 1, the main highway through Australia, I felt the shock of dry windy heat. With the wind behind me, it became effortless walking. Foxes were everywhere and as the sky grew black they slunk across the road like shadows.

David was beside me much of the time and I taught him the

rhyme I found so useful throughout my walk: the Kings and Queens of England. David's memory never ceased to amaze me. He picked it up in five minutes.

It began to rain heavily in the dark. We were together and laughing. It didn't matter that he was dry and I was not, it didn't matter that I was in pain and he was not. I found our bond to be an anaesthetic.

Day 41

A Day of Rest

No matter whether I work a five-day-week in London or have sporadic days off in Australia, it always rains at the weekend. The streams of condensation on the window, mirroring the rivers of rain outside, did nothing to hinder my enjoyment of my favourite rest-day pastime – sitting at the table, coffee steaming, smoking a cigarette, writing my diary. In London I longed for wild hair, body odour and bare feet; in Australia I longed for moussed hair, White Musk and high heels. Glancing at David's feet that morning, I noticed how unbroken and unblemished his skin was compared to mine; there was no skin left around my heels which was not blistered.

We agreed on new tactics for the walk. To avoid the heat of noon, we would break up the day into two main sections with four hours of sleep in the middle which made walking physically easier. But getting only four hours sleep at night was proving to be very difficult. I am largely a creature of habit – an unbroken eight hours is perfect – so waking after four hours' sleep was stressful for both of us and consequently, the final quarter was not getting walked. I needed a firm routine to cover seventy kilometres a day, which meant falling in time with the heat and finding shade to sleep under during the hottest hours.

My walking seemed to be taking on a new urgency. Seeing my progress to Port Augusta gave me the rewarding feeling of actually getting somewhere. The place names were becoming more important. I would see a town signposted, spend two or three days getting there, salute the town as I passed and would turn around occasionally to see from the signposts how far from it I had walked. I was ticking off the towns, pushing on for Port Augusta, the gateway to the outback.

There are three things which make a baby cry. And they were the things which the Wombat could always revoke – sleep in the bed, syringes for the blisters, and food. So it was that the Wombat took the form of mother, of womb. Womb-at-the-side-of-the-road. And since David was always in that place where all miserable things were taken care of, I looked to him for as much comfort, direction, judgement, encouragement and love as I would from my mother.

I always seem to be walking home. Always trying to reach the warmth. Watching the Wombat pull over ahead in the dark with the glow of guiding lights to mark the end of the day, I felt it then. But no matter how many times I reached those lights, I never got to the warm kitchen of my teenage home, where so many troubles were brewing. I seemed to be forever in the cold and dark – walking from the village after an evening in town, walking to the warm light far in the distance. And when I got there, I needed to ignore everything that was in that kitchen except the heart of the fire to warm my body. It was a transition walk from 'Ffyona, the girl about town' to the one who was clad with iron; the one who mustn't leak anything of herself to those who stood in that light, for a simple happy smile would be pounced on and I would be wounded. Always walking now, the longer the walk, the more time to make that transition; the higher the walls, the more time for the kitchen to be warmer and the things there to be righted, the problems solved.

Day 42

I began walking at 1 p.m. My head was pounding, I felt very sick having spent a merry six hours the previous night in a pub at Crystal Brook being bought brandies by the majority of its male shipping industry inhabitants.

As I was having a pee I was transfixed by the sight of giant ants which were digging and carrying pieces of sand and dumping the grains at the edge of a hole. I was to see them many times on this journey so that even when all the land looked dead, I knew the ants soldiered on; tiny dots of inconsequence, the cleaners of the land. The sense of failure I often felt at not raising more money was strangely boosted by these creatures; one person, no matter how small, *can* make a difference.

David made me a ploughman's lunch and, because of the late start, we ate as I walked. Without being reminded of my hangover craving of many years, he bought me a tomato, cut it in half, took out the insides and filled it with salt. 'Hey, good news. A new road is being built to bypass Crystal Brook.' That comment would have meant nothing to anyone else, but for me it was a blissful sign from the Road Gods. I could walk on it, far from the honking booming trucks, and cut a few kilometres from my route.

As the sun set, the 'private' road ended and I walked alone with the night traffic. The trucks were louder at night. I thought they might mistake me for a kangaroo and swerve to hit me. David once overheard a truckie boasting about his new roo bar: 'Now,' said the truckie, 'all I have to do is find me a few!'

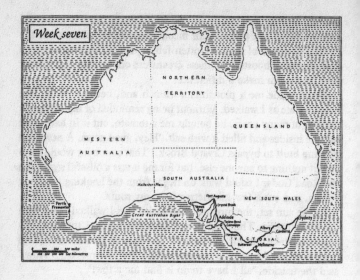

Week seven

Day 43

It was 40°C. David had left to take photographs of red sand dunes, admittedly at my request, but he used black and white film. At one stage I counted 135 flies sitting on my shoulder and countless more fuzzing around my face. I was determined not to be irritated by them. When a truck passed I could temporarily dislodge them by spinning around in the tailwind. But they soon found me again and buzzed more angrily at my attempted escape. I'm sure some of them had been following me from Sydney. I refused to wear one of these silly hats with the dangling corks, thinking they were just gimmicks for the tourists. But I later found that they were not just an Ozzie joke on the gullible poms and did in fact work admirably.

With the heat almost visible, my throat was as dry as the sand dunes. David left me out there for an hour and a half. When he arrived his hair was wet. I tried to be civil.

'Can I have some water, please?'

The liquid I gulped was hot and tasted of plastic.

'Why can't you keep the water in the fridge?'

'I've been on hiking holidays,' David said with condescension. 'I've had to drink warm, plasticky water. It's just one of those things you deal with and don't whinge about.'

'But David, there is a *fridge*! I'm not on a hiking holiday, I'm walking across a fucking continent trying to break a speed record. I don't like warm water so I got a van with a fridge. And why don't you put the water in a glass bottle like the hundreds we throw away every week?' All our attempts at a co-operative relationship were sucked out of us by the blasts of heat from the bitumen.

'The fridge will only work while we're hooked up at the caravan site.'

'Rubbish. It worked before. If it doesn't work now, look in the manual. If you can't find it, call Newmans. They even told us to reverse the charges.'

'Ffyona, it will not work.'

Months later when I returned the Wombat to Newmans it was discovered that the fridge battery was flat.

We ate lunch at Port Germein in a converted stone house owned by a fringe lunatic Dutchman with a grey pony-tail who produced under-risen bread and rambled on about battling with bureaucrats.

'Everything you eat here is organically grown.' The words belonged to him, they were his chant. David looked at his food. It was good but he picked up a piece of salami and asked, 'Is this organically grown?'

'Well,' spluttered the Dutchman, 'you've got to have something to add a little taste.'

It was cooler as we set out again and I let David participate in one of my favourite daydreams while he drove beside me.

'When this is over,' I began, 'I'm going to find a plot of land in Queensland and build a house in which to write.'

'What kind of house?'

'We'll get to that; first I must decide what land would be suitable.'

'You'll have to have fresh water; I presume you'll be out in the middle of nowhere?'

David became immersed in the dream. We discussed in great detail exactly how the house would be built, of what materials, to what design; we debated the merits of vegetables for the kitchen garden and the farm animals that would live in the yard. As the dream progressed, 'I' became 'we' and we imagined our life together after the walk; a cellar of wine, a jungle of plants, and two bedrooms which I secretly hoped would become one. As a means of getting me to the end of my journey it was a powerful motivator.

Time went slowly while we talked. I didn't care that day, I was happy to be with David. Despite my bitching, provoked by the heat, I was becoming very fond of him. Stopping for a break, David yelped as sharp thorns lodged in his feet while he was fetching food. He sat quietly and fiddled with the tweezers. I wanted to do it for him because he took care of me, but he wouldn't let me. I should have seen it then, that fierce independence, but I didn't.

I left him with his foot and stepped out again into the night. Silhouettes of mountains stood far across the water where I would walk tomorrow, beyond the lights of Port Augusta which twinkled on the horizon. The Half-Heart had begun to sink below the mountains. If there was a planet on the other side of that group of stars the inhabitants would see it as a question mark.

Day 44

I walked to the industrial and pastoral town of Port Augusta through the tip of the Spencer Gulf. The raised road was laid over the narrowest part of the sea, cutting it in two; the left half was blue, the right was purple. The Flinders Range curved away to the east, high and rugged, the last hills I would see for 2,414 kilometres.

In the town there was movement, people setting off for adventure, people returning with stories to tell and I, walking quietly, observing them, was part of it too. I asked a passer-by what made the water purple on the east side of the road over the tip of the Spencer Gulf.

'That's algae. The water's stagnant.'

'Is that because it was cut off from the sea by the road?'

'Oh no. The road's always been there.'

I discovered it was safer not to question the absurdities of natural phenomena in the desert.

An Aborigine was hitch-hiking. He was the first I had seen and I liked what I saw. He wore blue jeans and a thick checked shirt. An overcoat hung on a branch behind him. I liked his face, small yet broad, alive yet quiet.

'Where are you going?'

'Perth,' he said shyly.

'So am I! But I'm walking.'

'Can I come?'

'You couldn't keep up with me,' I teased.

'You want to bet?'

'No!' I passed him, and turned my head to catch his voice over the traffic.

'I think you're nice looking!' he called.

'I think you are too.'

The sun played on the water and it sparkled like a rough cut amethyst. The Wombat was parked in a truck stop where men in jeeps strapped khaki jerry cans to their dusty roof-racks, filled up with provisions. The sign above the garage read 'Gateway to the Outback'.

The airconditioning blasted as I opened the door. I squinted in the dark, David was ordering food. Maps of Australia, details of the Eyre Peninsula and the road to Darwin, hung on the wall. Sketches of echidnas, wombats, dingos and naked Aborigines with spears adorned the walls. I got a sense of 'beyond here, you be on your own.'

That was nothing new. We'd moved back to Scotland when I was twelve, to a small cottage which clung to the side of a windy hill. Getting to school meant a two-mile walk to the bus stop every morning, followed by an hour's bus ride and a further twenty minutes' walk the other end. If I'd had difficulty making friends before, four hours' journey time a day didn't make it any easier then.

The few kids who weren't put off by the succession of masks that I wore to hide my shyness – Miss Sporty, Miss Meditative, Miss Vegetarian and the rest – were put beyond my reach nonetheless by my father's insistence that I was confined to quarters on Saturday nights. I wasn't sure whether he wanted to protect his daughter, who had the mixed blessing of looking eighteen at age fourteen, from the less-than-local neighbourhood predators, or to protect them from me. Either way, he thought my yearning to go out and have fun abnormal, so my best friend was Big Boy, a rather majestic bull tethered in a field next to our house. I sometimes thought that Big Boy and I had a similar social life, except that from time to time he got invited out to parties.

Gordonstoun and the Marines left their mark on my father. They seemed to me to blame for the fact that he used his Robert Redford smile less as the years passed, and made life for all of us a lot like an endurance test.

'All of us' was me, my sister Shuna, and my mother, an exquisitely beautiful woman who could have been a model in the Sixties if she hadn't been too thin, even for that era. She provided the creative and musical core to the household, or could have done if her emotions too had not been increasingly checked by my father's overwhelming conviction that to show them was a sign of weakness. Ours was not, however, a house without passion. It was just bottled up in a way that rarely made life easy. I suppose that I inherited the best and worst of my parents' temperaments, and I suppose too that it was only a matter of time before I would find my own way of burning off the energy, the competitiveness and the sheer frustration that was my birthright.

I left home at sixteen, on the day of my last exam. Financed by a job as a nanny that I'd found through the small ads in *The Lady*, I set about finding sponsorship for my first big walk – from John O'Groats to Land's End. I set off two months later.

For all the emotional confusion that coloured that journey, I loved every step of it. I was still, effectively, alone, but somehow not lonely. I was *doing* something, not just for myself, and the bonds that grew between me and the people who supported me, and between me and the land I passed through gave me a new sense of strength that I have never entirely lost.

The top of the next hill was never far away on my British walk. Now, what emerged beyond Port Augusta was more dramatic than anything I had ever seen. The horizon was further than any I had walked to, and the brow of the road disappeared into the blue/red heart of a barren mountain, which split in two forming a narrow valley where I hoped the road would run. Behind me the Flinders merged into soft purples, paler as the range faded into the distance. The sky was bigger, the sunlit moon whiter and it looked more cratered than it did in the cities. The land was flat right up to the base of the mountains, red and dusty, with low spinifex and bluebush, dry and brittle. There were no trees. This was the land I had come to walk across – spartan yet beautiful.

Grasshoppers sprang up from the road as I walked through them, some jumped under my feet where I trod on them. They were too many to avoid. I liked the way they tickled my thighs when they landed there. I felt my body wanted to reach out and engulf the roughness of the land, feel the dirt on my skin, run my fingers through the prickles of the scrubby earth, walk barefoot upon it.

David and I went into the town to buy the last few provisions for the desert. We sat in a pink and grey café where a peach-haired waitress, smelling like a sweet shop, fiddled with the cappuccino machine and sneaked desperate glances at David behind his back. In a town this size in England one would seldom find a cappuccino machine, or even a peach-haired waitress. The standard of living was much more sophisticated than I'd imagined, perhaps the best kept of the Australian secrets. We ate our last fresh salad for many weeks to come, drank our last iced water and stepped out into the blast of the sun.

We had no need of a spray can to mark the road where I had left it, instead we relied on the distance markers which stood a foot high and were planted every kilometre showing the distance to the Western Australian border. The first was 987 and over the weeks that followed I counted them down, religiously, only missing number 675 because it wasn't there.

As the sun sank we turned right on to the road for Ceduna. It was the Eyre Highway, the road that would take us 1,662 kilometres across the desert to Norseman. Our senses sharpened as David turned off the headlights and we listened to the sounds of the land. Only the sound of our soft singing broke the vast stillness.

A truck, the first for many hours, broke the horizon with searching lights. Just before it passed me, I heard the tell-tale thud crunch of a roo under the wheels. The innards were everywhere, steam rising from them. I groped in the mess for a joey in the pouch but perhaps he had already left since a few paces further I spied one, small and velvety, split open like a pomegranate with its pink intestines embedded deep in the pits of the bitumen. I wanted to stay a while to see what monsters came out from the bush to clear the mess, but it was late and I walked on. I was unsentimental about death on the roads, having seen the remains of so many horrific accidents during my walks. I took a practical view; if the animal was alive, kill it quickly, if it was dead then take the opportunity to study the scavengers who might come to feed on the remains.

Day 45

Another blister had become infected. It was blue and bruised around the edges and oozing pus, but my pain threshold had risen after the previous infection and, popping an antibiotic, I managed to hobble along.

It was so hot that the thermometer shaft shattered on the outside of the Wombat and the mercury was gone. My ears thumped and the soles of my shoes stuck to the melting bitumen. I had felt that kind of heat in America, pushed hard through its barriers but never quite reached breaking point. I was curious about these 'walls'; what did dehydration feel like? I was searching for my limits – deserts are perfect places to find them.

The sun sapped my energy. I was sluggish. Birds nodded off in the thrumming heat as everything slowed around me. Discarded snake skins lay drying in the verges like parchment scrolls and the flesh of rotting roos curled away from bones and stank. All around me the blurr of scrub, blue bush, sky and sun. There were mirages and I must have sweated enough to look like one myself to the two road-trains that thundered past. They were the first I had seen – trucks hauling at least two container trailers, and I had been warned – they move over for no one. Their whiplash tailwinds belched the stench of burning rubber, heating the mirages. I was thirsty and lightheaded. The Wombat was like an oven when I reached it.

'No more,' I gasped. 'I will walk only at night.' I had to increase my daily distance and night was the only solution to avoid the sun.

We marked the road and drove ahead to Iron Knob where we knew there was a campground with a space for the afternoon. The park was a patch of cleared scrub where two gums stood, twisted and wizened as though they had squirmed over the years to find shelter from the sun. A 1960s caravan, of a type we endearingly referred to as a 'mouldy shower curtain', was parked under one, we stopped under the other. The sun was directly overhead.

Desperate to sleep, I tried to count sheep, tried to count flies, but only slept lightly. David tried to sleep cramped up in the front and I felt guilty. I had not asked him to, but the heat of two people on the bed, sweating and bumping into each other was not conducive to any kind of rest.

It was 7.30 p.m. by the time I stepped again on to the road. It was cooler now the sun had gone, but the wind that had crossed the northern deserts was still hot. The moon was so bright that if I had been walking the other way I would have needed to wear sunglasses.

Beyond Iron Knob lay the source of its name; a massive mountain of iron ore which is the principal source of raw material for the Australian steel industry. The lights from the mine could be seen across the desert for hours; I felt I was getting nowhere. David was tired and went ahead to sleep leaving me alone. I could hear my breathing and the even fall of my feet. The lights of a car extended my shadow in front of me. It slowed.

'You trying to get somewhere?'

'I'm on a charity walk.'

'S'truth. Good on ya, mate. Where ya walkin'?'

'Perth.'

'You've got a long way to go.'

'I've come a long way too.'

'Where?'

'I've walked from Scotland.' I liked to shock sometimes, and alone in the desert in the dead of night seemed the perfect opportunity.

He told me he was from Kalgoorlie.

'When will you get there?'

'Late tomorrow night, what about you?'

'I do sixty to seventy kilometres a day.'

'Well, I'll buy you a beer when you get there. That'll be about a month from now. Sure you don't want a lift?'

'Thanks, but I'm earning that beer.' A month and I still wouldn't be in Perth.

A fresh kill was sprawled across my path. A fox was eating it. He didn't run as I passed, but hissed and flashed possessive yellow eyes in the light of my torch. I put up my hands and spoke softly. 'It's OK, I've already eaten, thank you.' It was so still, so quiet the stars beamed above and the Half-Heart was there, guiding me to the west. The Seven Sisters pulled Jupiter across the sky in a formation I named the Chariot, racing the ancient planets to the west. To walk the other way would have been like swimming against the tide.

I passed a rest area where the dark form of a road-train loomed and then another. The drivers lay sleeping, oblivious to a small person walking by. Then one of them awoke, the engine started, the lights flooded across the land, so brightly that my shadow was fierce. The truck slowed as it reached me, but instead of seeing a friendly face looking down from the lighted cab, I could see nothing but an arm.

'I don't need a lift thanks!' I shouted up at the light and suddenly the arm threw something. Catching a shaft of light it looked like a cigarette butt; I dodged. It was an apple. I picked it up and waved after them. I rubbed it on my T-shirt and walked on, munching quietly.

Then there was no noise except for me. The skulls of roos lay white on the verge. A mouse scurried out from the desert, ran a full circle around me and then fled back into the scrub. Shooting stars ripped across the dome. How big everything is in the desert.

I reached the Wombat at 2.15 a.m. We tucked into a feast and I finished a cigarette. It was time to go. My feet were painful, the air was sleepy. 'Just one more, and I'll be off.' I lit another and supped my tea. Each movement sounded so loud in the desert. But there was nobody to hear a cry for help.

'You OK?'

'Yeah, I'm fine. Don't worry about me.' But David was my lifeline and I did worry about him. He was beginning to look drawn and grey around the eyes. He looked older.

I stubbed out the cigarette and stepped out into the night. It took a while for the light-headed nicotine effect to be replaced by easy breathing in the clean night air. Those bloody 'stink things'. I did try to give up but there were no other rewards at the end of the day worth walking for. I couldn't get fired up for a whisky because we didn't have any and the food was so unpalatable that I wouldn't have walked as far as the fridge for it.

During the fourth quarter the dawn came rippling through the scrub behind me with a luxuriously light breeze and Venus shone bright in its midst. I felt very sick as I walked the last six kilometres, perhaps from drinking coffee but perhaps, more probably, I was not used to feeling so tired at this time in the morning; my mind was saying, 'Oh God another day.'

Day 46

Temperatures inside and outside the Wombat were high. It was impossible to sleep for more than a few minutes at a time. Flies were everywhere and the bedding was soaked with sweat. Neither of us got the sleep to tackle another sixty-four kilometres through the night. David tried to sleep in the front again. A gallant gesture but he didn't realise that I'd gladly sacrifice half the bed so that he could sleep, ensuring that he would be awake to drive with me through the night, instead of dozing off at the wheel. Resentment was brewing in the silence which replaced communication at a time when it was vital to the success of the walk. David may have understood my rationale, but I suppose in the end he needed his own space away from my nagging demands.

Time to walk on. The salt water I had soaked my feet in had given the skin around my heels the texture of pork crackling. One enormous piece had been accidentally ripped off leaving the flesh red and raw. Absentmindedly I picked it up and chewed on it, easing myself back on to the road. The fading light cast the undergrowth in hues of turquoise and blue. The bushes looked like lavender but the most pungent smell was of rotting dead animals, like melting wax crayons. After a few hundred metres in the first quarter, David left me to drive ahead and sleep.

It was pitch dark when the sun sank – which brought a claustrophobic feeling. I kept looking around, my mind playing tricks, feeling self-conscious, sensing thousands of eyes watching me from the shadows, waiting to pounce with bared teeth. 'Childish!' I whispered and slapped my face. Where the hell was the moon? I had my torch but the battery was running low. I watched for every marker, counting them down. There would be fifteen to count till I found David.

I felt very much alone in the desert at night, but for all the fears, for all the weariness, there was something startlingly familiar about it, as if I had always lived there.

The shadows became darker. A truck passed me and I wondered how long it would be before it pulled up. Predictably, the red brakelights flashed, the white reverse lights went on and it backed up. This amused me. The truck was noisy and stank of burning rubber. The lights were so bright that I couldn't see up into the cab. I came parallel with the door and stopped.

'You just couldn't figure it out, could you?' I said, laughing up at the light.

'Na, curiosity got the better of me. Where ya ga'win?'

'I'm on a charity walk to Perth.'

'Aw yeah, I read about you somewhere. How are the blisters?'

'Bloody awful!' I stood and chatted with him for a while, I liked him, I liked truckies – the big brothers the Road Gods sent as guardians. Strange to hear another voice in the desert.

Many weary, weaving kilometres later, I reached the Wombat. David woke up, switched into semiconscious automatic and heated a can of Heinz Vegetarian Spaghetti and made tea with powdered milk. I felt even more nauseous with the stodge in my stomach and stifled a few tell-tale burps as David went ahead again to sleep.

The road began to undulate a little, scrub gave way to what looked like a grassy flat, all blue in the moonlight. The desert had gone, replaced for a while by agricultural land, suffering from the drought that had been raging here for four years. Another truck pulled up. We chatted until the demands of his schedule urged him to move on. But then I saw him pull over ahead, his arm hanging out of the window with a tin in his hand. I thought he was offering me a beer. 'I don't need a drink, thanks.' But he didn't retract it. I took the tin and the engine started, changing gear every few seconds until it had gone. The tin was full of money.

The Half-Heart sank, and the markers indicated David should be somewhere along this stretch. I looked to right and left; every shadow might be the Wombat. There, under the gum, was the Wombat. 'Oh you beauty!' I whistled softly.

The air was heavy with sleep. I had to keep awake. I nudged David gently, not wanting to startle him.

'Tea and soup?' And that was the last thing I remember until I woke up two hours later. It was dawn. The soup had been made and had congealed again and the tea was tepid. I felt that terrifying feeling of sleeping late and missing an important meeting. I ate and shot out to the road. It would be very hot soon; the precious hours of cool walking had been wasted. I was angry. But all that changed as we rounded a corner.

I started screaming, leaping and laughing hysterically.

'Look! Look! David, look!' There, ahead of us, was a map of the country with the words 'Half Way Across Australia' sprawled across the top. With new energy, I walked towards the sign, and hugged one of its legs hard and silently thanked the Lions Club of Kimba for erecting such a plaque. We took photographs of each other and then David and I solemnly shook hands. David was relieved, though he may have thought back over all the events of the last forty-six days and wondered how he could go through the same amount again. This is the curse of the halfway point, but I look upon it as being further than halfway, for just one step over that mark means I am closer to my destination than to my place of departure. The scales have tipped, for the first time, in my favour and now it should be a downward slope all the way to the end.

I was learning to deal with impatience. 'Never, never think of the end' was a maxim to strive for, never really attainable like 'love your neighbour as yourself', it was a Commandment of the Road. I was also learning self-discipline and self-worth, how to deal with pressures and with boredom. The road was a school of intensive learning where many aspects of life were represented in their simplest forms. Graduation from this school was a powerful motive in itself for walking across a continent.

I was longing for something substantial to eat having lived off canned food for two days. For the last twenty kilometres I had been eyeing the billboards advertising a twenty-four-hour truck stop.

At the back of the restaurant was a wire enclosure where two roos and an emu lounged in the shade. The emu was more than two metres tall with a bulbous body of scruffy feathers which looked so much like the desert gums that we renamed them 'emu-scrub-gum' in memory of her. The smaller of the two roos came hopping towards my outstretched arm. As I stroked his chest, he reached up with his front paws and gently clawed at my arm to steady it, before licking it clean. Concerned that the emu was feeling ignored, I asked David to distract her while I played with the roo. He placed pieces of barley on my head and the emu pecked at my scalp.

Day 47

While I was walking in the first quarter a truckie pulled over to check his load and I asked him if he needed help. We chatted a little. Just as I was beginning to think I was safe in the desert at night, he drew me to him and kissed my cheek. I pulled away, a little frightened. He asked me where I'd be on Sunday night and drove away.

Even with hindsight I do not think it was foolhardy to walk at night. Australia has a low crime rate and Australians are a fun-loving and sensible bunch who protected me more from myself than from each other.

In a field to the right I saw a black caterpillar about seven metres long moving over the stubble. It baffled me. But I was happy to accept it if that's what it was. Sections began falling off as a cloud covered the moon. I walked on, glancing across at it. When the cloud cleared the caterpillar turned into a line of sheep.

David drove with me in the second quarter. We tried to listen to the news. The radio was a link with the 'other world' through which we glimpsed lives influenced by governments, sex scandals and drug round-ups. The obligation to keep in touch, just to check that the country was not at war, became obsolete with that glimpse. We couldn't digest what we heard, the broadcaster didn't speak in terms of quarters and kilometres and his voice seemed to contaminate the land with the disasters of man. Switching off the radio was a statement that our way was preferable to theirs.

There came a point during the nights at which we identified a physical barrier, when loss of sleep and poor nutrition caught up with me: '3 a.m. exhaustion'. If I pushed on past that hour there was a chance I could walk through the dawn and out the other side. But my lack of control over even the most simple movements, like raising my hand to scratch a bite, was such that so much mental energy was needed to enforce the command, that it sapped what was left and I couldn't walk. So when a ruddy great mozzie sank his proboscis into my ankle, I fell asleep for three hours until the irritation had eased. Then I ate muesli trying to avoid looking at the happy family painted on the packet; syringed another seventeen blisters and set off again alone.

The flies were getting quite ferocious. I squatted to shit and watched between my legs as it came out; it was still attached to me when the flies attacked it, screaming with excitement, I could do nothing. There were no smooth stones or soft grasses to wipe myself with, and all I could do was thrash the flies with a bunch of brambles.

As I approached the Wombat David came to meet me. We walked the last few steps together and he took my photograph. But as I tried to stand still, battalions of ants ran up my legs, got into the holes in my shoes and bit me. There were too many to kill and opening the door, getting in and quickly shutting it was like trying to escape from a hungry shark. Food was low. I ate a tin of potato salad and drank coffee to keep myself awake.

I knew the next quarter would be hard. David was beside me for only a few minutes before I asked him to leave me alone. With the Wombat far away I would have no choice but to continue. I veiled myself in heavy mosquito netting, tied firmly around my neck with a strip of T-shirt cloth. My hat, still starchy from newness, hugged my head and pressed the coarse cloth against my sunburnt forehead. The flies were all around me, barely settling, circling furiously. The undulating and thundering road, the dirt, the road-trains that tried to steal my hat, the heat – none of it would go away unless I walked through it. The kilometre markers crept by, one by one. I tried to empty my mind of thought and focus on the new horizon, forgetting the flies until one got under the netting pressed against my face. It screamed and tickled and I scrambled to let it out.

My movement was duck-like, compensating for the pain. I could not think about the muscle damage it was causing when the end of the week was beckoning to me. My imaginary companion, Joshua, came to me and pushed me along so that my footfalls were echoes of his. And hours later, on a distant slope, blurred by the shimmer of the heat, was a small round shape.

It was the Wombat. I cried. Tears stung the sunburn and welled up in my glasses, and the flies were more attracted to my face. Veiled, my mouth shaped words I had long forgotten, a melody pushed through my lungs. Something stirred deep in my subconscious to release an incantation learned as a small child, standing before her God.

'The Lord's my shepherd . . .'

I reached the Wombat, and suddenly that was all that mattered. Not God. Not David. Not Australia or the world. Just sleep.

Day 48

A night of rest.

We visited a truck stop to buy the token bar of chocolate which truly marked the end of the week and drove down to the coast. We pulled into Venus Bay, a place where small boats can be hired for a day's fishing and ice cream is the most popular order at the 'bar'. The only thing missing was alcohol; there was no pub in the village and the local shop didn't sell it. However, we still had a warm bottle of champagne from the Scholl PR lady in Melbourne and this, we decided, was the moment to crack it.

As the sun set, we sat in the Wombat, drinking from polystyrene cups, toasting our success at reaching the halfway point.

'Here's to the next half!'

'Here's to Jan from Scholl!'

'Here's to the doctor in Adelaide who said, "No more blisters"!'

We sipped and spat the champagne into our cups.

'Here's to long distance buses!'

And as we got more drunk, we saluted all our sponsors in turn, all the people who had in one way or another helped us and for those who had let us down, we cheered and spat and the giggles bubbled around the Wombat in the dark.

Day 49

A day spent on the beach with David. We swam, surfed, and at no point did my feet touch bitumen.

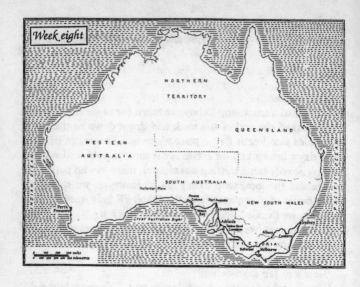

Day 50

The holiday had revitalised my spirits. The road was glorious; the distance ahead to the next bend was my world, and whatever lay further was of no interest.

David stayed with me and I babbled to him. He said little, just interjecting with a nod of his head or a question to keep me talking. It was the first time we had been together that I had not asked how far I had covered and a quick glance at the kilometre marker on the road told me it was time to break.

We sat in the Wombat farting cream of broccoli soup smells and our raucous laughter competed with the ripping noise they made. Bodily functions were the source of all our jokes; puns, wit and sophisticated quips remembered from the 'other world' were eclipsed completely in our exhaustion. We would bitch and bait and giggle and share secrets like brother and sister. But such jokes were not the only measure of our regression.

David left that night with the encouraging reminder that 42°C was anticipated for the next two days. It was vital, in order to break the record, that I push through the '3 a.m. exhaustion' barrier.

It was dark, the moon would not rise for a few hours, and I was alone. I became scared of silly things. My mind was playing tricks on me, thinking about vampires, thinking about wolves. As a child my nightmares were always about things with teeth, dark things. I would lie awake after a bad dream listening to the breathing of the wolves under my bed, smelling their breath.

'Should have told them about mouthwash.' My voice frightened me in the dark so I called out louder, 'Yo! Wolves and vampires, you've got bad breath.' Perhaps such weird imaginings are a warning signal in the mind when other signs of exhaustion are ignored. But, nevertheless, I picked up a stick, feeling uneasy. A kilometre marker indicated David was an hour and forty-five minutes away.

Trudging on, I looked cautiously into the night. I tripped on something and shone my torch on it: blood and organs of a fresh kill. I watched the gums for signs, and the squeaking in my shoes grew louder. 'Bloody sports doctor.' Something light was behind me, but it wasn't a car. I glanced around. It was the moon, big and shimmering like a melting butter pat with a slice cut from the top. I wondered if the other side of the world saw that slice. I had to look more closely in the now darker shadows for the shape of the Wombat. David may have forgotten to leave a light on. I cursed him and the irritation gave me power over fear.

But perhaps 'they' were inside the Wombat. I knew it was ridiculous and yet, as I ripped open the door, I was poised to defend myself. David was asleep. He woke up and smiled. I looked at his teeth; they didn't seem to have changed.

'Hullo.'

'Hullo, that was scary.'

'What?' It was silly now in the light.

'Walking alone in the night sometimes gets a bit frightening. What shall we eat?'

If he had said meat I would have attacked him.

'Toast?'

Again David drove ahead. I was too embarrassed to reveal my childish nightmares by imploring him to stay with me. I became numb, greeting every kilometre marker with a nod instead of an energy sapping salute. I accepted every noise; I was too tired to be scared. The Chariot turned slightly to the north, the sign for dawn. I looked around – yes, the sky was growing lighter there, the wind was fresh. The hell was over, the wolves would retreat. Soon the flies would come, the wolves of the day.

There was the Wombat. I was drunk with fatigue, my words were slurred when I got there.

'Ffyona,' David's tone was insistent, 'if you want to break the record you've got to push on and do another quarter.' My eyelids fell in confession of my failure. 'Ffyona, it'll be hot soon, you've got to push through, you can't postpone every quarter you find difficult, they're stacking up against you. You can't give in to . . .' His words became a hum and then there was only silence. I had been up for twenty-two hours. I slept for three.

I woke feeling groggy.

'What's it like outside?'

'Good Morning, Vietnam: it's hot. Damn hot. It's so hot I saw one of those little orange fellas just burst into flames.'

Outside in the 40° heat the flies came in heavy swarms but I couldn't face being wrapped in netting again. Before David went ahead to fill up with petrol, I took one of the pillowcases and cut holes for the eyes and mouth. It was hot under there, but the flies couldn't get in. I saw them, black smudges on my glasses and heard them. It was Hallowe'en and people in their cars did not hoot in happy greeting. I think they thought it was the Ku Klux Klan.

Day 51

Well over 50°C in the Wombat, the kind of heat that makes the skin under your fingernails sweat. I occasionally slipped into a doze but could not sleep. Out on the road, babbling incoherently to David, I asked his opinion about silly things, just to hear another voice, just to know someone out there was listening to me and when he replied, 'Do you really want me to answer that?' my depression deepened.

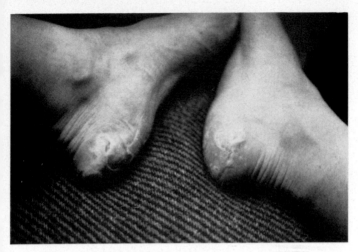

My feet, fired by infections as I walked

The Wombat displaying its wares in Balaklava

She'll be sloshing through the puddles till she's soaked

In the sandstorm that destroyed $9 million worth of crops
on the Eyre Peninsula

My first attempt at
warding off the flies . . .

. . . and my second

Halfway Across Australia: I saluted the Lions Club of Kimba
for erecting this magnificent sign

The week's end was always marked by a night of rest
and a bottle of red wine, as here in Point Sinclair

Checking out Bon Sato's rollerskates
on his journey across Australia

On the border with Western Australia,
the State of Excitement

Battling against the headwinds with Norris on the Nullarbor Plain

With Roger Scott who was a day from completing his walk
from Darwin to the Great Australian Bight

David, after the desert and my childhood had taken their toll

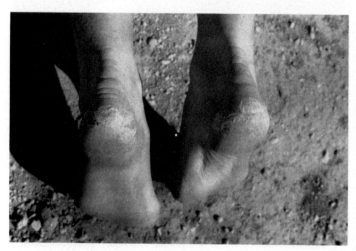

Near journey's end my glazing feet were deceptive –
pus still squelched beneath the calluses

If I had not been walking to beat a speed record, my dealings with David would have been very different. Because I did not have enough of myself to give him, I did not know how he was standing up to the challenge. In fact, I knew very little of him and because of that I couldn't rely on him to be my safety net and give me inspiration when I had no more strength. I was alone on that road; we were not a team.

At the first break I fell heavily on to the bed, head spinning. 'I need to sleep. I'll be OK. Just sleep.'

'You'll sleep all through the night if you do.'

'Please, David, wake me in an hour.'

I slept through the night, wasting all my precious walking time and woke at 7.30 a.m., terrified. David was amazed at my lack of will-power though he didn't say so. Instead he mimicked me:

' "I'm walking across Australia. I'm walking round the world." Ffyona, I know it's an enormous feat and the pain you've been through with the blisters makes it all the more admirable, but . . .' and he searched for the most tactful way of putting it. 'You've just got to push through this. I mean I know what you're like in the morning – it takes ages to get you up.'

I gnawed on an apple and glared at him in silence. Were the heavy dragging limbs of the night before just laziness? Was the road shifting under me my imagination? Were the spinning visions in my head just an excuse to opt out? David did not believe in me any more. I was furious.

Erratic sleep, extreme temperatures and poor food at odd hours were breaking me down, to say nothing of the blisters. My mind tried another trick to get me to give up, tormenting me with the memory of an article I had read about a marathon runner in Wagga Wagga, New South Wales. He ran a half-marathon in the extreme heat and the sun melted his muscles. One of his legs had to be amputated. I was frightened by my ignorance of desert conditions. I didn't know the warning signs and kept feeling my legs to make sure they were still sound.

David drove beside me as we passed a sign for a campground. It was not the end of the quarter but, for perhaps the first time, he was around to see the effects of exhaustion. He gave me a choice:

'D'you want to pull in here or continue and then drive back?'
After his accusations that morning, there was no choice.

'Walk,' I mumbled. 'Drive back.'

With the flies, heat, sweating and nausea, I was in real danger of
losing control. I misjudged every footfall, weaving on the road like
a stunned kangaroo. David went ahead to the end of the quarter
so that I had something to walk to. I should have asked him to
stay with me to calm me but I didn't know how bad it would
be. The world was swimming. I stumbled, fell into the verge and
vomited, ripping off the pillowcase just in time. There I retched,
flies swarming into my mouth and under my glasses to drink the
tears. As I tried to get up, my hands tore on the prickles and I
retched again, falling over with the spasm. Breathing deeply, I
wiped my mouth with the pillowcase and sucked on a pebble to
increase the saliva in my mouth to dissolve the acid. I crawled back
on to the road, fumbling to replace the pillowcase and sunglasses
against the flies. Sweat stuck to my face and itched. The blisters
shot pain up my legs at every step, and everything around me was
blurred in the blast of the sun.

I reached the Wombat. David said nothing and drove me back
to the campground. The temperature reached 48°C. The fan David
had bought that day only spun the hot air into thick wind and I
thrashed around in it. Exhaustion, heat, pain and flies would not
let me sleep. I gave up. An airconditioned truck stop with food
were the next best things for refreshment, so we sat in one for the
few hours till 5 p.m.

Over a Coke, David began talking about my treatment of him,
probably prompted by my depression and meant as a pep talk.

'In the beginning you were pushing me away and making me feel
guilty for intruding on your "special world", this great atmosphere
you had to create. "I need to be alone." Now you're saying you
want me to be more involved with your walking. All that stuff
in the beginning was just bullshit, right? I am not walking across
Australia with you, I'm just the support guy. If you expect me to
be an Olympic coach, forget it. I'm not going to motivate you;
you have to do it yourself.' He looked away for a moment, slowly
shaking his head. 'When we drive back to Sydney, you'll be going

through some serious shit. There's a lot of stuff I'm holding back on, you'll know about it then.'

Silence. His words had bitten deep.

'I feel like a really nasty person.'

He touched my knee and contradicted himself. 'No, you're not.'

Not only had I lost David's faith, I had also lost self-respect because I was consistently falling below the nightly distance required to break the record. I knew that nothing could give me energy except the one motivation I had fallen back on all my life and which the walk was supposed to quell: anger.

'Will you be around after the walk?' I wanted him to smash the fantasy. I needed to be angry.

'Oh, I'll be contactable, I don't know what my plans are.' Visibly revelling in the freedom he would have then. And then the truth slapped me as I knew it would, as I wanted it to: we would never live together in Queensland.

Outside the temperature was 58°C. It felt like being packed into the underground in rush hour in summer wrapped in blankets. I had slept for half an hour that day. It was time to go out again.

Day 52

The blisters were dressed, the throbbing, white mess of them, some so deep he had to stab many times to find the well. Rolling his finger over the surface of another to force out the last of the liquid, he suddenly leapt back.

'Fuck!'

Pus had shot into his eye. He wiped it away and continued. More streams shot out and dribbled down his clothes. I looked at him, confused, and wanted to hug him. He gave me so much relief from pain that I couldn't help but love him. My wonderful, wonderful back-up driver who must have hated spearing those tattered wounds for the ungrateful little bitch who grew them.

I eased myself out into that furnace without energy, without confidence, without the slightest chance of walking more than sixteen kilometres. But I was not sunk so far that I missed the lavish sunset, streaked across the sky like orange crayons slashed across a woodchip board. Though the heat haze distorted the familiar sparse gum and the arid land beyond out of all recognition, I could still make out the road signs for the next settlement – just a truck stop, a grocer's and shop which sold electrical fans. As darkness fell a film of dust clogged my nose before entering my lungs where it lay heavy and burning. The trucks no longer brought relief with their tailwind; it burned. I cowered from it in the dark scrub and became bad tempered. I sensed the land was bad tempered too. The insects flung themselves with more venom against the Wombat's headlights. What did they think lay in the light that they needed so badly? And the roos were nowhere to be heard.

A freelance cameraman stopped to film us to give the national stations an update on my progress. His collar and tie looked silly in the desert. It was dark, so he shot some footage using headlamps instead of tungstens, but wanted to film me walking towards him.

'Ffyona?'

'What?'

'Can you walk up to that post, about 500 metres, then turn and walk back to me so I can get the light on you?' He was such a gentle man, soothing me with his careful directions, but I was exhausted and treated him unfairly.

'No.'

When they'd finished they said they'd be back in the morning to film me at dawn having walked through the night. If I'm still alive, I thought.

'Come on,' I called to David, and hobbled into the dark. The lights of the Wombat shone on the open road, casting a clear shadow ahead. An ungainly shadow, not one I would want Hillaby to see; a shadow I would keep to myself. David revved up the engine but was getting nowhere. I turned and faced him, lights brilliant in my eyes.

'Come on!'

'I'm stuck,' he bellowed. I retraced the wasted steps. The sand bank had sucked the Wombat into it, the wheels digging deeper when he revved.

'Get inside and press very lightly on the accelerator.' We changed places. So, this is what it was like! He went to the back and pushed. I sprayed him with sand and gravel.

'Stop! I'll try from the other end, put it in reverse.' After much pushing and rocking, the Wombat came free.

It had wasted our energy. We would have laughed at it once, but now there was no laughter, only a grim acceptance. I asked David if he wanted to go ahead and sleep.

'No, I'll stick it out for a while.'

But after another kilometre, he said, 'Hang in there, Champ,' and was gone.

His vote of confidence melted my earlier anger towards him. I wanted to reach out and touch him, show him I loved him. I probably accelerated my exhaustion with all the energy I expended over these sudden swings of emotion.

The light from the moon was glowing on the straight, pale grey road. The heat gnawed at my consciousness, forcing my eyelids to close. I rested them for a while and stumbled, losing balance. Using my fingers I forced my eyes to open; with saliva from my mouth I moistened them. But the wind dried them again. My body was trying to sleep but my mind could keep it awake. The atmosphere was too oppressive for song; poetry would keep me awake. I thought of all the pieces I didn't know well and puzzled through them, repeating them like the motion in my legs, up and over and down again. Drunk with the weeks of walking, my words began to slur. 'With all its sham, drudgery and broken dreams . . . broken dreams . . . broken dreams, it is still a beautiful world.'

There, in the dark shadows, I saw something under the trees that didn't move with the wind. I had repeatedly asked David to leave a light on in the Wombat but he rarely remembered to do it. So I then did not know if I had passed it or whether I would have to turn back and search the shadows again.

The food tasted of dust and of tin can. I was tired and annoyed with David and became even more so when he told me he was exhausted and would have to sleep. I let him go but knew I wasn't going to last long. I was afraid. I had no lifeline. I didn't care about wolves or vampires, but I feared the wind, feared that it would lull me to sleep. The only thing that would keep me awake was pain.

I began to crawl on my hands and knees and forced them to draw blood from the thorns of the desert floor. But when there was no more energy to enforce the pain my body took over and I vomited. Then, like an animal, I crawled on. 'The Lord is my Shepherd, I shall not want – I shall not want – He leadeth me . . .' All I knew was which way I was going and that I had to get there before dawn.

My stomach convulsed and left me paralysed. Crouching there helplessly, I heard a voice in the wind, clear and strong.

'Come on, lovey, one last ditch effort.'

'Ma?'

'Just one last ditch effort.' I straightened, lifted my head and strained to hear her again. When no sound came but the rasping of my breath I pressed my palms on the road and moved my legs straight behind me in a push-up position. From there I bent my knees and drew my hands and feet closer to each other. And stood.

A pale glow of a kilometre marker in the bush told me there was an hour and fifty minutes to go, but longer if I didn't walk faster. Whenever I was tempted to fall and vomit, my mother's voice beckoned me westwards. I fell into a trance, knowing nothing but her calling until the Chariot turned north in the sky.

Dawn. A fly landed on my lip. Then another stuck to my tear duct, followed by swarms. The noise of a car horrified me; if they questioned me now I might break. In my mind I implored them not to stop.

'Lovely morning!' It was the camera crew. 'Where's David?'

No answer.

'We'll go ahead a-ways and catch you with the sun rising.'

I realised, even then, that I could not let them film me in the shoes I wore. They were not Adidas. I tore them off when the crew were ahead and walked barefoot, but the lack of shock absorption added a new dimension of pain. I had no choice but to wear the shoes I had with me. But once my feet had been unharnessed and spread to their normal width, I put them back into my shoes which were now too tight and this brought fresh energy from pain. And I walked. Thud, thud, thud.

'Ffyona?'

Thud, thud, thud. Thirty minutes to go. Thud, thud, thud. I *will* make it. I conjured up my father's face so that hatred would drive me on.

'Ffyona, can you just wave the flies away? We can't see your face.'

I was in a trance and acknowledged only the brow of the road.

'The flies, can you just wave them away?' The words were a hum, and even if I had heard them, I could not raise my arm to brush away the swarm. I knew fear. What if David had forgotten to press the mileometer and was further ahead? But the trance was too strong for thought and I thudded again, aware only of the road. Twenty minutes to go.

Something was obscuring my view of the road ahead. Something was waving its arms and had long hair.

'Ffyona?' A death adder was in my path, I stepped over it. 'Ffyona?' The obstruction was very close. 'Can you just walk in the middle of the road, I'll watch out for cars?' Ten minutes more. 'Ffyona? Can you hear me?' No, lady, I can't hear you. Thud thud thud.

I blocked out the hum and steadied myself to look only at the horizon. The object with hair had gone. I strained to search the horizon for the shape of the Wombat, but I couldn't see further than ten feet. As I rounded a corner, David appeared at the side of the road and I found myself trying to form the words. 'Oh my God! My dear God, David!'

The television crew were clapping. The last few steps brought an almost uncontrollable urge to hug David.

'Hullo, Fee.' He was cold and stepped back, handing me a bottle of water. I stumbled suddenly but could not see to reach out and steady myself.

'Can we do an interview now?'

'Of course you can,' said David.

'Did they wake you, David?' I said.

'I was already awake.' They moved away to get their equipment.

'Be nice, please.' The feeding of the flies continued and the sun blazed as the microphone edged towards me.

'Right then, Ffyona, why are you walking across Australia?'

Day 53

As far as I was concerned, the interview I gave that morning was the best I'd ever done. If the cameraman wanted to send back a report of what it was like for me on the road, then that's exactly what he got. The purpose was to stir the public into donating to the charity. Throughout the interview, David kept interrupting me, nudging me; he thought I was being too harsh. I seemed to be blaming the Australians for the very fact that I was walking across their country. 'I walked all this way, I'm in all this pain and you still can't get off your arses and give me a round of applause for effort by donating to a charity which is for the benefit of your own children.' It didn't swell the coffers by a cent, and I can understand why. I didn't realise at the time how foul-mouthed I could be, since swear-words had become our only adjectives. The interview was probably so full of bleeps that nobody could hear what I was trying to say.

A breeze lifted from the Bight and brought a storm which calmed me. Black clouds suddenly flashed and flickered with white light. Forks of lightning exposed the ground from every direction as if it were day. It was a display to walk in time with, to take my mind off the road. I felt David near me then, near my world, a world moving forwards, never stopping to savour a moment. We both spoke of a time, one day in the future, when we could stop and watch the sky. But not now. Bound by endurance, which was all we had in common, David and I were able to lower the walls of the walking relationship to tell secrets and become, at least temporarily, friends. It was mutually understood that nothing we heard or spoke of must ever be brought up again. But in moments of despair, I mulled over the words that David had spoken and the strength they gave me compensated for the loneliness of perseverance.

Watching the Wombat trundle away into the dark didn't evoke

resentment; my emotions were at the mercy of the elements and tonight they were merciful. I slid into a lullaby of balanced walking conducted by the cool wind and the spinning and flashing of the world above.

Because the Wombat, and all that was in it, registered relief from pain, so David became the symbol of walking without pain. And as the desperate pleasure I drew from that lilting movement grew, David became so inextricably bound to it that all my joy of walking focused on him. But this was dangerous, I could no longer think of peace and pain-relief without thinking about David. I became confused and, without realising it, I was building David another pedestal, higher, because of the pain before, than the others had been. But perhaps it wasn't such a bad thing after all.

David was softly sleeping. I entered quietly so as not to wake him. He murmured a greeting.

'Ssssh, don't get up,' I said. 'I'll make some breakfast.' It was the first time I had not demanded that he get up and make me food, the first time I realised how exhausted he was and how valuable to my success. I was careful to be quiet while I made breakfast, dawn was so peaceful in the cool drapes of yellow light. He sat up slowly, I felt him so warm and drowsy beside me.

Day 54

Saw our first sign for Perth! Yeeeeeeha! The bad news was, it was still 1,964 kilometres away.

The road into Ceduna was dark under heavy cloud – a good temperature for walkers and for spiders. Big black ones scuttled around and froze in the beam of the headlights. They crunched underfoot but remained whole. Perhaps aeroplanes should be built of spider skin.

The small coastal town of Ceduna with its fishing jetty and pizza cafés was named after an old Aborigine word meaning to sit down and rest. How I wished I could but from here on we were on our own. The real test was about to begin. There were no towns until Norseman except truck stops which, although marked on the map as villages, consisted of one building whose existence was only justified by travellers. There would be petrol pumps, coffee machines, a snackbar/restaurant, sometimes a telephone that worked, sometimes water if it rained, a motel and a patch of dried scrub called a caravan site. Before us stretched the Nullarbor Plain, that much talked of, little known about, expanse of desert that I had longed to walk across.

It was easy walking – the road was so flat that the occasional fan of headlights in the sky could be seen twenty minutes before they passed. The trucks seemed more urgent to get somewhere, and the cars fled off the plain as though they were being chased. And fear they might, for only a few months before, the strange stories of unidentified flying objects had reached a head with tales of a car being picked up, showered with ash, turned round and being deposited back on the road. Everyone was aware of the American space-tracking station at Pine Gap near Alice Springs, but nobody knew what went on there. The truckies believed all the stories. Some claimed to have seen 'things'. The way they spoke in the truck stops suggested I might have to rethink my conviction 'Beyond here you be on your own.'

Day 55

I slept while David drove me around Ceduna like a baby in a perambulator, re-registering the Wombat, picking up more supplies for the desert: Fruit Loop cereal and biscuits. Both of us longed to be back on the Hay diet but fresh food supply wasn't available. Food was chosen for its entertainment value rather than for nutrition.

The last few rays of daylight painted the desert colours on my mind; I would remember through the night that yellow existed. The wind was from the ocean and chilled me into action. The Half-Heart didn't stay above the horizon for long at night now, but I felt if I walked fast enough, I might keep up with it. In its place the constellation I came to call The Prince of Wales Feathers was my focal point when walking south-west.

The profundity of thought people assume a walker attains never materialised for me. I felt obliged to have a bash at it – being in the desert under all those crosses in the sky, and going through pain barriers – but I failed miserably. Never got further than thinking about being profound, wondering what the hell I was doing out there at 3 a.m., and how I could lay my hands on a gooseberry fool.

A car which had passed me slowed, turned around and then stopped at an angle across the road interrogating me with its headlights. All I could hear were the thumps and shouts of drunken men. I stepped off the road into the bush – Lord knows where I thought I was going, but anywhere seemed safer than the road. Someone called, 'G'day,' and I turned to see the silhouette of a tall, Atlas-like man in a ten-gallon-hat get out of the car and walk towards me. I felt threatened. I didn't return his greeting. The yells and thudding of the drunk men grew louder.

'Yous garna carry on walkin' or yous garna to stop and talk?' I stopped, uneasy, but feeling the cold night giving me energy to run if I had to, though I wouldn't have got far on all those blisters. He held up his hands a little to show, it seemed, that he was unarmed.

'Don't be jumpy, just wanna know why yous walkin' down the road with a torch.' The pitch lifted at the end, in typical Strine and turned the statement into a question. My first reaction was to answer, 'I'm walking down the road because I want to get somewhere and I'm carrying a torch so that I don't bump into anything on the way.' Instead I said simply, 'Because I'm walking across the country.' Never had those words sounded more improbable.

'Sorry!' His hands flipped up in a sarcastic gesture of despair. 'Won't bother yous again, mate.' And he climbed back into the car. It was then that I saw the markings on the side. He was a policeman.

My rule of 'be defensive, apologise later' was checked by guilt. The police have a tough job patrolling the desert roads and even with his hands full of troublesome drunks he had stopped to make sure I wasn't in trouble. It was too late for apologies and I turned back to the darkness.

I walked through the smattering of buildings that was Penong and the light which had shone out across the desert as a golden crown was none other than a Marino restaurant at the truck stop. It was safe in there, full of Them, but I didn't stop as a traveller would. Penong was a village for travellers with a video library which, at 4 a.m. still had a neon 'Open' sign switched on outside. I looked in at the empty moonlit shop and wondered if the business suffered much from unreturned films. And then the last building in the village, a school. The silhouette brought back the fearsome memory of being a new girl yet again at my fifteenth school. I felt the anxiety of always being monitored by the other children, who were looking for ways to belittle the newcomer, mistaking shyness for snobbery. But I was on the outside now, looking in. I'd never have to enter there, and with belated relief I walked on. It was one of the blessings of a speed record attempt; nobody could force me to stop and participate – in anything.

About three kilometres out of Penong, I heard it. First, as a kind of wind moaning through railway tracks or an old barn. But there was no wind. It began low and got higher like someone running a finger up a vibrating guitar string. It was a metallic noise which turned into a twanging sound like a Jew's Harp. Then it came again, this time from a field on my left. I tried to think of all the possibilities but the one which stuck in my mind was that a group of Aborigines were engaged in a tribal ritual in the darkness. I knew that some of their rituals could only be witnessed by those who had been initiated so I was careful not to explore, but kept my distance. I walked without my torch, stepping as lightly as possible, keeping inside any shadows which crossed my path and trying not to slip on dead animals. I was learning not to fight the blackness nor be frightened by the unfamiliar, but to accept the give and take of the road. The fact that I thought someone was following me became rather more comforting than frightening.

David had remembered to leave the torch on so I saw the Wombat under the shadows of gum on a long stretch of pale grey road. It was so peaceful sitting there – it was asleep, waiting for me – and I crawled into bed convinced that I would wake up and walk through the dawn and the fourth quarter. But we slept on and by the time we woke, it was far too hot to continue.

Without asking me, David got up, marked the road and drove back the way I had come. It was a cop-out; I should have pushed on further in the knowledge that a night of rest would follow. I'd let myself and the night down.

Day 56

A night of rest.

Lord knows how many kilometres and weeks we'd been at this, I couldn't even think to divide fifty-six by seven. Lying on the sofa as David drove back to Penong to pick up some provisions, I felt frustrated – we hadn't 'shaken on the week', there had been no 'Good job', those two words of praise David had uttered at the end of previous weeks. It hadn't been a good one.

I was getting bored. Each quarter seemed one last ditch effort with an anticlimactic snack and the mumbling of some desultory conversation at the end of it. To David I felt I had become the puppy which needed feeding and putting out for the night. He had once leant across the table in a pancake café in Canberra and said, 'Thanks, Fee, thanks for getting me out of Hong Kong.' But that acknowledgement of freedom and his jokey good humour had also subsided into boredom.

From Penong we drove south for the night of rest to Point Sinclair on the coast. In the distance the saltbush was suddenly transformed into white glacial mountains. I gasped. David remained unconcerned and silent. I studied the topological map but was shocked to find they weren't marked: they didn't exist. In fact the 'mountains' were brilliant white sand dunes sculpted like the surface of a meringue pie. No porcupine grass had grown to anchor them, and they blew and recreated themselves at will.

The camping area at Point Sinclair was a cornered-off maze of cleared scrub without electrical hook-ups or water. The site was dotted with tents and 'mouldy shower curtain' caravans; and in them lived the original, no frills, no fakes, beach bums. They came to windsurf on the best coast in Australia. Their cars were older than they were, their hair was uncombed and wild, their skin brown as hazelnuts. They breathed the life of the waves. Any other bum would stink and be unfit, but these were beautiful.

David sped away on the motorbike, our emergency back-up which we pulled on the trailer, to play, and I went down to the sea. With all the sun and wind in my life it was unnatural to be cooped up in the Wombat and the chance of a swim was irresistible. The white dunes shimmered with a strange iridescence from a fine dusting of Mother of Pearl. The breeze whipped cuttlefish into life and tangled them in fingers of seaweed which lay in rims of tide. Beach bums in wet suits harnessed the wind and sliced through the waves as I swam and slept and swam again. Lying there, that day in the sun, I waited without anxiety for some greater impulse to drive me on.

David startled me with an ear-splitting yell as he sprang from a sand dune and sprinted down the beach in his swimming trunks. I casually glanced after him but was shocked when I saw the state of his body. He had grown stubby and fat. He hurled himself out of the water and came plodding up the beach, patting his belly. 'I'm a cute little dumpling, aren't I?' It hit me hard; he refused to walk with me – he, a former aerobic instructor and model, preferred to lose his figure rather than walk with me.

I awoke after our boozy night at 9.30 a.m. I had meant to get drunk but I hadn't meant to sleep for fear of messing up my sleep pattern. As I cleaned out the Wombat David put up the map banner and added a few more footprints to mark my progress. I was overwhelmed by a sense of inadequacy. I needed to calm myself and not dread the walking, so I looked at myself; monitoring the positive developments of my body was not only a superficial boost to continue but also the very type of motivating force I was walking to develop – positive observation as opposed to my life-long friends, resentment and anger.

Although my cycling shorts had rubbed the hairs from my thighs, leaving them bald and blue-white, I was feeling good in my clothes and my legs were becoming sleek and strong. Muscle tone had improved along with circulation and my skin was clear. It felt good to put on some lipstick and brush my hair free of tangles and dirt. I wished I had done it sooner for when David came in he looked at me and said, 'What have you done? Brushed your hair?'

'Yes.'

'It's amazing.'

But my interaction with David had largely become a series of complex ruses aimed at getting more than a monosyllabic answer, if any. And he in turn would lure me into asking interested questions about something he had been doing, only to snap a snide remark at me and I would deflate. Deserts and shared experiences make either firm bonds or fierce enemies. We had become like brother and sister in that we knew where to jab the knife and where to twist it, but the days of secret sharing were over. Coupled with the power struggle of who was leader, the unspoken plutonomy of our relationship screamed between us forcing us to prove we neither needed sex nor found the other attractive. The suppression of accepting ourselves as human and of the opposite sex caused us to channel the charge of those desires into resentment. It was by far one of the most self-destructive hardships of the walk, and one which time and again led me to lose confidence in even the most natural of my abilities. If I failed at this, what chance did I stand of using my body unnaturally?

I became aware that David's confidence was also ebbing when I heard him say to a dark-haired surfer-girl: 'This is a great place. Ffyona once told me she could find another back-up driver at the drop of a hat – I think I'll stay.' I decided to let him vent his spleen; after all, he'd heard an update of mine every two and a half hours.

Attempts at sleep in the 45°C heat were futile. I dressed and began packing everything away.

'Let's go,' I said.

'Too hot?'

'No, too boring.'

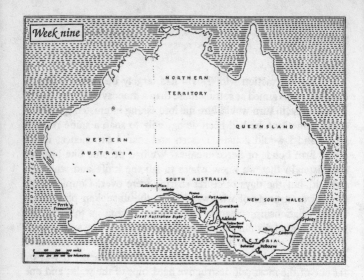

Day 57

We sat in the truck stop in Penong, ignoring each other and waiting for the day to cool. The root of our silence was the drinking water; Penong had none and neither did we. I couldn't stop thinking about Shuna. She had been in my mind for the last few days and I wondered if she had been thinking about me too. I missed her so much, missed her laughter and our own private jokes. I took out my diary and wrote her a note, trying to explain what I was going through, hoping that by thinking about her she might sense what I was writing. 'Forgive me my confusions. I have been in a wilderness where pain and majesty walk hand-in-hand beside me.'

After five hours the temperature eased but the north wind blew hotter with the setting sun. It was time to be moving on. A truck driver gave us water and as a result I felt powerless to insist that David should not rely on such a source. He never listened to me.

David drove with me during the first quarter. I knew he didn't want to be there; he didn't want to be on the walk at all.

'I owe you an apology.'

'Oh?'

'I said I could replace you if I needed to.'

'Yeah?'

'Well, I'd like you to know it isn't true. I could find another back-up driver if you left, but I couldn't replace you. I'm sorry.'

'That's OK.'

And I leant over to kiss his arm and smiled as though it would solve everything.

A couple of cars slowed and shone their lights on us but didn't stop or call a greeting before driving off. David drove three kilometres ahead to make the first meal. And that was when I saw it first.

The night was dark and cloudy but on the horizon were intermittent fan-shaped flashes, spraying faint white light repeatedly in the same part of the sky. There were three lights: one in the centre of the road at the brow which turned out to be a car, but the other two, one on each side, did not pass me. I thought perhaps there was a disused road ahead where kids were driving their cars around in circles. Or maybe it was a lighthouse since the flashes came in pulses and pauses. We were near the sea, it was possible. It could be that the road meandered sharply up ahead and those were the lights of cars going around the bends. But why would a road through the desert have twists in it like that?

The light display grew more violent as I reached the Wombat. David suggested it was heat lightning – distant lightning reflected on the clouds, usually accompanied by thunder. There was no thunder but since there seemed no other explanation, I accepted his opinion. But when he left me I felt uneasy.

A heavy fog fell and a fierce north wind blew the cloud tightly around me. But even through the dark and the cloud, the lights continued to dance and flare with purples, blues and pinks. I could hear nothing over the wind, I could see very little through the fog and felt crowded and captured. Cars sped past from nowhere, but they didn't stop.

My shadow suddenly leapt out in front of me. I spun round and saw the heavens split open, flash green and then close. The lights were playing havoc with the horizons, penetrating the fog. Again there was a flash and I was lit up in green light.

I thought of nothing but getting to the Wombat as quickly as possible. But the markers said David was almost two hours away. I began to sing, but my words were lost in the wind. I thought of poetry but it was all too safe and distant. Nervously I shouted, 'Take me! Take me!' But the joke fell flat. I could hear a few things by turning my good ear away from the wind, but what I heard made me turn quickly back again. Something was screaming. The Road Devils were having a field day.

For the rest of the time on the road I jumped and shuddered in my uneasiness, stumbled and slipped in the wind, lit up by strange green shafts from above. Eventually, tired, scared and confused I reached the Wombat where David lay oblivious to the turmoil outside. I moved close to him, quickly checking his face to make sure it wasn't green with the odd antenna sprouting through his hair.

I slept fitfully while the wind battered against the Wombat, making the cups and plates rattle in the cupboards. After two hours I crawled out of bed in the strange lights of early day. I covered my eyes with my hands, tightly pursed my lips and stepped out into a dust storm. My body bent against the west wind. It was hopeless. I fumbled with a piece of cloth and tied it around my head, covering nose and mouth, and pulled my sunglasses down to meet it. My breath came in gasps and my nose became too clogged to breathe through. It was hot, over 55°C. The whole world was red and brown, furiously spinning around me. Bush and small shrubs suddenly hurtled out of the red, flying a foot off the ground, I dodged them, trying to keep my head up to watch for them. David had no problems; the wind was not blowing from the north into his window and he sat there staring at me.

'Go ahead and see how far this lasts.'

'You want me to come back or stay at the end?' Oh foolish question.

'Come straight back.'

I felt terribly claustrophobic. The vast horizons had shrunk to pockets of pale red through which I could see no more than two metres. The sand in the wind scratched my bare thighs and arms and I lost balance many times from holding my hands up to shelter my eyes. The storm was angry, picking up rubbish and throwing it at me. My eyes were raw from grit, and the restrictive cloth on my face was sodden and caked with red.

Out of the corner of my eye I suddenly saw the front of the Wombat. I leapt aside in case he hadn't seen me.

'How much more of this?' I screamed over the wind.

'It doesn't stop.'

When I ripped off the mask to breathe again, David was astonished at what he saw; my face was a mess of red dirt, and globules of it lined the runnels of sweat. He made me stand there for more precious minutes while he fumbled with the camera. I could barely see the Wombat though I was less than a metre from it. He got out, clicked and dashed back to escape the mess of it.

We couldn't survive in the Wombat so we spent a precious $45 and booked into a room at the Nundroo truck stop motel. I stood an hour in the shower, everything I touched was streaked with red and I wasted another hour cleaning up the mess. It was cool in the room and the walls were thick enough to muffle some of the storm outside. With thoughts of the Aboriginal reserve which had to be crossed tomorrow, I fell in time with David's snores and slept.

Day 58

Sitting in the motel room at the back of the truck stop was the first time my feet had been syringed in hygenic conditions since the last visit to a doctor. Even though I could hardly walk after the operation, I felt they would heal better. We were careful to use our supplies stringently; there would be no way of replenishing them until Norseman which lay twenty-three days' walk ahead. There were four clean syringes left. To prevent infection we would require three per day. Instead, David re-used each syringe until the needle channel became clogged with pus and Betodine.

We sat in the airconditioned restaurant, an oasis in the desert marred only by the lack of cold Coke, and waited for the storm to die down. David had taken advantage of the shower and looked clean and dashing in a jacket from the 'other world', but he looked drawn.

We talked of the Schedule. David had calculated that if I carried on at this pace, I would not break the speed record. Our funds were also running low – another reason why I would have to push myself harder every day. But I was well rested from the few hours' sleep in the cool and I resolved to make this energy last.

Back on the road, I met a real wombat, solid, squat and thick-set, and I trotted gently beside her. Unsure of what to do, she reversed and scuttled back into the darkness. She was a fool to fear me and not the road. Wombats lined the verges, upturned and dead. The roos were back; their thudding echoed in the night and vibrated under my feet. They held no respect for the road and they paid the price. I flashed my torch and growled to warn them of approaching trucks, but the tell-tale thud crunch proved it was futile.

David was sneezing and mumbling through heavy mucus. Shadows cast by the headlights emphasised the sunken hollows in his grey face. I fed him paracetamol and fruit juice. I had to keep him healthy; I could not allow him to pass anything on to me. It was my turn to take care of him and he seemed to give in to it, though a little reluctantly at first, and drove ahead to sleep as soon as I stepped on to the road again.

During the last five kilometres of the quarter my eyes began to jump. I could no longer focus steadily on the horizon. The loose muscle in my right eye would always double my vision when I was tired, but now that vision bounced. My head hurt, my skull clicked, my eyes throbbed. It worried me. Was I going blind? It couldn't happen to me, there were enough things to go wrong: my lower back, my hips, my feet, but not my eyes as well. I shoved the fear back in its place and concentrated on David. In my mind he was with me in every step, his presence was warm about me, and a sudden desire filled me just to be with him and compelled me to walk faster and faster, counting the markers with new urgency. Although well aware of our common battle, the battle to end it all and go our separate ways, that night I didn't care what would happen at the end. I just wanted to be with him and lie with him and care for him.

A warm tenderness filled me, a feeling of unusual compassion. I was not tired as I stepped into the darkness where David lay. When he woke and suggested he make me some food I said, 'No.' He lay on top of the duvet and I undressed and lay beside him, pulling the second duvet over us. We fell asleep with my face nestled deep against his shoulder. He woke me with the sound of his cold. I nudged him softly.

'Ssssh, you're snoring.'

'I'm sorry.' And we slept again.

The sun came up and it grew warm in the Wombat. David woke and reached up to open the flaps. When he settled I moved towards him again and rested my cheek on his shoulder. Uninterrupted sleep seemed to be what his body had craved. When he woke he was playful with me, attentive and laughing, and stuck dressing tape to my nose and smiled, a smile that I could only respond to with a welling up of absolute happiness. His old practical jokes returned; he seemed to have emerged from the storm with a lighter heart, the old David, the one who wanted to play.

He drove back to Nundroo to buy supplies and I walked that wonderful road bursting with some strange emotion. The sun was warm, the land was red and coarse, and the smell of it when I knelt to press my face on it was sweet and rich.

At the end of the last quarter, we marked the road and drove ahead to Yalata, a truck stop on the edge of an Aboriginal reserve. The road was narrow and cut through banks of thick mallee that transformed the open plains into a heavy tapestry of blue and green Oil stains in rainbow circles patched the concrete of the truck stop, wasps hovered over the rusting five-gallon drums and the air lay still, heavy with the stench of old drains.

Aboriginal artefacts covered the walls inside, but there was no money for the artists because the road brought no tourists. The word from other truck stops was to keep clear; Yalata was a danger zone. I ordered a Coke and sat in the corner, watching.

The bell tinkled over the door followed by a scuttle of two pairs of bare feet on the linoleum, drawing a sigh from the cashier. The young Aboriginal woman was tall with long thin legs, ankles the width of my wrists and a flash of white on her soles. Heavy breasts protruded through an orange sweatshirt which nudged the band of her pleated burgundy skirt. Her face was knotted and silent. A small naked boy skipped beside her and he surveyed the sweet counter solemnly. He dragged a wooden chair from one of the tables set for lunch and launched himself on to it. Small brown fingers delved into the jars and caught a bunch of chocolate drops in a fist that was too big for the neck of the jar.

A few old Aboriginal men in varying states of ill health scuffed through the door and took up their places at a table, slouching against the wall. There was no movement amongst them; they each chose a focal point on the floor or wall and simply observed. Something in their observation kept them interested in living. They were neither bushmen nor western men; they lived on the edge, a displaced desert tribe brought to the thick gum land of Yalata. With money every month from the Government, the convenience of the truck stop replaced their interest in gathering bush tucker.

One of them was white. His face was sunburned, his hair was yellow and he hummed a few bars of a pop song and tickled a fat brown baby whose hair was the colour of desert sand. The man was an albino Aborigine. He had graduated from university in Adelaide, but had returned to the bush to live, not to talk.

I wanted to sit with them and learn from them for they were the masters of walking. Their ancestors had walked across this land in lines, singing the world into being: the grass, the trees, the gullies and creeks. The earth must be continuously walked and sung, as the ancestors did, to heal it. But were these men slouched against the wall so far from their tribal lands of the desert still able to walk their songlines? And if the land had the power to heal them, could it also heal me as I walked across it and sang to it?

Day 59

The precious hours of coolness and light were upon us. But before we left the truck stop we asked the cashier to stamp our witness book.

'I know all about you.' She grinned, stamping the page and dating it. 'I've just been reading in a magazine.' David and I exchanged glances. Magazine?

'Can we have a look?'

She pushed it towards us, open at the article. We had never seen it before. It was nothing to do with David. It was full of lies and badly written. I looked at the cover and was shocked. David laughed. Despite all my attempts to be taken seriously by the media, I was rewarded with a centrefold story in a semi-pornographic magazine. I had already warned David, back in Sydney, that I never wanted to see my face in such a publication. He snatched it away and pored over the pages, occasionally thrusting it in front of me to add insult to injury with pictures of half-naked, pouting women. I resented him more that day than any other. He would never appreciate me if he could laugh at that magazine, laugh at my effort, prefer their sexuality to my determination.

I walked out and sat on the driveway. Old Aborigine faces peered out at me from a battered Holden. My anger and resentment subsided when I saw them.

'You the one walking?' one of them said gently. They were such kind people.

'Yes.'

'How good is it?'

'Bloody awful.'

'I'd like to walk to Perth with you.'

'I'd love your company.'

They didn't find my walk absurd or abnormal but accepted it as a natural desire. The Aborigines understood the need to make a journey, they did not have to ask why I was doing it. And perhaps young Australians have learnt from them for they all take time to travel in their youth, discovering more than their everyday surroundings.

David came out and we waved goodbye to them. Back at the starting place I told him to go ahead, not to aid his convalescence but because his attitude to the magazine revolted me.

But in the failing light I still had the road as my companion. I began quietly to fall in love with the desert, kissing the land with my scars, feeling lonelier than ever and wanting to stay that way.

The night was black, the white line shone and gave me direction. I knew the Aborigines were there as I walked through Yalata, I felt them watching me not as wolves but as wise men, nodding at me in the dark.

It came as no surprise when I heard footsteps behind me. I knew I had been followed. There was no fear. Two songs beat out a rhythm, teaching me until two became one song, one knowledge, something deeper than any spoken word. He left me after a time but the rhythm of the night carried me through the first fourth quarter for many days. My body was weakening towards the end but my head was strong and filled with a new certainty.

Day 60

The sun melted through the trees, and the rough land glowed. No amount of ill feeling could contaminate such an evening as this. My feet and body, rested from sleep, carried me across the land protected from insult and resentment in a honeycomb casing of sunlight.

We had both been suffering from constipation. Yalata had provided us with dried prunes which we set about eating with humour, sucking the sticky sweet flesh from the stones and blowing them out. It was easy for me to turn my head and 'Pa!' out would fly the stone, but for David there was only one place, and that was in my direction. He caught me a few times before I realised it was intentional and suddenly we were grabbing and fighting over the fruit to gobble the flesh and fire whole mouthfuls at each other. When I became over-enthusiastic and forgot the power of my mouth, he would press his foot down on the accelerator and hang out of the window laughing and preparing another mouthful for when I caught up with him. Our clothes were smattered with black and purple dye and for weeks we discovered dried prune pips in the most inaccessible places around the Wombat. However, the constipation continued.

We had spoken many times over the past week about the

diminishing money supply; I had not budgeted for the walk to take more than eighty days and it appeared that ninety to ninety-five days would be more realistic. Neither had I budgeted for the amount of dressings needed for my feet which, because they didn't manufacture them then, had not been donated by Scholl.

There were only two solutions: to walk faster or cut down on expenditure. If both of those failed, I would approach my financial sponsors for a small amount each to make sure I reached Perth.

Our expenditure fell into two main groups: food and fuel. We could be more careful not to drive ahead or back to a truck stop; if it was possible, we could stay in the desert to sleep during the day. As for the food, we had been eating at truck stops because they were convenient and offered us a variety of food and space in which to eat. But we had a trailer full of soup and spaghetti donated by sponsors which was being ignored. Thus, we decided, we would only spend money on perishables like bread and absolute necessities such as powdered milk and muesli.

However, after the heat of the final quarter of the morning, it was our one reward and almost a motivation in itself, to sit in an airconditioned truck stop and sip an ice-cold Coke. Back at Yalata when I had asked David to fetch me one to sup in the Wombat before sleep, he had refused because I didn't need it and we had to save money. He had then gathered all the loose change and made a call to a girlfriend of his in America at $7 per minute. Coke was $1 maximum. I thought this needed addressing.

'About the money situation.'

'Mm?'

From my experience with previous back-up drivers I knew they needed to have a break from the demands of the journey. During my British walk I was supported by a fifty-year-old reporter from my newspaper sponsor who would arrange the next evening's accommodation at a suitable Bed and Breakfast, drive back to give me directions then leave me alone for the rest of the day at my request. It wasn't an arduous job but he had a family back in London and needed to spend time with them so during my rest days he would drive home. The two men who supported my American walk were old friends, they could escape from the walk by going out dancing if we were near a town or simply by playing Pac Man. But David and I were so far from any means of escape and running so short of cash that there didn't seem any way he could have a day off. I suggested he might like to take the motorbike for a scramble in the desert but he wasn't enthusiastic.

'For all you've put into the walk I feel it is only fair that you have an outlet but we just don't have enough money for international phone calls. Calls for PR are the only ones we can afford. D'you agree?'

'Yeah.'

'So will you stop calling America?'

'No.'

'OK. Then will you please refrain from telling me I cannot have a Coke at the end of a hot day.' He was caught.

'Ffyona,' it was his whine. 'You don't need Coke, it's sugar. You can walk without it.'

'I will give up Coke if you give up international personal telephone calls.'

I don't know whether the deal stuck.

The land lent itself to the game of figuring out why I was walking, and recharged my assumption that somehow I was on the right track, for what other message could the dawn be bringing with such gentle fingers of early blue light? Somewhere through the night, the high dark banks of gum had melted into open desert plains. Low, stunted bluebush stretched to all horizons, there were no trees, it was absolute in its flatness. It was as if a plane had been sliced from the curve of the globe. I worshipped its simplicity and spread my arms wide to feel the vast nothingness, nothing of man, save the road and the litter of bottles and cans beside it, no fences, no bore pumps. Twigs and scrub clung to the earth, there was hope in the desert where nature lay naked.

David was with me. We had been silent for over an hour, occasionally communicating through looks that meant, 'Give me water,' and 'Thank you.' But something small and dark on the horizon gave him cause to speak.

'I think there's a rollerskater over there.' I jumped; I had heard about the Japanese rollerskater and had been longing to meet him and talked of little else to those who had come from the west, asking them if they had seen him.

'D'you really think that's him? He must be insane to skate in this heat. We must give him some water and some food, what d'you think the Japanese like to eat?' I tripped along happily staring hard into the distance as the black blob grew larger. All the things I wanted to ask him and to give him filled my mind. Once we had toyed with the idea of writing him a message on the road in case we passed him in the night, but the spray can had run out and we had no way of knowing if he could read English. David knew a few Japanese symbols, but he didn't know what they meant. He strained as I did, I could tell he was excited.

'Bet he hasn't had a shower for yonks – where's the next truck stop?' He pulled out the map and calculated our position.

'Nullarbor! It's no more than ten kilometres away. Fee, we're on the Nullarbor Plain!'

'We *are*?'

This was it! The real desert, and Lord, it was more beautiful than they had said. I was so glad then that others didn't know; how spoiled it would be if there were thousands of walkers walking here, staring across the shimmering land.

'No, no I don't think it's him, he's moving too fast.'

'He's on skates, remember. He's probably pretty good at it by now.'

'It's a cyclist.'

He was a bearded Australian called Pete, cycling from Perth to Melbourne, 'just for the hell of it.' We replenished his supply of water and gave him a bottle of Campbell's V8 juice. I asked him if he had seen the skater.

'No I didn't actually see him, but I know I've passed him.'

With that wonderful piece of news I walked into the melting white horizons and the ungiving heat.

A sign from the most blessed of the Road Gods loomed in the distance: WELCOME TO THE NULLARBOR PLAIN, EASTERN END OF THE TREELESS PLAIN. I hugged it, we videoed it, we photographed it, all in the presence of a handful of tourists who had stopped to do the same. We shared a bottle of our V8 juice and congratulated them on three days' hard driving from Sydney.

Between the sand-ridged Great Victorian Desert to the north, and the vertical cliffs of the Great Australian Bight to the south, lies the Bunda Plateau. it is one of the most featureless areas of the earth's surface stretching for 75,000 square miles. Within this plateau practically dead flat, bone dry and completely treeless is the Nullarbor Plain, derived from the Latin, *nullus arbor* – no tree. Upon it lie relics of old river courses, fossils from the dinosaur age and blowholes which lead down to catacombes of limestone caves. Although everyone refers to the 1,205 kilometres from Ceduna to Norseman as being the Nullarbor the road only touches the southern tip of the plain for about twenty-eight kilometres.

When the tourists had gone and I was alone for a moment with the land, there was that sense of belonging again. And I felt the land knew I loved it. That feeling took me back to the Cairngorm Mountains in Scotland from where I had begun my first solo journey. I was fifteen and taking a break from 'A' level studies by cycling 500 miles to see a friend. I pedalled a three-geared bicycle piled high with camping kit over those mountains and south to Newcastle. There I stayed for a day then headed back on the three-day return journey. When I reached the foot of the Cairngorms again, a howling sleet storm had blown up, forcing me to grind even harder up the steep, meandering road. After several hours I reached the top, threw down my bicycle and roared with delight. But the sound of my voice seemed to pollute the storms around me and I was silent looking at the craggy grey peaks of the old granite. I bowed to them, showing my respect for challenging me so hard. I sat for a long time up there, quietly getting to know the feel of the mountain.

The old road ran along the right and I walked on it in a heat-conquering trance, away from the cars and the road-trains. The road was cracked and overgrown with dry weed and small blue bush, and avoiding the split bitumen rubble prevented me from lifting my eyes to the featureless horizons. Slapping my face and thighs, I spurred myself to walk faster, furious that my limping pace kept me longer on the road.

A change of texture under foot, a few more steps and I reached the Wombat, parked under an awning in the shade beside a solitary track. Just as I turned to slide back the door, something caught my eye. I turned to face the restaurant and there he was: a tall, tanned, Japanese rollerskater walking towards me, grinning.

Day 61

He held out his hand, a broad smile splitting through his wiry goat beard, a silent oriental face of immense dignity. I took his hand and shook it with delight.

We herded ourselves into the bright modern café and ordered Cokes. It was a celebration! He also thought he'd missed us and had been receiving an update on our position from all the truck stops he passed. But when I began walking at night, the accounts seemed to have been mixed up with the mythical Nullarbor Nymph, a naked female said to wander the plains of the desert seen mostly by amphetamine-pumped truck drivers.

The restaurant air was so cold and refreshing that there were no thoughts of sleep. The rollerskater and I eased ourselves on to the seats, occasionally stretching out a limb to massage the tightening muscles. His name was Naoyasn 'Bon' Sato. He was twenty-two and alone in a country where he spoke little of the language but our gestures sufficed. We conversed in 'endurance language', and by his facial contortions, I knew he'd had it bad. He had been on the road for sixty-two days, a day longer than us, and had begun in Perth. He had chosen to skate alone but it was hard; he carried a fifty-pound pack on his back which made him lose balance in the tailwinds of trucks. He turned over his palms and we saw raw sores and gouges made by skidding on the gravel. His knees too were a mess of layered wounds, never able to heal before he fell again. And yet he had shown no sign of flinching when David and I had shaken his hand so fervently.

It was impossible for Bon to skate at night; his movements made the truck drivers mistake him for a kangaroo and they might swerve to hit him. So he would wake at 4 a.m. with the very first rays of light and finish around midday having covered an average of thirty kilometres. Every half-hour he stopped for water and food, eating muesli bars and dried fruit for immediate energy release. But there was no comfort for him at the day's end; he had to haul himself off the road into the bush, put up his tent, cook his food and sleep in the heat.

His courage was far beyond my comprehension; although we shared the same stretch of road, ruled by the same elements of discomfort, there was a silent strength in him that I knew I could never share.

We ate together and then I left to sleep while David took Bon to the bar. It was a hot day. The white plains were sterilised by the sun, and the Wombat was scorching.

When David woke me at 11 p.m., five precious hours of cool night had been wasted. He stank of beer and was so drunk he could hardly talk. Bon was smiling innocently and stayed to watch a very poor performance of the Ceremony of the Syringe. It was all I could do, in front of him, to stifle the screams. I finished the dressings as they both swigged another beer and, leaving them laughing and singing in the Wombat, I stepped out into the thick night.

The lights of the truck stop were visible behind me for over an hour. I did not know when David would come. He got so tired when he drank that he might sleep through the night. What would I do? A few cars passed at half hour intervals and I thought of walking to the kilometre marker that would indicate the end of that quarter and hitching back. But what if he came while I was in a car? He'd search the plains frantically.

While I was puzzling over what was to be done, a car slowed beside me. Remembering the incident with the policeman in Penong, I stopped. As two men staggered out of the car towards me, I realised too late that they weren't policemen. Drunken, drawling Australian accents cut the night.

'You got any money?'

'Shut up, Jeff! Whatcha doin'?' They were still moving towards me.

'I'm on a charity walk.'

'You got any fucking money?' There was anger in his voice. I wanted to walk on but I didn't want to turn my back on them. Someone inside the car hauled himself into the driver's seat and revved the engine.

'We need some money for petrol, we're out.'

'I don't have any.'

'You fucking bitch, I'll . . .'

'Shut ya face, Jeff, let me handle this.'

But that was all I was going to stand for. Furious at being confronted like this alone in the desert, my temper was high. I stormed off into the night hearing their shouts of abuse over the engine. But it wasn't over. They got back in the car, skidded on to the hard shoulder, turned around and then chased after me. I leapt into the bush and the car could easily have followed but instead it went some 200 yards ahead, did a shrieking handbrake turn and roared towards me again. The car attempted to mount the bank into the bush but skidded at the last moment. For a split second I didn't know if they'd made it. My hackles were up and I prepared to run. They span round, raced up the road again and then back, cutting so closely to the verge that I was hit by a shower of gravel. Shouting more abuse, they roared away.

Shaking with fury, I ripped out a bluebush and swung it round and round my head, freeing great clods of earth, and screamed in the direction of the disappearing red lights. I growled and spat. My breathing was quick and heavy as I got back on to the road. How dare they! And how dare David get drunk while I was out walking! What did he think he was doing? Spending all that money and abdicating his responsibilities. Even if something more serious had happened with those men, David was bound to shrug off any blame. And where the hell was he? Three hours had elapsed and still there was no sign of him.

Lights were behind me again, I climbed the verge into the bush. The lights were on high beam and they slowed. David never used high beam when looking for me. I picked up another handful of bluebush and grabbed as many stones as I could feel in the dark. When the lights were close I spun round.

It was David, a smirk on his face.

'What are you so annoyed about?' he mumbled. I glared at him, and wanted to smash him with the bluebush.

'Pull up over there.' With little co-ordination he manoeuvred the Wombat on to the bank. When I reached it, perhaps thirty seconds later, he was fast asleep in the front seat. I was by now overwhelmed with anger but realised that even if I could wake him there was no way I would allow him to drive ahead. So I could do no more walking. I lay under the covers and scowled.

The first lights of dawn woke me. I painfully syringed all the blisters and re-dressed them, brushed my hair, cleaned my teeth, ran a wet rag over my face, ate breakfast and woke David before setting off. He came alongside me soon after; it was obvious that he had a hangover and was on the defensive. I could see him waiting for the right moment to say something but I refused to give him the satisfaction of an argument. Nor could I bear him beside me, so I sent him ahead after gulping as much water as I could hold. It was not an easy day in which to be consumed with hatred; the sun scorched everything, sucking the night's moisture from every surface and the road steamed and shimmered.

The desert spread around me into flat nothingness. Something moved to the left, and I eased my head to look at it. It was a dog, trotting twenty feet away, staring longingly at me. I was furious that someone had abandoned a dog out there. I called out to it, patting my thigh in encouragement. It stopped and looked. It didn't respond but trotted off again, stopping every so often to look back at me. I suddenly realised it must be a dingo and found myself calling out to him more gently. He was alone in the desert as I was.

The Wombat's small white and blue form broke the far horizon but for the first time on the journey. I didn't want to get to it. I didn't want to get there because *he* was there and I wanted nothing to do with him. He had abandoned me, I hated him and I hated the Wombat: the smell of it, the luminous clock by the rear-view mirror, the dried flies suffocated in the muesli packet, the box cupboard with all its Betodine-stained syringes, and I hated the noise the Wombat made, grinding along on the hard shoulder and that blasting stream of heat it chugged out by the front wheel where I walked.

I hated needing someone who was prepared to abandon me, to leave me when I really needed them. So there he was, silent alongside me again and yet not with me. The heat was intolerable. I was dehydrating.

'I've got to stop,' I gasped. David looked at me, a look of superiority which forced me to lose my hold. 'You don't know how hot it is out here.'

'Well, Ffyona, I mean, what d'you expect me to do about it?'

I fell silent again and pushed on for another few, agonising kilometres, the blisters pulsing in my shoes, hot and wet through the blinding heat, everything white and moving. I could have vomited then, but David was there and, like my father, would be unable to sympathise with my weakness. Eventually I had to stop. My very soul seemed to have evaporated.

Bon was still at the truck stop when we drove back; he had to wait for new rollerskate wheels to be delivered from his travel agent sponsor. David consoled him, sympathising with the state of his hangover, and ignored me. I wandered back to the Wombat and tried to sleep.

The heat was much stronger than the day before, so I returned to the road house and sat in the airconditioning, talking to Bon and trying to tire myself enough to sleep. He, too, had gone through penetrating self doubt, confusion at his motives and wished it was over. But because he covered much less distance daily than I, he wouldn't finish until March 1989, another five months against my six weeks.

Then I noticed David was flirting with the cashier, asking for change.

'You went through quite a lot last night, didn't you?' she giggled. 'Playing that video game all afternoon until the bar closed. I saw you two!' I shot David a withering look but he avoided my eyes and called to Bon.

'Want a beer and another game?' Bon excused himself and followed him. At the door David turned and enquired if I would like to join them.

'No, thank you. I have to walk tonight. And please remember that the police want you to drive with me through the night in case I get run over.' I felt embarrassed that this confrontation had to take place in front of Bon, but David didn't seem to mind, he just smiled, a smirking, confident twist of the lips.

The only way I was going to show David that he was out of line in spending so much money, was to openly spend it myself, on trivial things. I ordered a hamburger, a hotdog, two Cokes, a banana split and a double ice-cream, none of which I wanted.

Day 62

'See you,' said Bon in the Australian way, and then added, 'later.' That afterthought tore at my heart; I didn't want to leave him alone in the hell of his endurance. We had given him what we could: a bottle of V8, cans of soup, dressings for his wounds, a tube of Deep Heat rub and a good nourishing meal in the restaurant, but I longed to give him a small phrase that he could constantly think about and draw strength from, a gem.

'Never, never think of the end.' It was what Hillaby had told me. I offered him this and leant forward and kissed his cheek. 'See you on the way back.'

Bon had suggested that I change back to walking in the day, using the middle hours for the lighter sleep I usually kept till night. The days, he said, were bearable. Although I had reservations about this, I longed to walk again in the day, to see what land I was walking through, to see the colours of the desert and the expressions of the people who passed in their cars, to return their waves and smiles again. I wanted to see yellow every day.

In the first part of the day David had been nursing his hangover. However, in the early evening he had woken me gently from sleep and his eyes were full of concern.

'We aren't getting along too well, are we?' I said softly.

Out in the desert night, I suggested he go ahead because he looked so unwell. I found him, a few hours later, curled up with a book and looking miserable. I now felt guilty, felt my bitter resentment after the drunken episode had been unnecessary. He'd only tried to have a break from the restrictive space of the walk, he hadn't spent time with another male since Venus Bay and he needed it. I sensed his weariness and helped him with the food.

'Heinz turns a lettuce into a salad,' he read from the can. 'If you ask me they turn a lettuce into a disgrace. Look at this.' Globules of mayonnaised carrot and peas slithered off his fork, the cue for a good fight. Tired as we were, we managed to laugh as we flicked pieces of 'disgrace' out into the desert.

The second quarter was walked mostly alone. I was especially careful to move into the bush when a truck passed. The truckies had reported their concern for my safety to the police; apparently they often fall asleep at the wheel and only the noise of the truck launching on to the gravel will wake them. By that time it would be too late for me.

As I walked, I realised I would have to treat David more carefully. He may have been irresponsible but he was helping me achieve my goal. He didn't want to be there but had stuck it out for me. I climbed into the Wombat and settled my body against his to sleep for a few hours.

Day 63

David pulled out the semolina and we mixed up a new variety of 'Trans-Australia Walk Style' gruel. We depipped the remainder of the prunes. For both of us, laughter was so important that to do without it, as we had done for the past few days, was as damaging as going without water.

Out on the road we munched on a few fruit sticks from Heinz which were meant as teethers for 'toddlers and children of all ages'.

'You're not getting the full benefit of the flavour by wolfing it down like that; you have to suck.' And he demonstrated. I thought it was a little suggestive but I played innocent and tried to be as unselfconscious as possible. With a piece melting in my mouth I adopted a most unflattering lisp and recited a poem my father had taught me as a child.

'My Mummy theth I lithp, my Daddy theth I lithp, but I don't think I lithp, do you?' with an enquiring look at David, dribbles of cherry-flavoured saliva erupting from my lips. I grinned at him and he playfully pushed my face away with his hand.

In high spirits, David demonstrated his acrobatic driving skills by sliding as close to the white guide posts as possible. Over-confident, he hit one, scraping the sides of the Wombat with a most astonished expression on his face. 'Oooops!'

I was too busy laughing to think of any damage. In any case, it had only left a layer of white paint on the van body.

He put me in an even better mood when he announced that if I kept up a minimum of fifty-nine kilometres a day (which was five kilometres less than four quarters) we only had twenty-seven days to go! Excited as I was, I didn't really believe it would ever end, I still couldn't imagine there really was 'life after walk'.

David's back had begun to irritate him. He couldn't turn his head without shooting pains running down his neck but he was determined to keep it to himself. I could tell when it was bad, because his eyes glazed over and he became snappy. He almost lost his temper at the first break, when he went out into the windy evening to search for the can of tomato soup I requested. Ants had bitten his legs and when he climbed into the Wombat, bulbous-bodied moths swirled around his head, getting caught in his ears and up his nose. As he lashed out at them, he winced from the pain in his back.

It was actually raining in the second quarter. A good headwind blew and I waltzed with it in the rain. I had forgotten about rain. For the first time in weeks, I felt cold. To me it was a source of refreshment. David pulled out a tape to distract him from his pain, but it didn't work. We didn't sing with it – it didn't lift his spirits. I decided he'd had enough. I knew he wouldn't allow me to stop before the end of the quarter on his account, so I threw him some feeble excuse that my hips were hurting and he pulled up ahead. It had been a long week.

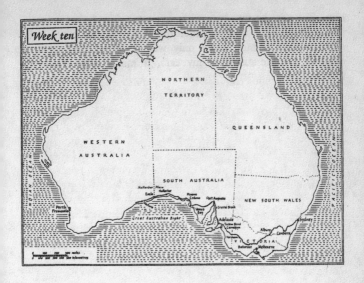

Day 64

A Day of Rest.

During our rest day rocketing winds lashed the Wombat with raindrops the size of gum nuts. We were in a state of doldrummed suspension, best summed up by David's Quote of the Day: 'Here we are, parked in a puddle.'

'If it wasn't raining outside, I'd go out and gather stones and write my name with them on the desert sand,' I twittered, glancing over to David who was engrossed in Graham Greene's *Brighton Rock*. No response. 'I must get rid of these warts, they've been on my fingers for four years. But I do rather like them.' Silence. 'Often, when I am alone at night, I walk on the road without my clothes on.' I raised an eyebrow at him; he hadn't heard me.

I switched on a tape to annoy David. It was one I had listened to at the beginning of the walk when I thought differently about him. But now he was here with me, not a friend, not a lover, just a David. The beat reminded me of how I once could walk in time with it but now I only walked to my own beat, I couldn't tolerate music in my ears, it muffled the sound of my thoughts.

Part Three Glazing

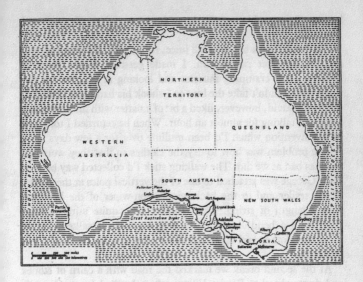

Day 65

The new schedule of walking through the day which Bon had suggested could not have begun in better weather. Grey bumpy clouds raced across the sky and covered the sun in a thick mossy shroud which it tried, with little success, to burn through.

Our conversation in the first quarter consisted mostly of taking the piss out of *Sinbad the Sailor*. But when we listened to a tape of *The Little Match Girl*, there was a painful silence between us. I was desperately trying to hide a few tears only to notice that David had reached for his sunglasses in an attempt to do the same.

Amusement in the second quarter appeared in the form of an English cyclist from Portsmouth. During the summer months in England he sold ice-cream to tourists who arrived at the beach for their annual week of sunshine which, thanks to the greenhouse effect, was hot enough to make him rich. In the winter months, he set off to test his muscles in such places as New Zealand and Australia.

We dispatched a bottle of V8 juice, replenished his water supply and couldn't get rid of him. I made gestures in the form of stretching my cramping muscles and looking at the sun for the time, but he didn't take the hint so I shook his hand and turned to the road. David, however, liked a bit of a natter with his desert and remained talking for almost an hour. When he returned I told him of my invention which I'd been mulling over for a few days.

The problem was how to dry the clothes so that they wouldn't smell as bad as we did. The walking stick I'd collected way back at Lake George was attached to one of the vertical poles at the corner of the trailer and to the back windscreen-wiper of the Wombat with a length of string. The Wombat had, quite miraculously, come with a handful of clothes pegs so while I walked, David hung the clothes and came trundling after me like a third world caravan.

At the second break we marked the road with a cairn of stones and drove ahead to Border Village where I called James Capel & Co., my major financial sponsor. We were very short of money. The PR girl in Sydney was the first person I tried, just to test the water. She was encouraging and said she'd fax the 'appropriate department' in London but wouldn't be able to give me a reply for at least three days.

I went back to the truck stop, gathered the last of our change and crossed my fingers as I called Adidas.

I was given the brush-off by someone's secretary and told to call back in an hour. When I did so the man still wasn't out of his meeting.

'Is there someone else I can talk to? I'm in a pay phone on the Nullarbor and I need an answer as soon as possible.'

'You can talk to me.'

'Um, who are you?' She sounded remarkably like the secretary I had spoken to earlier.

'I'm in charge of the walking budget. Are you the girl walking across Australia?'

'Yes.'

'You can't have any more money. We've used up the whole of the budget. Sorry.'

'There must be another budget . . .'

'No.'

'Perhaps I could speak to someone else who . . .'

'No. I'm sorry. Goodbye.'

She couldn't possibly imagine how much grit it had taken to get this far as she sat in her airconditioned office on just another day. I had only just begun to accept the mental battles of the walk, learning to deal with daily pain in my lower back, the torture of the blisters, and to think that the walk might come to an end through no fault of mine was not acceptable. I would never give up unless I personally failed – it would be a waste of all that pain.

As I walked alongside David, making suggestions, a black sports car pulled over and stopped ahead. A woman, dressed in what looked like a Dior suit, began teetering towards us.

'Good God, she's not going to try to keep pace with me in that get up, is she?'

'Knock it off, Fee!' I walked in front of the Wombat to greet her. If I couldn't get any money from my sponsors to continue the walk, I was damned if I was going to let the charity suffer if the walk ended prematurely. Anyone who stopped now would be pressed for a charitable donation for Care Australia, to hell with being embarrassed.

'Hullo.'

'Hi, I work for one of the clearing houses in Perth associated with James Capel. I'm on your arrival committee.'

'I doubt if there will be any "arrival",' so you'd better disband your committee.'

'You don't think you'll make it?' She asked sympathetically, puffing a little by this stage. I sped up just to prove my point.

'Oh no, that's not it, I'm fitter than I've ever been. I've been slowed down by bad blisters so it's going to take about a month longer than expected and I don't have enough money to finish.' I told her about my call to James Capel. 'But since you're part of the system, as it were, perhaps you could put in a good word for us somewhere. We've been on the road now for sixty-five days,

I've been through some pretty bad experiences and the only thing that has driven me on is the vision of actually getting to the end. And now,' I heaved a sigh, 'it looks like I won't.'

'I'll certainly see what I can do.' And she winked. 'Don't you worry.'

Then she slipped herself back into the airconditioned, leather upholstered sports car and waved goodbye.

Out of the desert scrub, ran a black cat and shot across the road like a small velvet rocket.

'Did you see that?' gasped David. 'It's very bad luck when a black cat crosses your path.'

'I've always thought it was good luck.'

Day 66

I had counted down every kilometre marker since Port Augusta where they'd begun at 987. We had stopped the previous night at number 11, and so during the first quarter today, I reached kilometre marker number one. And hugged it. Ten minutes later, I walked into Western Australia, 'The State of Excitement'.

The hard shoulders, far wider and redder on the other side of the boundary, edged a narrower tarmac strip. The trucks had to drive half on, half off the road. Emu-scrub-gum grew with twisted trunks bearing ragged clumps of dry and yellowing leaves; blue-bush carpeted the red land dotted with a thin spread of dry twig and stunted sandalwood. The small white sea shells I had found scattered throughout the Nullarbor and its neighbouring plains were in greater abundance on the red land. The flint and white chalk of the last hundred kilometres gave way to a thick russet clay which smelt of England. Roadworks had been under way to build drains under the road for the rain, and where there were trenches, the clay was wet and dark red in the puddles.

I had been looking forward to stopping at Border Village for a shower but David insisted I finish the quarter before stopping. The carrot of being clean was whipped out of reach by the stick of his words and I erupted into a storm of spite for being cheated. Screaming some obscenity at him I stomped away like a spoilt prima donna. David shouted after me, 'Don't walk away from me like that!' It was one of the few ways I knew of provoking him. But as soon as he'd driven past me to the natural end of that quarter, I felt very guilty.

I looked around the bush for a gift for him, but there were no desert flowers on that side of the border, only red clay in small puddles. I bent to scoop a great handful of the clay and played with it, moulding it into a sphere. I tried to keep it moist by spitting on it but it was fired by the sun's heat and caked my hands and fingernails with red powder. I hid it behind my back as I approached the Wombat.

Looking sheepishly at David and without saying anything, I drew my hand from behind me and presented the small gift. He looked at it curiously, picked it up and rolled it around his palm. He seemed pleased with it.

'Do I need to keep this?'

'No, you need to accept it as an apology.'

I took it back, made it into a thumb pot and placed it in Tag where, by the day's end, it had crumbled to red dust.

I changed into an elasticated black and white striped top from Adidas which I hadn't yet worn on the walk. It fitted me snugly, emphasising the new firmness of my body, and as I stepped out on to the road, David called after me, 'Wow!' It made me feel sleek and aerodynamic in the desert heat. I scuffed along in the red dirt, bending sometimes to cover my hands with powder clay, rubbing it through my hair to make me feel part of the land.

There had been a time-zone change in Border Village, but the names of the hours didn't matter to us – we lived by the sun. When the bush shadows pointed westwards, we woke; when there were no shadows, we rested; when they lengthened to the east, we knew coolness in walking before sleep.

The prunes sat in my digestive system for several days before deciding to launch themselves. That day I had the screaming, burning shits. The first onslaught poured out when I had no lavatory paper with me. The bush was too coarse to use and there was no water; if there had been any flies I would have gladly let them clean me, but when I needed them there were none. I walked with the remains rubbing between my buttocks until David arrived. By that time the skin had become raw and red, making it uncomfortable to walk even after lavatory paper, water, talc and prickly heat powder.

A curious semi-circular bend lay ahead on a road which had no reason to be anything but straight. I decided to find out what the obstacle was by walking due west through the bend instead of around it on the road. I took my hunting knife from the Wombat and instructed David to wait for me ahead.

Moving between branches of scrub and gum, I picked my way over clods of earth and clay. Away from the road, it was darker, rougher; I longed to spend all my time walking through such desert. I held one hand on my knife handle feeling like a hunter, looking through the twisted trees for signs of prey. How could I have ignored this virile beauty, crossing the continent on sterile roads? I vowed never to do it again. In Africa I would walk off the beaten track, supported by expedition professionals, and follow a schedule dictated only by the rise and fall of the sun.

Then I came upon the cause of the diversion: a crater as deep as the Devil's Punch Bowl in England. There were no traces of the meteorite that must have formed it. I joined the road again and handed back my hunting knife, wishing I could kill my food with it.

A curious sign from the Road Gods appeared at the side of the road: STEEP DESCENT. I had no fear of shin splints then, so it was with great amusement that I walked towards this sign, wondering just how steep a descent it could be on one of the flattest plains in the world. A police car pulled up beside me.

'It's a long way to Perth.' I wasn't sure if he knew who I was.

'Yes,' I agreed. 'But it's even further to Sydney and that's where I've walked from.' Nobody ever said 'You've come a long way.'

'You're kidding me?'

'No I'm not.'

'Where's your gear?' I was tempted to pull his leg and say I never carried any.

'In my back-up van, about half a kilometre behind me.'

They'd seen me on the television. People always look different in the flesh, they said, and they wished me well, urging me to keep on the right side of the road as I 'went down'. I still hadn't seen what all the fuss was about. But there, around a corner, stretching far below to the west, lay a spectacular valley of the flattest land I had yet seen.

The plain is technically a beach, formed by the bight's erosion of the sandstone which, on that stretch, composed the continental shelf. The beach had been anchored by vegetation but in the distance, at the edge of the sea, were mountainous white sand dunes like those at Point Sinclair. This phenomenon was one of the 'three plagues of Eucla' which had been caused, in a roundabout way, by rabbits. Armies of them had swarmed across Eucla in 1898, devouring all vegetation and honeycombing the area with warrens.

To combat the rabbits, the Adelaide government had deposited hundreds of cats in the area. At first the cats gorged themselves, but then, tiring of rabbit meat, they turned to birds and lizards for a change of diet. Then came the kittens and Eucla's second plague – cats.

Finally, exposed to the strong southerly winds with no vegetation to hold it in place (sandalwood had been felled in great quantities to be exported to China as incense), the sand began its relentless encroachment. The original Eucla settlement was being buried as . ambled down the cliff path with the sea breeze in my hair.

The road, although a narrow strip of bitumen, was vast: the hard shoulders of white chalk, small flint chips and shells, stretched ten feet on either side. The sterilised bones of carcasses scattered the verges, picked clean by dingoes, foxes, ants and sun. The skin that had been cooked and cooled since the animals' death was brittle and it filled the wind with a stench so strong it seemed to kill the plant life in its path. My eyes could no longer focus on anything, it was as if I was looking through a film of thick mucus.

We returned to Eucla, a truck stop some ten kilometres west of the border, which had once been the busiest non capital telegraph communication centre in Australia. Eucla had fallen prey to the advance of technology in the form of a telegraph line, built around 1920 along the railway. I didn't suppose the station hands minded the closure, with four inches of annual rain, temperatures in excess of 123°F and 1,280 kilometres from the nearest amenities. All that was left to set it apart from the other truck stops was a few olde worlde signposts and a thick fall of tourist litter. We showered in saline bore water which would not foam the soap. The water was hot which was a blessing, but to keep it flowing, 20c pieces had to be fed into a metal box above the shower head. Slimed with soap and ready to plunge under again, the water would suddenly stop and I would grope for more coins. Even after a good rinsing I stepped out covered in a film of sweat, salt and soap.

While I showered, David had called Newmans Campervans in Sydney. I had secured the Wombat for three months, but the walk would take at least two weeks longer. We didn't have the $70 a day to rent it. He had a generous response from the owner:

'You're doing well, take her for as long as you need, I'll probably sell her in Perth.'

There was no need for us to drive it back to Sydney if we couldn't afford to. But it had been a motivation in itself, to one day drive back the way we had come and often we would wave goodbye to the owners of a truck stop with the words, 'See you on the way back.' It was our way of expressing our confidence that we would succeed.

I had longed for these flat, open roads where I could pick up my speed. But the new unmoulded shoes collected from Adelaide had proved to be yet another disaster; they were not wide enough across the width of my toes. The knuckles of my little toes had swollen and when I tried to straighten them, they roared. The heels were too wide and rubbed badly. The Second Skin had run out. We were using the syringes over and over again, cleaning them with Betodine but the chances of infection were so high that I had to inspect the wounds at least twice a day to reassure myself. The nearest chemist was still thirteen walking days to the west.

The border had done away with the kilometre markers, but I didn't really need them; I could judge how far I had walked and their presence had been as damaging to my freedom as my watch had been. Now I was free to dissolve into the road and let each far horizon be the only regulation of distance. I began to feel sensuous with the land; every part of my body seemed to be focused into the centre between my hips. For me, it was the Centre of Forward Motion, just as the halfway point between the wings of an aeroplane is its Centre of Lift. I thought about the bumble bee. Its wing span is too short for its body weight, technically it should not fly, but nobody told the bumble bee.

By the time I reached the Wombat at the end of the third quarter, I was almost crawling. There were no tears, just fury that I lacked good shoes to do justice to the road. David was in bed as I ripped off the dressings and surveyed the mess.

'It's snuggly and warm in here, Fee.' So I left my feet open to the feeding insects and the cooling breezes of night, and crawled in beside him.

Day 67

My feet left deep imprints in the molten bitumen, just as the cyclists had left their tyre tracks and Bon the gouges from his skates. Flies flew up my nose and into my ears, but I let them.

Tap, slap, tap, slap, tap, slap, tap, slap.

'Have you noticed how the flies eat the roos? They start by eating through their anuses and then get inside to eat the intestines.'

'Mmm?'

'Mmm.'

'Bit hot today.'

'Water?'

He fetched it, I drank.

"kyou.' Handing it back. 'I wish we had some gooseberry fool.' I picked my nose and wiped it on my singlet.

'You know something?'

'Mmm?'

'Almost everything you do annoys me.'

'You can go away now.'

So off he drove to the end of the quarter, leaving me tap slapping in the desert. The dream of the night before returned under the pulsing sun, a dream that left me aching to be touched. The sun grew wilder and hotter, caressing my back, the muscles tense under its touch, and the skin burning as the caresses grew

183

stronger. Drops of moisture slipped from my hair and tumbled down my spine. The demon thrashed every part of my flesh that walked exposed, pounding my body, drinking my sweat and raping my very breath. I longed to fall upon the land and feel its thumping heart against mine. I wanted to ravish it, feel at one with it. By loving the land, the white line and David, I was protecting myself from the reality of their challenge. If I *had* realised how hard it was going to be, I might have succumbed.

I replaced my singlet as I reached the Wombat and cooled myself with water. Breath came in gasps as I drank. It was over 45°C. I could not walk in it again. But sleep led me back to the yearning of my dream. I sensed David beside me, the firmness of his muscles, the curve of his spine, the round hollows of his buttocks. He was much broader than I, bigger, taller, stronger – he was male. I heaved my body to the far side of the bed and pressed it against the cupboards so that I wouldn't be tempted to reach out and touch him. Lying in a pool of sweat from our bodies, I slept.

When I woke I re-dressed my feet and put on some new shoes which seemed to fit better. I would know after a few quarters if they would work. Eat the road, Fee!

Straight into our song. 'It's a wonderful, wonderful life, no need to run and hide, it's a wonderful, wonderful life . . .' It was our song, the song of the walk, a lilting, melancholy song that filled me with a desire not to let it end.

'You smell.'

'It's the clothes.'

'What are you washing them with?'

'New improved Bold.'

'First there was Bold.'

'Then there was Bold II.'

'Then there was Super Bold.'

'Then there was Down Right Brave.'

'Soon there'll be Fucking Courageous.'

'It's a wonderful life with Fucking Courageous!'

Gradually the heat eased off the day. A light wind sent the

stench of the roadside carcasses. to us long before we could see them.

In the second break we drank great quantities of water which had been desalinated from a bore pump. It tasted like an algae-covered billabong. The blisters were syringed before we ate and by the time I was ready to leave again, they had refilled. We had only two syringes left.

The night was cooled by a light breeze from the ocean, and everything lay calm under the pounding of my feet. But I was anything but calm. The pain, though I had endured it during the heat, now became unbearable and the last ten kilometres were hobbled in tears. I distracted myself by talking with David, but when I shot him one word answers or bitched at something he did, he retreated and became silent.

In the distance, the sign above the petrol pumps of Mundrabilla showered the indigo night with streams of red light. We amused ourselves by trying to read the sign but after a few guesses fell silent again. There was nothing to see when we got there, only the truckies slumped over meals of canned stodge, their trucks big and dead in the shadows and the faint barking of a dog at the kitchen door. We slid back into the thick desert night. I stumbled and slipped in the guts of a fresh roo kill and David laughed at me. It didn't smell bad, but was like a good country smell on the farms of England so far away.

Day 68

Bumbling along, thinking about my joints, I was distracted by a movement out of the corner of my eye. Turning suddenly, I found myself staring at two six-foot 'Big Red' roos poised to leap away. But when they caught sight of me they seemed amused at the limping, sweating blob, panting under a floppy slouch hat and stayed to watch. Roos in the daytime were so unusual for me that I felt compelled to stop and study their slender pointed faces so out of proportion with their rotund red bellies and thick muscular tails. But instead, I charged at them, screaming frantically and waving my arms. They took the hint and elegantly bounded away a small distance into the scrub to turn and look at me. I didn't want them to be interested in the road, they had to learn to fear it. Even though the roos remained no more than three metres away as I walked, they faded into the colours of the land so that I could no longer distinguish their shapes from the gums and scrub.

On the road I was caught by a sense of forward motion. It was movement enough to bring back the Road God of Daydreams, and my fantasies centred on a new desire – lethargy. I lived a life where all daily tasks were cunningly executed from the comfort of an armchair with the help of remote controlled robots.

There was no wind, the temperature on the road surface was approaching 50°C. I had not noticed I was dehydrating until my lungs simulated an asthma attack and I could not swallow water when David arrived. I took a wet cloth and 'washed' my arms, stomach and legs, absorbing water through my skin, until my breathing became even again. Then I lay down in the Wombat, while David drove us back to Mundrabilla to make the vital call to James Capel.

The PR girl had no news but urged me to call the original sponsor in London. It cost $7 a minute to call London from the desert and when I got through, the sponsor was on holiday for four weeks. I explained the problem to his assistant, asking her to find out who else could authorise further sponsorship and gave her the phone box number to call me back.

Outside in the searing heat I sat waiting while flies shot up my nose and fed there. Eventually the telephone rang; it was the operator. He tried to connect me to the assistant in London but she must have left her desk after the call was requested because a man answered and hung up.

Another hour passed. I knew a Capels' employee would not let me down so I moved into the shade of the truck stop veranda where I hoped I could hear the telephone.

Two heavily laden bicycles were propped against the windowed walls of the restaurant and a motorbike, almost submerged under the weight of luggage and,camping gear, sat in the shade. Nearby, a black and white sheepdog dozed under the bench, occasionally snapping at a fly that ventured too close. He softly thumped his tail on the concrete as his mistress's hand felt under the seat to pet him.

She was a native of Alice. Her blue jeans were oil-smeared and ripped at the knee, but her face was carefree and open. Sam was touring Australia by motorbike, looking for the character of her country, with her dog. Her relaxed manner made me realise how my walk could have been, if only I had not been in pain.

The two cyclists had not been travelling together for long. I had to listen carefully as the man recounted the journey of the woman because she was so androgynous, and his speech so muffled, that I wasn't sure if he was referring to a 'he' or a 'she'. Sam sensed my confusion and piped up with introductions.

Lenore was a grandmother of fifty. Her squat, box-like head was topped with a short back and sides haircut and her teeth slanted backwards giving her a permanent expression of frankness. She had cycled from Cairns via Melbourne and was heading to Perth. Up until Adelaide she had cycled with a tour but there they had stopped and she decided to go it alone across the desert. Lenore had been on the road for six months and didn't let anyone forget it.

It was in this state of depression that she had met Norris, the other cyclist. She had been sitting in the bar in Penong, when the barman, probably in an effort to get rid of her, pointed out of the window at another cyclist. Norris, halted by her yells, agreed to let her ride with him as long as she didn't slow him down. Lenore was used to ninety kilometres a day; Norris averaged 120. So far, she had kept up.

After five minutes of her chatter, I felt great respect for Norris. He seemed a man of unlimited patience. He was an attractive middle-aged Briton who had set off with his bicycle to give his wife 'a break'.

The four of us sat in the shade, occasionally swatting an aggressive fly, watching the trucks pull in and pull out. To the truckies Mundrabilla was a pit stop; to us, an oasis. Some of the car travellers recognised me and wished me luck, but none of them gave a donation.

It depressed me that so little money had been raised from the general public, by that time perhaps $400. This wasn't because Australians were mean, in fact from the wads of notes truckies handed me on the road I knew they were quite the opposite. It was largely due to the media. When they reported the story, the charity was often omitted and even if it was mentioned, the systems for donating were not. The fundraising effort for the American walk had also been hindered, but then it was because I didn't have a facility for telephoned credit card donations. I thought I had solved this problem by arranging such a facility through Care Australia but what was the point if the media didn't include the number with the story? I have now resolved to link up with one newspaper to follow my progress in Africa. This system worked very well on my British walk when the London *Evening Standard* published a donations coupon every day. Within seven weeks I had raised £25,000.

Fed up of waiting for Capel's to call me back, I plucked up courage to reverse the charges. Miraculously, the girl accepted the call with the enthusiasm of a much wished for birthday present and explained there had been a constant fault with my phone box which was driving her frantic with worry. Apparently the only person who could give a decision on sponsorship was the Chairman. I was transferred to his secretary who said he was on his way back from Paris, and was then flying off to the Middle East for two weeks. Ah. Perhaps she might catch him before he left and explain the situation? She would try she said, and I was to call her back in a couple of hours, reversing the charges.

I slept lightly, which tends to make me talk in my sleep. For the first time I dreamt of making love with David and because I found it disappointing, I had a feeling that I called out his name and asked him for more. We had long since agreed to tell each other what had been said in the night; David spoke almost as often as I did. So I asked him if I'd called his name to which he replied, 'No, you didn't say *that*.' I was too mortified to ask what I *had* said.

The sun was setting by the time I called Capel's again. David was at my side, feeding his favourite Chunky Beef soup to a mangy dog and enticing a fiercely independent cat to join in. He seemed oblivious to the importance of Capel's decision.

When I got through, the secretary had informed the Chairman who said the manager of the Sydney office was the only person who could make that decision. Damn. Sydney was closed and the next day was Saturday. All that time had been wasted.

Having to depend on a bureaucratic organisation was annoying but I'm sure they are no worse than any other. I didn't have the kind of time people do in their world, no time to drive around the desert trying to call someone between meetings.

It was pitch black by the time we set out again, despite an opaque ring which circled the sliver of moon. I sent David away to get some sleep; I wanted to be alone to mull over how I was going to salvage the walk if Capel's wouldn't oblige.

Even if I got rid of the Wombat and continued alone, I wouldn't have enough money for food to see me through to the end. On top of that, I had grave doubts that I would make it anyway. I was tiring, and could manage little more than fifty kilometres a day. No more than twice a week could I walk the full fourth quarter.

I always carry the burden of my walks' organisation alone so there was no base camp in London to raise more funds on my behalf. My only other chance was borrowing and, having spent half my annual salary for 1988 on finding sponsors, I had nothing but my contract with Heinemann as collateral. But that contract was dependent on me finishing the walk. I realised that if Capel's could not help, I would have no choice but to walk until the money ran out. I felt at that moment that I wanted a hug – a simple hug, a no questions, no expectations hug – or even a piece of good news.

When my body told me the end of the day was near, I searched the verges for the shape of the Wombat. David had forgotten to leave the torch on to guide me and I passed it. If the wind had not blown a cloud from the moon, I would have carried on in the desert, searching, confused. David woke as I entered and when I lashed out at him, he sank back and snored.

Day 69

Another curious sign from the Road Gods appeared ahead: DUSTY ROAD. I had walked on many dusty roads before but had never seen a sign for one.

Gargantuan earth-moving machines were digging trenches some fifteen metres into the bush; other enormous creatures whose function wasn't quite clear would hurtle out of the bush on to the road surface and charge towards me, then suddenly skid their three-storey hulks across the road, revving their engines, and kicking up arcs of red dirt before driving back again. A man with a pink fluorescent waistcoat walked down the middle of the road, seemingly unafraid of the monsters that charged around him. I followed on his heels. He was wearing ear mufflers against the terrible din, but he guessed what I wanted to ask.

'Don't,' he shouted, 'do anything sudden, just walk in a straight line. If they don't get out of the way, then make for the nearest place of safety.'

The 'nearest place of safety' was hard to identify; no sooner had one monster roared past than another would appear from nowhere moving in the opposite direction. So I just barged through the centre of them for over two kilometres, battling against the headwind, covering my mouth with my hand and blowing my nose on my singlet. I stumbled to reach the Wombat, wiping the filth from my eyes so that I would not miss it.

David had suffered too from the road works, his head was pounding from the noise and he could hardly breathe through the dirt-saturated air. We ate quickly and David went on ahead.

I walked bent double for three hours, charging against the dust-filled wind. The sun's rays, although seemingly filtered by the red cloud, were no less ferocious with the wind acting as bellows for his fire. Mulga trees in shapes like the boomerangs they once supplied were permanently bent in homage to the north.

The wind made it difficult to pee; no matter which way I

faced, it always blew back at me. Peeing on my shoes was a standard joke between us, David always knew it had happened when earth or sand was stuck to them. But out in the desert there were no bushes over a foot high and all the gums were too thin and scrawny to provide any cover from the cars caught waiting by the roadworks. After an exceptionally strong threat from the Road Devil of Small Accidents, I decided I'd better 'do it quick'. I climbed up the bank into the bush and looked for a good spot. Always trying to overcome my phobias by facing them head on, I deliberately squatted over a rather large hole on the desert floor, thinking that if a spider did leap out, I could easily dodge it before it had time to climb up me. The cars hooting as they went past did not lessen my sense of achievement when no spider appeared.

My hips began to grate in their sockets – a sure sign that the second quarter was over. I scanned the horizon for sight of the Wombat; with my eyes so sore, I was in danger of missing it. But there it was beside me, tucked away behind a peculiar row of overgrown bush that formed a natural shelter. It amused me to come upon the Wombat unexpectedly, as though I was on a daily treasure hunt, the treasure being food, drink or whatever was foremost in my mind. That day it was shelter and water.

Flopping inside, hot, sticky, tired and covered in red dust, I looked out and spotted a slab of concrete under the bluebush covered with graffiti. It looked rather like a Youth Hostel noticeboard with a message in spidery blue letters which read:

Hi Pete (Push bike bloke)
OLE!
11-14-88
Hate that headwind!

It suggested this shelter was often used by Trans-Nullarbor cyclists.

While I slept, Norris and Lenore stopped for a chat with David. Even though they had left at dawn, it had taken them all day to get to this point. It was very satisfying to know that I was faster than two people on bicycles.

There is no place better for bellowing out a song than in the desert. Out there I sang everything that had bottled up inside me. My feet did not hurt, the headwind had eased with the setting sun and the walking was better than I'd known for weeks. I kept jumping in the air, waving my arms to hug the sky and offering it kisses. This was real walking – pure motion!

A white pillar, like a large guide post, appeared in the distance. Only when the object was within one hundred yards did I realise that it was a person. I chuckled at the thought of it being another walker, perhaps going to Sydney from Perth. He was only ten feet away before I realised it was David.

'Hullo!'

'How's it going?'

'It is so beautiful out here! I can't get over it, I'm just so happy!'

There were two dictating forces which either hindered or helped me achieve the goal of 'pure motion'; pain and the weather. If I couldn't stretch my stride in harmony and balance because the wind pushed me around, I grew furious and irritable. When the weather changed, often suddenly, to a climate in which I could reach that goal then my mood changed with it, just as dramatically, to one of elation. Time takes on a different perspective on the road, each minute is lived to the full, days seem like weeks, so I wasn't aware of how quickly my moods were swinging, I thought I had been happy for days. David didn't understand this, perhaps because days dragged on, changing his perspective of time in reverse.

We walked together to the Wombat, singing Bruce Springsteen songs which always began with an off-key cue from me: 'I gatta dollar in my pocket!' and from there I'd let him take over because I couldn't make out the words.

David climbed in the Wombat, and drove beside me. A noise like a badly tuned radio came from the Wombat. David looked startled.

'What was that?' I asked, looking around quickly.

He still looked startled, an exaggerated surprise that could only mean one thing.

'You dirty bastard!'

'I thought it was rather a good one. I think I'll call it "The Ripper Zipper"!'

The fourth quarter was walked alone. There was such peace over the earth and I moved upon it with ease, feeling awake to the colours and textures of the desert night as if for the first time. I had been guilty of wishing my walk away because of pain, never daring to relax and absorb the beauty for fear of losing self-control without fury to spur me on. For the first time in sixty-nine days I had no pain in my feet and I had no pain in my body. I sang and sang again through the moonshadows and they seemed to reach out and hold me and dance with me.

'Sail on, silver girl, all your dreams are on their way.'

Day 70

5.38 a.m. in the desert, solemnly eating prunes. As I stepped out, the headwind was even more fierce than the previous day but at least it kept up a steady attack without throwing me around fitfully. It also brought rain, which blanketed the world in thick, clammy folds of fog. I passed Madura truck stop tucked in the trees where cavalry horses and polo ponies were once bred for the Indian army.

Then the road shot straight up the northern continental cliff to the Hampton tablelands which, even without the driving gale, was a tough climb. Out of energy from battling without altering my pace, I reached David but it was not time for a break. He pulled along beside me, opened the window and stuck out his arm.

'What are you doing?' I laughed.

'Testing the wind.' I'd never heard anything so silly.

'You can't judge it unless you're out in it.'

'Yeah, I simply don't know what it's like out there.'

'You being sarcastic?'

'Mildly.'

'Go away, I really don't have the energy today.' It was all I needed; a backseat long distance walker. But I grew lightheaded and kicked myself for baiting David instead of asking for food. When I found the Wombat again later, I stumbled to it, sticky and sweating under the waterproof. And as though I would not get food unless I were submissive, I abased myself with demonstrative apologies.

David stayed with me for the second quarter, listening to my chat but he was so far removed from what I was going through that he couldn't possibly understand my swings of mood or measure what tenacity I had left. As we moved forward an old red car pulled up ahead and waited for us.

'Stop and say something, don't just ignore him.'

A young man with pasty white skin sat staring at me through steel-rimmed John Lennon glasses. I called out over the wind in my friendliest voice, 'We're OK, thank you, we haven't broken down.'

'D'you want some money?'

I saw he waved a note, like a peanut for the monkeys.

'Oh! Yes!' I walked off the road towards him. 'Sorry. So many people ask if we've broken down, I've just come to expect it.'

'I saw you on the telly in Brisbane . . .'

'You're English!' He was from 'saf' London and had the complexion to prove it. Standing in the buffeting wind, we talked, rather bizarrely of the stock market – we had nothing else in common. Our conversation was interrupted when the heavens opened and down fell raindrops the size of mung beans. Considering John was from England and David was testing my dealings with donors, I thought it prudent to invite him into the Wombat instead of continuing to walk. The three of us sat cosily, drinking steaming cups of tea while rain battered the sides of the Wombat.

'Where have you come from this morning?' I asked.

'Madura.'

'Ah!' piped David. 'Did you see a couple of cyclists there? They may have left early.'

'Funny you should mention that. Last night there was this woman, oldish, funny shaped head . . .'

'Lenore!' chimed David and I simultaneously.

'Yeah, and she was trying to chat up these two truckers at the bar. One of them left after five minutes and the other just turned and started talking to someone else. I saw her this morning, looking a bit hungover. She was on her own all right. She kept asking these two cops if they'd seen "the walker". But they hadn't seen you, and she looked really betrayed.'

The rain stopped, and as I clambered out again, John roared away in his 'Big Red'. The wind gave me something to push against, something which replaced the pain of the last seventy days. David suddenly broke off from the sci-fi story he was making up and said, 'What are we going to do about Lenore?'

We assumed that Norris had gone ahead without her because she was tiring from that hefty headwind and couldn't keep up his pace. Her decision to go on across the Nullarbor alone after her cycling tour disbanded in Adelaide was one she had made with us in mind. Lenore knew of the walk and that we would meet somewhere in the desert. If times got rough, she thought, she would ask to join us to Perth. These thoughts she shared with us in Nundroo. We were all endurers on this road, sharing the same horizons, the same anxieties, the same laughter, fulfilment and tears. 'We, of the same mettle.' I battled with myself over giving Lenore the chance to reach her destination but at the expense of losing the rest of my walk to her dominating personality and constant chatter.

After much deliberation, David and I decided on a compromise, if she did join us it would be for two days tops to give her a break, a boost and some company. Besides, if Capel's didn't come through with the money, we wouldn't even make it to Norseman. Just as we finished arguing, David noticed a red-clad, head down cyclist in his wing mirror, battling furiously against that headwind. For once I didn't envy them, wind has very little effect on the speed of a walker.

We hurriedly affirmed our plans and tidied our smiles to meet her. But it was Norris.

'Hullo! Hate that headwind.' He told us that Lenore was waiting to join us as we walked through the Madura truck stop. But she must have missed us – we were gone by 6 a.m. We would have to flag down a car to deliver the message of where we were. He hadn't stopped cycling as he panted beside me, if he couldn't go much faster than my pace, Lenore certainly wouldn't catch me today.

Norris pulled over for a pee and David went ahead, three abreast, he said, was dangerous. I set a strong, even, pace and when Norris eventually caught up with me he commended my speed. His battle was more ferocious than mine and resulted in him cursing the elements and not enjoying it at all. He was used to cycling at twice this speed and he was constantly in danger of falling over.

To give him something to work towards I shouted over the wind, 'I'm stopping in twenty minutes for a break, would you like to join us for a cup of tea?'

'I was just about to say I'd better try and push on, but you've twisted my arm on that one.'

'Can you go any faster?'

'I might.'

'Try and get to the van before I do.'

He changed gear and struggled on against the wind, gaining very little distance on me even though I could see he was pushing himself to the limit. I reached the Wombat a few minutes after him. David was making tea. I glowed with pride when he warmed the pot first, especially since we were entertaining an Englishman who offered us 'chockie bickies', as he called them, a phrase which I always thought was peculiar to my family.

Norris was clearly worried about Lenore and we promised to send her a message.

'Just as long as you let her know,' and he gave me a rather penetrating look, 'she'll lose another day if you don't.' And with that, he thanked us for the tea, shook us gravely by the hand and headed out into the wind again. We watched him, zigzagging across the road to get his speed up, until he was too far in the distance to make out. I turned to David, it was a relief to be alone with him. The day had been rather too full of guests for my liking.

I am a loner. In London I change as the city demands but only to a point. If I worked with people in an office, I didn't want to go home to an occupied flat. I go for weeks without returning phone calls, and cancel social invitations in favour of delicious weekends alone with my thoughts. Walking gives me space from the toils of other people's troubles, the further away I walk from their lives, the more I want to keep going. But at the end of each walk, I have retreated so far into myself that I have lost not only my communication skills but any desire to become involved with people. Fitting in again with the demands of society was a challenge I faced when I reached Los Angeles. It took me two years. My desire to be alone may be a problem on the walk through Africa; there I shall not find many uninhabited pockets of solitude.

Another black cat crossed our path in the third quarter and there was a rainbow, brighter than the last, when the rain called a truce. It was cold as the sun set below a bank of thick, black cloud and the wind began to ease, as it always did at dusk. My thighs felt powerful again, at last they were able to thrust forward to their full capacity. I thought of the woman in Venus Bay who had offered us a fish. 'The currents are very strong in the bay, the whiting have to fight to swim out. They are leaner here than anywhere else in Australia.'

In the darkness, David switched on the cab light and read me a short story from a Roald Dahl collection. Almost at the end of the story, I glanced at him and suddenly realised why beauty is so highly prized. His face was so pleasing to look at, all honey-coloured and smooth. I wanted to possess that face, take it in my hands and kiss it very hard. He paused from reading, realising that I was looking at him and smiled, knowing that he had the power to change my moods with a teasing gesture.

'*Pain au chocolat!*' he whispered.

'Oh you knuckle-head, don't start. You've just made me think of those tiny French cafés on cobbled streets in Paris with the sun shining and frothy cappuccinos.'

The delights of French cuisine were batted between us, testing our imagination and we grew hungry but not just for food. We longed to be back among things less raw, less primitive, away from testing endeavours. Yet there were still weeks to go until we finished.

David drove ahead for the last six kilometres of the week because I wanted to walk them hard in the knowledge of what rewards the end would hold. For once *pain au chocolat* had usurped gooseberry fool.

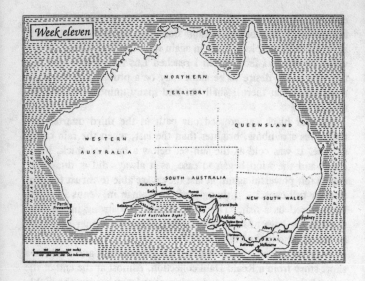

Day 71

A Day of Rest.

Degeneracy on a day of rest: a cup of coffee, a peanut butter sandwich and a cigarette in bed at 8 a.m. Bliss.

I picked off the scab from the first infected blister. It was completely healed except for the two blisters which had formed snugly beneath it, using the scar as a disguise. Had I thought about it, I would have saved all my pieces of skin and put them in a test-tube marked 'Injuries Healed from Wars of the Road (1983–1988)'.

We built a cairn marker and drove ahead to Cocklebiddy truck stop to shower the dust and grime of the last six days. I longed to feel feminine again so I blow-dried my hair, touched my lips with Vaseline, and dressed in a red and white Cacharel skirt and a white cotton top. The effect was far from the sun bleached urchin who walked the desert highways. When I drifted into the restaurant, David glanced up from his reading and surveyed me with what I took to be a cool desiring look, and said, 'Look at you!' Nothing else. It was enough to colour my cheeks as well as my daydreams for a few more days.

The tailwind blew a new arrival into the restaurant – Lenore. She was saddle-sore and, dipping a hurried nod in our direction, headed straight to the bar where liquid anaesthetic flowed on tap. We also moved into the bar, I to a comfy chair to write my diary, and David to a corner conveniently inaccessible to Lenore's constant interruptions which, with alcohol, became increasingly boisterous and incoherent.

Lenore set out on a rampage of the drinkers at the bar, airing the story of her achievements and prompting them for praise. Watching this woman, I was struck by a startlingly familiar pattern. This was exactly the way I behaved towards David. I would tell him what I'd accomplished in order to receive a pat on the back which I would use to fuel more kilometres. And I, too, would twitter away to him about whatever came to mind just to keep me going. In those few hours of observation, I had a glimpse of what David had suffered over the past seventy-one days. I was at once astonished and full of a sudden admiration for my back-up driver as well as disgusted with myself.

Sitting in the bar that evening, we met the producer of a documentary which was being made about the cave diving expedition to the Pannikin Plains. As we spoke, teams of divers were lowering equipment into the caves in preparation for an attempt at the world's longest subterranean cave dive. Some of the team members already held the current record of six kilometres which was set in these caves in 1986.

The producer, an Australian with all the characteristics of the Hollywood stereotype sans the attitude, invited us to spend New Year with him on his houseboat in Queensland. His invitation shook me awake.

We were making exciting plans for 'life after the walk', we wanted the walk to end quickly so that we could be free. This apparent contradiction led me to realise that I did not want to get to Perth. For seventy-one days I had been squeezing my eyes tightly shut in self-preservation and by wishing away the next twenty-four days, I would be oblivious again to what I was experiencing. This would be an obvious admission that I was walking for the sake of the re-telling and I could only find satisfaction in that if I could make my audience vicariously live through the walk. Which was impossible. The challenge of meeting the week was now seen from a new perspective: I wanted to get back on the road to experience its challenges with all my senses alert, not endure them from the window of a cocoon.

Day 72

The Nullarbor lay under a blanket of gentle grey clouds. There were no barriers to push against: no wind, no heat, no pain, no vicious arguments with David to spur me on. We moved across the desert in sequestered tranquillity. It was a day like tepid milk, our last day of solitude before meeting up with Lenore at Caiguna. A time for us to remember we had each other and for that, she was a mixed blessing.

The sound of a cat mewing in the bush caught my attention.

'Hey David! Did you hear that? Maybe it's a tame one that someone dumped. I should rescue it!'

I called to it as I moved, half bent, across the bush, listening for another mew. But the one that broke the silence came from the other side of the road where the Wombat was. I looked up. David was trying very hard not to laugh.

'You!'

'I can't believe you fell for that.'

'You making fun of me?'

'Yes. Meow. Meow.'

'Bastard!'

During the second quarter we passed Cocklebiddy truck stop and the old stone ruins of an aboriginal mission. A few cars had pulled in for petrol, and families were easing themselves out, shaking out the crumbs and creases of long-distance travel, breathing the warmth of the day but blind to the breath of the desert that lay around them. They had no time to think, no space to be alone, but worse, they didn't seem to want to be.

A curious vehicle was parked alongside the far wall of the building. It was a cross between a small truck and an army jeep, with swaying radio antennae and dented roo bar. The roof racks were laden with bundles and the sign painted across the top read: Transcontinental Safaris.

'That's a real expedition, Fee,' David sighed.

'Yeah, setting off into the outback with a group of Nikon-clanging Japanese. Very exciting. We'll have to drive back at the end of this break to phone Capel's. This is it, David, if Sydney says no, we are fucked. Understand? Finito.'

'I know. What are you going to do?'

'I'll cross that desert when I have to, I'm more concerned with crossing my fingers and bracing myself for a not very happy phone call.'

David drove ahead to mark the road for the end of the second quarter. As I watched the Wombat trundle into the distant verge to wait for me, I was aware again of the feeling of always walking home. 'Home', as a six-year-old at boarding school, was defined by my mother as being 'wherever Mummy and Daddy are', but at that time of endless house moves and occasions when my parents had no fixed abode, this idea had been too intangible to give any comfort. And it struck me, as I walked towards the Wombat, that in all my own wanderings and phases of 'no fixed abode', I had created a capsule which encompassed all the yearnings those early years had left unfulfilled – safety, support and escapism. Instead of spending weeks away from it, the homebase followed me wherever I walked and was there every two and a half hours, at my request. I had begun this walk by resenting the intrusion and the dependence the Wombat symbolised, but now that I understood the need of it, I was able to let go of some of the resentment I harboured towards my parents – no matter how unjustified – for those years of insecurity.

We drove back to the truck stop where I pulled on my James Capel sweatshirt for good luck and gathered up the change. I first called the PR girl in Sydney to check on the state of the stock market and therefore the mood of the person I wanted to speak to. The market was stable; it was a good day. Waiting to be put through I tightly crossed my fingers but there was no time for prayer. I explained the situation, what my chances were of breaking the record and how much money I needed. There was a sharp intake of breath at the amount, a pause and then he said, 'Because we are one of your four financial sponsors, we will give you a quarter of your requirement.'

Yippee!

'Thank you *very* much.' I put the phone down and returned to the café with a little skip in my step. In anticipation of this response, I had quadrupled the amount required to $2,000. If we strictly rationed everything, the $500 from Capels might just get us to Perth.

As I burst in to tell the news, I found David talking with a werewolf-like man of considerable body hair – I could hardly tell which way he was facing. He was dressed in a dark blue singlet which stretched over his barrel chest and made the grey-brown tufts of hair on his shoulders stick up like a couple of hedgehogs. A beard hugged most of his face and all of his neck. He stood up.

'You must be Ffyona?' I shook his enormous hand. 'M'name's Chris. I'm part of the support crew for Roger Scott. Heard of Roger?'

He went on to explain that Roger Scott was walking 3,500 kilometres from Darwin to the Eyre Bird Observatory, following the old stock routes.

'See that track? Roger came down there about an hour ago. He wanted to meet yous so we kept a look out while he had his first shower for seventy-five days.'

'Where is he?' My voice squeaking with excitement.

'He's walking down to the Bird Observatory. He's finishing the walk tomorrow.'

'Oh my God! Can we go and see him?'

'He should be done the day in half an hour. He doesn't have people walking with him so you'd better wait for . . .'

The werewolf was broken off in mid-sentence by the hearty sounds of someone getting very drunk at the bar. Shaking his head, he mumbled, 'That's Gary, he's part of the crew, but he's only been with us two weeks, can't stay away from the drink.' Chris turned again and bawled across the room, 'Gary, get over 'ere mate.'

Cloaked in a black beard and floor-length oilskins, Gary looked like a pirate whose shoulders weren't wide enough for his parrot. Stumbling towards us, his face split in a wide two-toothed grin. He lifted one hand to tilt his slouch hat.

'Struth! What'cha got 'ere, mate?'

'This is Ffyona, the walker we's bin waitin' for.'

'Aw yeah? Haven't seen a blonde for a while. Sorry, I'm a bit drunk.' He beamed at me, pouting his lips, seducing me with his silliness.

No sooner had I told David the good news about Capel's than the door opened and another expedition entered from the wings. John Larkin joined our table. David had spoken with him last night; he was writing the narrative for the documentary on the cave diving expedition. As he sat back in his chair and watched us, he became fascinated by the situation David and I were in as a couple and asked us questions about our relationship.

David talked only of the difficulties he faced every day when driving at six kilometres an hour beside me; how uncomfortable, how boring and hard to stay awake it was. He seemed to have no vision of the land we were so close to, no relationship with the desert, as though he wasn't part of the adventure. But maybe he didn't want to discuss his feelings with John; he certainly never discussed them with me.

John told us the divers were directly beneath us, waiting to push forward through unexplored tunnels, hearing the booming sound of the trucks overhead. I thought of those men, waiting in trepidation while the colours and lights of limestone formations glinted through the green of the water. The plump woman from Sydney in the corner and her half starved husband knew nothing of this; for them Cocklebiddy was a place to get petrol, have a brush up and a coffee. But adventurers were sweeping through all the time. There had been Lenore, a fifty-year-old woman cycling from Cairns to Perth; the Pannikin Plains Cave Diving Expedition attempting to break a world record; Roger Scott, walking from Darwin over the deserts to Eyre, and then there was me, walking around the world. Someone mentioned we would see a man riding a windsurfer on wheels across Australia, he was another fifty kilometres to the west. Cocklebiddy was a lesson to them in not judging a truck stop by its pale blue formica table tops; things were not as mundane as they seemed.

We drove back to the Bird Observatory and down the dirt track. We passed the Mog, their back-up vehicle, and the crew eagerly waved us on. There, at the end of the track were three figures, one of whom was Roger.

I leapt out and walked straight towards him; I knew which one he was.

'Roger?'

'Ffyona?'

We shook hands firmly.

'What a task you have!' he said.

'Nothing compared to what you've been through.'

I removed my sunglasses so he could see my eyes, and I felt him warm to me. We talked 'walk-talk' for a long time: blisters, distance per day, swellings, horizons and hallucinations.

He'd been on the track for 109 days, but his voice was steady as he stood lithe, clean shaven and spotless in a cotton shirt and running shorts. His Adidas shoes had taken him the length of Australia without blisters.

Then we talked of the toughest days.

'Was it bad?'

'Yes, it was bad.' I knew my eyes were watering. 'And for you?'

'Not good. But, you know, I always say to myself, "I'll only pass this way once, I'll never have to relive this moment." That was the gem I had wanted, a part of him from his own worst days, something to carry with me, to mull over and draw strength from, to be what Hillaby had been for me so many years before: standing on Hampstead Heath in London, he had gripped me firmly by the shoulders and fused his eyes with mine. 'You have the spirit of a lioness and the physique to go with it, but never, never think of the end.' Then he nodded, satisfied that I would succeed with my British walk and turned his attention to a pair of swallows that were mating on the wing.

Once the Mog had parked for camp, I walked a few paces with Roger through the bush to reach it. I treasured those steps. He was a little stiff and there was a very slight limp but I knew he was a better walker than I.

'Will it be a sad day when you finish tomorrow?'

'Funny you should say that.'

But he said no more. Through the thin branches of patchy emu-scrub-gum we saw the Mog. Gary was lying on the ground. 'He's having a rest. Only been with us two weeks, can't stay away from the beer.' I marvelled at Roger's even disposition; there was no resentment, nothing of the acrimonious bile I so readily vomited over David. Walking gave him peace. There are some questions which walkers do not ask each other. One of them is 'Why?' Why is a word we hear as often as love, people ask us because they want to put their finger on what makes us tick, typecast us to understand something of themselves from what we are doing. But why should we be so different from everyone else? If we had figured out the meaning of our lives we wouldn't be scrambling all over the continent in the first place. I wouldn't have dreamt of embarrassing Roger by prying into his private thoughts, but if I had, I am sure he would have held up his standard press response, whatever it may be. The more we are asked why we do it, the more we give false answers. It doesn't take long after that to start believing them. I felt a very strong pull to Roger, something more than for Bon and I did not want to leave him.

Later, I sat in the truck stop and thought of the divers. A few kilometres away, Roger was bracing himself for the last day of the walk.

And the weary people came in for coffee, for cigarettes, for a break from their travels across the desert, looking around at the truck stop and seeing only the cake trays, the menus, the folded paper napkins and the glass tanks of orange and lemon squash.

And David and I, who had shared all of their worlds, were ready to set out into the darkness to cover our distances.

And tomorrow we would face Lenore, a woman who had cycled from Cairns and who seemed not to notice the world around her.

And a Japanese man on a windsurfer heading our way. Oh Lord, I thought, it is a busy place this desert land, perhaps I should call it The Comic Strip. And us, the 'Comic Strip Gang'. David too, had been affected by the oasis of people like us and perhaps he saw his role more clearly, perhaps he was glad to be part of a walk.

'When I tell you that you don't know what it's like out here,' I whispered to him as I walked in the night, 'it's not that I'm being derogatory; it's because I sometimes need a little encouragement.'

He reached out and touched my shoulder,

'That's OK, Fee, I know, but I'm glad you told me.'

I could have cried for us then.

We were so tired that when David began hallucinating and swerved violently to avoid a display of garden furniture which turned out to be loose bundles of tumbleweed, we knew it was time to sleep.

Day 73

We paid the price for our midday adventuring the day before by waking late, and I had to set off in the fierce heat. The east wind was strong but it had no impact on my speed, only irritating my exposed flesh with the sand and dirt it carried.

Although the elements were against me, my experience with Roger brought out a greater strength to continue without complaint and to talk with David in a more balanced way. That night we talked of attention-seeking. I was aware that the only way I could face a crowd of people was to be the centre of attention. It was a way of hiding my fear from them. From an early age I felt the odd one out with my contemporaries and at home I felt I had to be masculine and boisterous to hide my early femininity. In our house the only acceptable human being was one without emotions. To have them was weak, and to show them was 'wet'.

Still as I walked every day I carried with me a fear of people who stared and mocked me. By walking around the world, I realised I was the centre of their attention again, but I was using it to make them cast doubt on themselves as they had done so freely and so often to me. This crazed and distorted logic was one of the things I was walking across Australia to understand and to reverse.

As I explained this to David we both felt rather uncomfortable. Although the desert was a land mass seemingly without boundaries, our space when we talked was very small.

When we arrived at Caiguna Lenore had already packed up her gear. The tailwind was what she needed to push on alone and although she feared her first night in the bush, I reassured her that I had walked for many long nights alone in the desert and never once felt uncomfortable.

'I doubt if you can be this safe anywhere else on earth.' Hearing those words, she shook my hand, kissed my cheek and made ready to leave. Although I did not like her, I felt she needed a boost.

'Good luck to you. You are a woman of substance.'

'You're not so bad yourself,' she retorted. Fear made her words sound hollow. I understood.

And away she went to battle against the kilometres. When my spirit was almost spent, I would remember that lonely woman's determination.

I slept in the thick tide of heat and grime that flooded the Wombat. When I awoke, two short and fitful hours later, David greeted me with a smile and a piece of apple pie.

'Oh, David, you are a darling!' I bit into it, sucking on the refreshing tartness. 'There is nothing more heavenly than a piece of apple pie in the desert.' It was the little things David did for me that made me so confused about him; I knew he was my support man with responsibilities to keep me fed and watered and tend to my wounds, but he often went beyond his duty, like this slice of heaven I held in my hand.

'You know something?' I ventured quizzically.

'Mmmm?'

'I quite liked you on the day when you were drunk.'

'I know!' And he gave me the most endearing smile of the trip. 'I'm a sweetheart, aren't I?' Then, to add to my confusion, he gave me the rest of his apple pie.

The new shoes I was trying out were narrow, snugly fitting my heels so that there was very little rubbing, but squeezing my toes together like red blistered sardines. I changed into an older pair to let my toes ease back into their proper shape and decided to rotate the shoes as soon as my heels began to burn again.

I walked into a sunset which was a perfect display of melting fire. When the violet blanket of dusk had slipped to the west, the moon eased herself above the torn horizon of mulga and beefwood where the land looked lonely, naked under her silver light. My shadow stretched out in front of me bouncing about in an abstract motion that some call walking. It became a night of many songs, sung not to inspire me or to drive me on through barriers of pain, but to celebrate quietly how far I had come. It was a good feeling.

The warm light of the Wombat lay in the distance. I had seen it some time back but I wasn't walking to it. If I reached it there would be a few moments of anticlimactic refreshment and then it would leave me, to go and wait on another horizon. By slowly growing away from walking just to get to the Wombat, I was learning to accept the Time of the Road and to experience its adventures. I had invested too much in that home, expected too much. Now I wanted to search for the home within myself, but that was going to take longer than a walk across Australia.

As we passed by the Caiguna truck stop in the third quarter, a police car pulled up beside me.

'I've got something for yous.' He pulled out a box from the boot and gave it to me.

'For me? It isn't my birthday yet – is it, David?'

'I don't know what month this is any more.'

Ripping the box open I found a note from Roger:

Dear Ffyona,

Reached Eyre and the southern ocean at 0800 hours this morning. I have sent this box which contains only an assortment of leftovers (I'm sorry). However, you may be able to use them. You'll definitely need Glucodin and Staminaide to replace electrolytes. Peaches and the rest use if you want – hope they are helpful.

Good Luck and God Speed.

After two to three days – start checking post offices etc. on your way, I shall send you some messages until you reach Perth.

Good walking,

Regards,

Roger Scott

I was tremendously touched. Roger was the greatest desert walker I had met and I felt flattered by his generosity. Other people had given me food, had invited me into their homes and wished me luck, but I had not been receptive to them – their lives were so different from mine.

I moved on in the desert night alone and my thoughts went out to Roger. What must it feel like to suddenly have the choice to change your movements, to get up and walk around in a circle and then sit down again and know you can do it as often as you like? What did it feel like to play tennis, to run and jump and twist and use your whole body in lots of different ways? What did it feel like when the road fell into the sea, when the walk was gone?

Gunshots ricocheted through the desert silence. People killing roos. I wondered if they were shooting for fun. Did they not know that scores of roos lay writhing in pain beside the road and needed the gun? I felt revulsion springing up and I pounded it out on the road, wishing I could crush Them under my feet and burn Them with the fire that scorched my heels.

During the fourth quarter we entered the long straight stretch of the desert land on to a road that had no curves for 181 kilometres.

Rabbits played on the road with their families, but they

209

became mesmerised by the lights and sat there staring as the cars approached. They did nothing, the driver did nothing. They died. David drove ahead and honked his horn to clear the way but he caught the ears of one and they whizzed around in the fan.

Three dead roos lay in the middle of the road like wet cardboard, all in a row. Mummy Roo, Daddy Roo and Baby Roo. Bam! Bam! Bam!

Day 74

We were now entering the domain of Diprotodon, the largest marsupial to walk the earth. His fossilised remains had been found with giant wombats and roos, bogged down in the mudflats which once surrounded the natural rock hole dams. The water lay to the north and had once supplied the engineers who began to build this road in 1941. It was finally completed in 1969 but people I met said it wasn't fully sealed until 1980. I wondered how those men had dealt with this stretch, 145 kilometres of the straightest road in the world. Perhaps they thought only to the next horizon, as I did, but for me it only took twenty minutes to get there.

David hauled me out of bed at 6 a.m.: 'Come on, Fee, we've had a lie in, time to get up now.'

I felt drunk. Stepping out on to the road I was dizzy and low on energy even though I had eaten plenty of peaches from Roger's stores. My thoughts and speech were slurred and my eyes would not focus.

'What d'you think it might be?' It came out as a lilting sing-song rather than my usual brisk voice, it took me by surprise. David merely ignored the question. I had a feeling he thought I was being weak.

An off-side tailwind crept up which took some heat off the morning. I was thankful for its presence since my body was behaving so awkwardly; my right knee kept seizing up, my pelvic girdle was rubbing at the ball and socket joints and sending a sharp pain down my thighs. Realising I could not go on after the end of the first quarter, I fell into bed and sweated profusely.

'You want me to read you a story?'

'Oh that would be lovely.' David lay beside me and read me a Roald Dahl 'Tale of the Unexpected'. I fell asleep before he'd finished, an exhausted and anxious sleep. What the hell was wrong with me now?

I awoke two hours later and lay listening to the even, heavy breathing of the man beside me. As I eased myself to a sitting position I became aware of a pool of sweat which had collected on the sheet from my body alone. I prodded David awake. It was time to eat and move on.

'I know you don't want me to have sugar, but I feel lousy and I have no energy. I think I should use the Staminaide and Glycogen from Roger's stores.' This speech took a while to get out and left me feeling dizzy and drained.

'Try it, but don't blame me if you go into a lower trough after a few hours.'

I opened a can of creamed rice from Roger's box and mixed it with a teaspoon of powdered glycogen. The sweetness was foul but I felt it was the only hope of getting me back on my feet. I drank a few very diluted glasses of Staminaide while David prepared for the Ceremony of the Syringe.

I stepped out on to the road again, determined, no matter how bad I felt, to get through the quarter and carry on for another. The wind picked up from the east and was gently nudging me towards my destination. Had it been a headwind I doubt if I could have walked more than a few hundred yards. As it was I walked eighteen kilometres instead of sixteen and a half in the second quarter, just to prove to myself that I still had tenacity.

A truckie climbed out of the vehicle that had pulled up ahead. I was glad of the opportunity to pause for chat.

'Ya doin' well!'

'Thanks, are you going to Perth?'

'Aw yeah, come from Adelaide this trip. Saw yous at Penong I think, 'bout two weeks ago. I thought I'd missed yous, didn't think yous walked that quick.'

'I don't really. They'll be calling me a Whingeing Pom if I don't hurry up!'

'Na! You be 'right. Heard about the blisters on the radio, if yous can walk this far on those feet, I wouldn't call yous a Whingeing Pom.' He pulled out a wad of notes and pressed them into my hand. ''Ere's sam'thin' for the kids.'

'Thank you very much, that's very generous of you.' He heaved his chest out, embarrassed, and drove off.

'Feel like a story?' David asked gently as the red tail-lights were swallowed by the night. He knew I was moved by the truckie's kindness – a passer by, someone I would never see again.

We immersed ourselves in the stories; wishing we were anywhere but here, and pretending to be people we were not. David's reading became a relaxation for both of us, it evened out the pressure between us and distanced us from the story of our journey.

Day 75

While making the breakfast cup of tea, David made an announcement.

'Go easy on the water.'

'Why?'

'Because we've only got two pints for the next three days.'

'Why didn't you fill up?'

'I forgot.'

He didn't bother to apologise.

I was feverish as I stepped out on to the road and wondered if I was suffering some bug caught from people in Cocklebiddy. Somehow, I had to force myself to push through whatever barrier I was hitting.

The land was scattered with gum whose yellow bark was scribbled with markings made by parasitic insects; grey and acorn mallee formed a canopy with their crowns above the saltbush scrub; slender trunks of small cooba and hop-bush grew so thickly that they blocked my view of the horizons to the north and south. The arrow straight road with a few undulations helped me to focus on covering the distance, breaking up the quarters into lengths to the horizon. I almost fell over the body of 'old man' kangaroo, stripped to the bone of flesh and skin. His kin who had crawled under a blanket of spinifex that marked their grave, steamed and stank as they rotted.

At the first break we mixed the last of the muesli with reconstituted milk. It was a standing joke between us that the muesli was actually dry dog food. I looked at the tin of powdered milk, reading the label for distraction while David read his book.

'It says here not to give this stuff to babies, I wonder what happens to them if you do. I know that if you don't feed them enough their poo comes out green.'

'If you don't feed them enough they die.'

For some reason we found this hilariously funny. Our stomachs were raw, our faces ached and tears ran down our cheeks as we weakly punched each other. It was by far the most intense exercise we'd had together for months and I felt much better for it.

The kilometres flowed under my feet without battles until the gum grew thicker at the roadside and offered an ideal place to pull over and sleep for a few hours, midday. Feeling a little woozy, I gently took off my shoes and the dressings and inspected the morning's damage. Water was too precious to use for a saline soak so I left them to the open air, despite the flies. David was beside me reading a book when we heard the sound of a truck pull off the road. He looked up.

'It's Roger!'

I sat up and sure enough there he was with an enormous grin all over his face.

'Hi!'

'Hullo!' we chorused.

Roger seemed a little hesitant, seeing we had been in bed, but I got up and sat on the edge while David stepped out and shook his hand. The Wombat was a mess, so were we. I had the feeling of a woman whose house is filthy when the Queen drops in unannounced. My feet were bare; I didn't want Roger to see the wounds so I tucked them under my bottom.

Chris came up behind him.

'Hullo!' we called. 'This is a surprise, what are you doing here?'

'Ah, it's a long story . . .'

'You're looking so well. What was it like at the end?'

'That last ten kilometres were probably the hardest of the whole

213

walk; the sand dunes were enormous and the wind was directly from the south. But we got there and drank champagne . . .'

'Did you swim?'

'No, I didn't, but some of the others did.'

'You're one of "them" now.'

'Not quite,' he laughed, 'I've still got to walk around Tasmania before I'm really finished, but it feels great to be in a car.'

'Getting stiff?'

'Yeah, I'm stretching as much as I can. But how are *you*?'

'I ran out of energy for a day or so, but I took some of your Glycogen and Staminaide and I'm feeling fine now. Thank you very much for the box of goodies, we've been stuffing ourselves silly.'

'Is there anything we can get you in Norseman?' David and I exchanged excited glances.

'Might you be going to a chemist?'

'Of course, if you need something.'

'We desperately need some dressings for my feet, I'll show you the things we use.' As I reached over to the First Aid kit in the cupboard, my feet slipped out from under me and Roger saw them. When I turned back, he was looking at them and reached out to take one in his hand.

'Oh, lovey,' he said gently, 'you have been through it.' I had to fight back the tears.

David and Chris returned from filling up our water jugs from the truck's containers. They had to get moving.

'See you same time tomorrow. How far will you be?'

'About seventy kilometres west of here.'

We waved them goodbye then turned back to our world and slept an hour in the heat, less anxious now that I knew I would have new dressings to ease the pain.

David had the road map out when I woke and greeted me with the bad news that the daily minimum had to be sixty-three kilometres (one less than four full quarters) in order to break the record. There could not be a day when I slipped behind. How the hell can I keep up that pace? I mused to myself. Certainly not by thinking about it.

The night draped around us a cloak of drizzling rain. With the headlights turned off, the darkness seemed impenetrable, thick and forbidding like a fairground tunnel of horrors. David must have sensed this for all through that quarter he would silently climb out of the door while the Wombat was still moving and start howling, or shine the torch under his chin to light up his face in horrific Frankenstein expressions. I kept shouting, 'Stop it, stop it!' All this had a terrible effect on my bladder and twice I had to change my shorts.

We ate at the break. David was restless, and danced around with a can of tinned fish, bashing it against his head. The contents was dubbed 'scrag end of salmon' which he took great delight in slurping in front of me, opening his mouth to reveal the grey paste. I wouldn't touch the stuff, the smell was so bad. He took a box of matches and set fire to his jeans, he raged and growled and whipped me with a drying-up cloth. I took this as my cue to exit and ran out into the night.

I heard a thrashing noise in the bush about a hundred feet to my left. I called out to it thinking it might be a wombat, but when nothing appeared I went into the bush to investigate and at the end of a trail of pale pink liquid lay a young roo whose tail was covered with blood. It was alive, but very much in pain. I shone my torch on it and spoke soothingly.

'It's OK. It's OK. I'm not going to hurt you, just lie still and let me see if I can finish you off.' I moved a little closer while she flipped on to her back and snorted heavily, breathing hard against the pain. I looked around the bush but there was nothing I could use to kill her. There were no branches thick enough or long enough so I slowly backed away, helpless.

I got back on the road, feeling wretched. The road was covered in blood; carcasses littered the verge every fifty feet and stank like damp carpets. Nobody seemed to care that the animals didn't die instantly from a hit. They lay in pools of blood with wounds that caused them to die slowly, in agony.

I reached the Wombat with the thought of asking David to drive back to the roo I had found and help me kill her. But the tinned salmon had taken effect and half-paralysed him with stomach cramps. I couldn't ask him to drive through the desert at 2 a.m. to kill an animal. I closed my eyes in the soft comfort of my bed but saw only the snorting, suffering mess of her. A number of times I almost woke David to drive me back there, and for months afterwards suffered great guilt for not doing so.

Day 76

I hardly noticed the airconditioned sports car that pulled over beside me until a tanned middle-aged man leant out of the window and bellowed, 'You 'right?'

'What? Oh! Yes, yes, thank you. I'm on a charity walk.'

'D'you want to hop in the back? Or would that be cheating? We wouldn't tell.'

'If I wasn't happy walking I wouldn't be doing it.' I was boiling inside. These were the ones who afterwards would swear I had cheated. I stormed down the road at a fearsome pace. The car overtook me and hooted merrily. I turned and spat not realising at the time how funny I looked.

During the second quarter, right on cue, Chris and Roger pulled up. They walked towards us, leaving the truck on the verge. I wanted to ask Roger to walk with me but wasn't sure how he would respond.

'One kilometre?' I implored.

His pace was exactly in time with mine, neither of us was lagging or straining which is one of the most aggravating problems when walking with company.

'How are you? I mean inside, d'you think you'll make it?'

'I'm keeping steady. I can't allow myself to listen to David making plans for the end, it's still three weeks away.'

'I know.'

'I've had a frustrating morning . . .' I stopped myself, wondering if I should burden him with the arguments that had been raging all day with David. 'I really hate myself for lashing out at him, I understand it when I'm in pain, but this morning I did it for no reason, I just wanted to push him like I'm pushing myself.'

'I always have two back-up people,' he advised, 'so they can vent their energy on each other when I'm exhausted at the end of the day.' It was a sound piece of advice and I resolved to follow it on my walk through Africa. 'Don't worry too much about baiting David; he's a strong guy, he'll bounce back. You can't expect yourself to be restrained with all the pain you're enduring.' We had caught up with the Wombat but Roger waved it on. 'I often pick up a stone or a few sticks and focus my negative energy on them and throw them away.'

All too quickly it was time for Roger to ride back to the truck and be on his way. I wanted to embrace him but the energy I felt in his handshake was more powerful than a simple hug, then he pulled me to him and kissed my cheek. I turned back to the road with tears in my eyes and waved goodbye from a distance. When I knew he was out of sight I sobbed. He understood. Why was it that I had to find what I wanted in the middle of a vast desert, 12,000 miles from where it should have been all the time? Why couldn't my father have understood me? Had he done so I would not be looking for it so far from home.

Roger had walked beside me, encouraging me with words of wisdom from his own experience. I didn't feel monitored by a critical stare, nor dismissed because I stumbled. In the eyes of one who knew, I was not a failure. Roger allowed me to believe in myself, he knew how important that was in striving for a goal, but his encouragement also showed me that I didn't need to prove myself to anyone. My father's scrutiny was not born of any defect in *me*.

Over the next three kilometres I buried my face in my hands and left my legs to blunder on.

David's face was lit up with glee, he was holding something behind his back and then suddenly produced it. A banana! A ripe, fresh, delicious, sweet yellow banana! He revelled in the joy of surprise.

'It's from Roger, he gave us a whole bunch of them and some other fruit; jams, chutney, fresh bread, drinks and all your medical things.'

'He is a darling. I hope he let you give him some money.' His face fell.

'Oh fuck. I forgot to ask. Shit. Shit. SHIT.'

'I doubt he could afford it.'

'Fucking hell, Fee, how could I have been so stupid? I just didn't think.' We scoffed the fruit like half starved vagabonds, both of us feeling very guilty.

'I expect he was rather surprised you didn't ask.'

'Damn.'

I took off my dressings at the break and glared at the wounds on my feet. They were so unhealthy, they displayed my inner feelings, laid bare and oozing.

When we woke at twilight, the heat had gone from the day. I took delight in rummaging through Roger's gifts; rubbing calluses with Lanolin cream and wallowing in the comparative joys of the Ceremony with brand new syringes. Clean dressings with cloth plasters adorned my feet and I slipped on a clean pair of socks.

Roger's kindness and thoughtfulness had eased my pain. I felt ready to walk around the world.

Day 77

I woke at 5.30 a.m. itching to be back on the road. A breeze was fanning through the trees, swaying the shadows as I stepped through them.

There was something very strange about the hard shoulder; as always it was gravel but these stones were perfect spheres. Some of them were split in half and inside were rings of different colours – red, ochre, grey and white. I couldn't imagine what had made them. I put them to good use by picking up a few as 'patience-beads' and concentrating my negative energy upon them. As a result, negative thoughts were as far from my mind as Perth was from my feet on that golden morning.

After a time David pulled up.

'Hey, Fee?'

'Hullo!'

'You'd be really proud of me if you'd heard that interview I just gave.'

'Good one?'

'It must be all the reading I've been doing, I've suddenly become articulate.' A radio station in Kalgoorlie had requested an interview which would be played every hour over the next few days. David had offered to give it on my behalf.

'I hope it wasn't as awful as that one in Hong Kong. "Mr Richard," I mimicked, "what will you be contributing to the walk, in terms of your former experience as a physical instructor?" "Well, I'll be like, keeping Ffyona stretched out."'

'Oh, and what about one of yours in Sydney; "So, Ffyona, what's David's job on the walk?" "David will be co-ordinating all the media on the road, cooking all the meals, advising me on my diet. Just generally handling me across the country."'

'Freudian slip.'

'Ditto. Oh, I nearly forgot. The guys at the Balladonia truck stop went looking for us late last night with a crate of beer! They didn't realise we were parked in the front.'

'That was decent of them.' Somehow my reserve was never a hindrance where a group of Australians gathered in a pub and I looked forward to getting disgracefully drunk tonight before the rest day.

David went ahead to prepare food for the first break and I wandered on alone, part of the solitude that engulfed the land. One large and insanely inquisitive wasp joined the swirling party of flies and circled me in ever diminishing spirals. Soon it was hovering around my thighs. Occasionally with the back fling of my hand I hit it mid-air and it seemed to buzz more aggressively and dart at my body in kamikaze nose-dives. I tried running at full pelt down the road only to find it had overtaken me. Angry and tormented, I arrived at the Wombat and burst into shelter. Inside, David was in fine form and, picking up a few of the spherical stones, began to entertain me with a juggling act. Soon there were four stones flying in the air under his concentrated guidance.

'I didn't know you could juggle! I can do three, but what's the secret with the fourth?'

He grinned. 'You keep it in your hand.'

Outside again, the heat was a constant pounding on my head even though I was protected by my slouch hat; the air was so heavy it seemed to burn my lungs. Wisely, David had driven only two hours ahead and when I reached him I was dehydrated and dizzy. I couldn't go on in that heat.

Once he had marked the road, David drove me back to a clearing in the mallee but even within the dense forest, the air was burning and stagnant. We tried to keep cool by splashing water. We stripped off to a bare minimum and lay on top of the white cotton duvet cover, but still we suffered. Sticky and irritable, we stayed there, squashed together in the tiny space of our home for two hours, until the heat had eased and my body had rehydrated. I needed as much stamina to rest as to walk. I wished I had a Mars bar.

After eating canned veggies I stepped out again, my feet merely touching the road on my toes because the blisters had again secured a stronghold on my heels. The road was wildly undulating and thick with gum, not the emu-scrub of the open plains but tall silver-clad giants Australians call ghosts. The golden moon rose with a slice cut from the upper edge as I walked into the week's end.

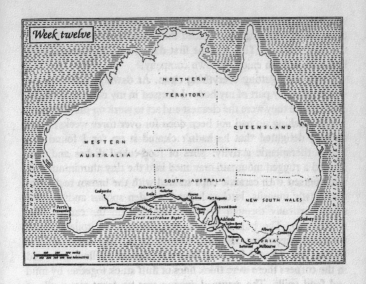

NORTHERN
TERRITORY

QUEENSLAND

WESTERN
AUSTRALIA

SOUTH AUSTRALIA

NEW SOUTH WALES

Nullarbor Plain

Eucla
Cocklebiddy
Madura
Penong
Ceduna
Port Augusta

Perth
Fremantle
Coolgardie
Norseman
Balladonia
Great Australian Bight

Crystal Brook
Adelaide
Yellow Sand
Coonalpyn
Albury
Canberra
Sydney

VICTORIA
Bordertown
Melbourne

0   100   200   300 miles
0   200   300   400   500   600 kilometres

Day 78

A Day of Rest.

The clearing for the Balladonia truck stop was a pale yellow acre of compressed dirt. It stands alone in the dry forest of the Fraser Range. From here to Norseman is the longest stretch without petrol or water, 191 kilometres. Everyone stops here, a hundred cars a day, and the petrol pump attendants don't need to ask how much they want. Small wooden picnic benches divided the areas for electrical hook-ups. We parked under a large ghost gum and I pottered around my home. I made a washing-line out of the branches, improvised with the bench as a two-tiered dresser and moved around with my hair tied up, humming like a contented woman in her woodland kitchen. It made me realise that I was not intimate with any one place in the desert, but I wanted to be.

David had gone to wash the mountain of clothes which had taken over the whole of the back shelf and was smelling very rank. He was having a pleasant morning, reading John Fowles' *The Magus*, occasionally reaching up to reload the machine or rinse and wring the clean clothes. This was the first day of rest during which we had been able to enjoy our own company.

I was busy getting everything clean. At dawn I showered and scrubbed every part of my body. I dressed in my clothes of yesterday because they were the cleanest and set to work on the Wombat.

The washing up had not been done for over three weeks; I was secretly delighted that he hadn't cleared it up for I found it a highly therapeutic activity: piles of food-caked dishes and pots formed a rugged mountain crammed into the tiny aluminium sink interspersed with ceramic cups stained with the brown residue of tea, plastic utensils, kitchen knives, wooden spoons and spatulas stood vertically through the mess like ribs on the carcass of a rotting roo. The box cupboard that we used for toiletries was a mess of ripped or discarded wrappings and the oozing goo of leaking jars. The tan linoleum floor was originally yellow ochre and in the corners there were thick lines of fluff stuck together by mud and food spills. The cramped driving area up front was a pile of maps, press releases, books, camera equipment, sunscreens and hair bands, all sprinkled with the brightly coloured wrappers of Heinz cherry and pear fruit bars. Our bed was a mess of sweated sheets, duvets and thin cotton sleeping bags which I draped over a washing line. It gave my little place in the desert a few defined walls and made me potter even harder.

I cleared all the rubbish out of the Wombat and scrubbed it completely. Very pleased with the immaculate, antiseptic result, I showered again and re-dressed in the same clothes because the others were still on the washing line. I took my diary into the restaurant, ordered a Coke for David, delivered it, and then settled down in the airconditioning to write.

'People go to the circus to see somebody get hurt. I wonder if that's the same thing that makes the people in the buses turn and stare at me as the driver announces, ". . . and on our left, the English girl who's walking around the world." Maybe, if they're lucky, they'll be the ones to see me collapse.

'Yesterday as I stepped out for the beginning of the third quarter, dressed in my pink skirt, summer halterneck, and shoes which are larger than David's, I carried the last of the bananas. I peeled it and was shoving a great length into my mouth when a car pulled up from the opposite direction. The windows were tinted and closed and inside sat a prim-looking couple in their late twenties. They stared at me for a few seconds without rolling the window down. The woman leant away in horrified disgust as I opened my mouth and oozed the banana between my clenched teeth.

'I know I am close to breaking now. My body and feet are sore and worn out. The effort it takes to get out of bed or stand up after a rest is worse now. Roger asked me if I was relaxed – that's indeed what I must try to be. These last few weeks I need to toy with new daydreams and let the road take me. Somehow I haven't got the energy to get excited about the end. I have walked over four thousand kilometres with just less than a thousand to go. I must still walk the distance Inverness is from London and here I am, thinking I've almost finished. It is the simplicity of the roads on the map which is deceptive: turn right at Norseman, up to Coolgardie, turn left and then straight on till Perth. I've thought of throwing myself in front of a truck to end it all and save face.

'I must care for my feet, soak them in saline solutions twice a day, get back into the habit of cleaning my teeth every morning, wearing clean clothes, brushing my hair and washing my face. It is so easy to get filthy in the desert without a shower at the day's end. It is this that could finish me before I have a chance to reach Perth. Deep down I think I will get there for if I don't my walk round the world is over. I won't have a chance at Africa, nobody would sponsor me again if I fail at this. Africa, two and a half times as long as this! Oh Lord, maybe I should pack it in now.

'A week of walking is always rewarded by a day of rest, a bar of chocolate, a cheap bottle of rough red wine for me and a couple of beers for David. Wine always makes me think. It's thinking that makes me want to walk and walking that makes me want to think. I have yet to confront the real reasons why I live on the road. I talk of it often – but my thought waves are small and lapping and only briefly do I come across a breaker to ride on. But then the undertow pulls me back again to confusion and I wander out there undirected.

'I have decided I will walk two quarters on my last day of rest so that I can arrive in Perth midday. It was I who suggested this for the sake of the media and surprised myself as well as David. I have a nagging feeling, perhaps 'walk intuition', that someone is going to donate a large amount of money to the charity and for this, I will sacrifice my day of rest. God help me to raise that money and God help me to stretch out my money to last to the end of this walk.'

The barman was chatting to me, I told him I had lost the art of conversation and almost my ability to think.

'Just as long as you don't stop communicating with each other.'

'It's hard.'

'But keep your talking with him going, your marriage will suffer badly if you don't.'

'I am not married to David! David and I are . . .' and he looked up from the pool table, we smiled at each, 'just business partners.'

Everyone assumed that David and I were a couple and we had begun to race to be the first to correct this error. And yet I couldn't help thinking that if the way we acted towards each other did not suggest a firm 'relationship' this assumption wouldn't be made at all.

The direction of our conversation was changed by a well built woman who radiated good humour. Her mouth couldn't stay still and she laughed and chattered with the truckies at the bar. We all had something in common, and it bridged the gap which would have existed in an English pub where people go in cliques to socialise under the ambiance of oak beams and copper warming pans. Here the men sat at the bar in stubble and work boots below the airconditioning fans which spun in the atmosphere created by people united in a common goal – getting somewhere else. The woman knew of the walk and our troubles in raising money and brought out a tin box she had used to gather funds for John Perkins who, after a severe head injury paralysed parts of his body, had cycled across Australia. From each drinker at the bar she extracted money as I'd never seen it flow, and they enjoyed giving. By the end of the evening over $100 had been collected. We wanted to buy them drinks in return for their generosity, but they would have none of it.

Day 79

Creamy yellow and as fluffy as the chicks they would have been, were the scrambled eggs we gorged on at 5.30 a.m. Stepping out in that dawning day was an enchanting feeling. Without the joy of those first few hours of the new week, I would never have lasted as long as I had. The first quarter flew by leaving me wondering what was so difficult about walking across the country. But the week was young. I knew what was coming.

It was 32°C as I stepped out for the second quarter and, although warm, it was not hot enough to slow me down. The heat shimmered from the road and intensified as the quarter took its course.

A tiny dragon lizard leapt up on its hind legs and fled at terrific speed into the undergrowth. There was grass all around, tall, wild and brown and it moved like fine velvet in the tailwind of a passing truck. This road was very different, almost like the winding lanes of England, except the colours were burnt umber instead of brilliant green. I had always felt the most joy for the open land but these twists and turns added a new sense of adventure; what would lie behind the next bend?

We laid bets over what we might see; a dead fish, a roll of Sellotape with the end clearly marked, a gooseberry fool factory, or maybe a coconut tree which could have provided the husks in the water I drank, it tasted so bad. There was no refreshment value in it.

The heat sucked me into it, enveloping my skin in a thick woollen blanket.

Red and sweaty, I reached the Wombat. Oh God, what relief to see it there tucked into the bush. How blessed I was to have these sudden eruptions of pure happiness in reaching my short goals, and finding shelter from the heat. But the Wombat was oven-like and the water was as hot as the day.

We distracted ourselves by catching bulbous black and brown striped flies; they used devious cunning to catch us unawares and shove their enormous probosci into an exposed piece of flesh. When they buzzed for mercy under David's thumb, we grinned and marked up the points. With covers torn from books we fanned the air, taking it in turns to cool the other, and talked of everything which reminded us of the cold: skiing, facemasks, numb feet and fingers, frozen water pipes, clean cut blue mountains, long horned cattle. But the stark reality was that we were in the Australian bush in over 40°C heat.

A light breeze picked up as I watched David prepare the food. I couldn't help but notice how he'd changed from the honey-coloured, muscle-bound stranger who had met me at the airport in Sydney. His hair, once blond from the Hong Kong summer, had mellowed to a dark auburn, his skin was a dirty brown and his body bore the marks of sitting for long hours without exercise. His troubled eyes looked out from shadowy sockets, echoing the strain that I and my escape from childhood had forced upon him.

We were together at the beginning of the third quarter as the sun set and the breeze picked up to a wind.

'You've changed,' he said.

'I have?'

'In the beginning you were so concerned with building this "perfect world" around you in which to walk and I wasn't allowed in lest I disturb the equilibrium. Now you're just walking, you're just doing it without all the superficial shit.'

Now that I understood it, I was able to explain to him that the 'superficial shit' was to psyche myself into believing the walk was the most wonderful experience I could ever set out on. Walking on lies, I know, but it kept me going and so I didn't really care how I did it.

David had been observing me from his silent seclusion while I had been watching him distance himself. I wondered what had made me push him away so hard in the early days. I walked close to the Wombat and rested my hand in front of me on the side view mirror. Looking across at him I caught his eyes for a moment. Tears welled up. I leant towards him and brushed a kiss on his shoulder.

'This is my wonderful back-up driver.'

Then in a deep Ozzie accent to disguise the real feelings, 'You 'right?'

'Yeah, I'm 'right.'

I was alone with the shadows of the bush and the cold wind. Cats cried out and spat at each other, marking out their territory, until the sun rose and the time came to purr together.

Stumbling over spherical stones in the pale white beam of my torch I was conscious of the movement that had carried me so far across the continent. My feet no longer paused slightly on the road at the end of a step, they automatically left the surface and pushed forward for another. It was the most natural motion for my body. But some of my muscles would never learn to accept their daily punishment; tonight a shooting pain in my right thigh made me lurch sideways, my leg folding under the strain when the pain stabbed through. I couldn't let it affect me. I had to keep to the Schedule rigidly or else there would be no record and perhaps no end.

I sat for a moment, tore off my shoes and studied the toenails which had been hurting during the last few kilometres. One of them came away in my hand.

David's soup was revitalising and warmed our spirits.

'Good shit.'

'Mmmm.'

'Do another quarter?'

'You bet.'

And when we'd finished and I had re-dressed my feet, we turned to each other and said in unison, 'Rock 'n' roll!'

David caught up with me after clearing the supper things and he talked of *The Magus*. It was an extraordinary story but I lost concentration in that prolonged bout of listening and began to doze. I tried to pace myself and keep steady but when David told me I still had an hour and fifteen minutes to go, I almost crumbled. The white beams of the Wombat's headlights picked out features of the landscape which I had seen a thousand times. I was enduring time and pain to cover distance which seemed to have no meaning. Pushing myself ever harder, counting down the minutes, I kept a watchful eye for the appearance of a rest area sign.

Eventually, I saw one gleam in the darkness ahead.

'Is that what I think it is?'

'Yep.'

That glowing sign for heaven drew me to it with such concentration that if Perth had popped up out of the bushes, I wouldn't have noticed it.

I remembered my promise to myself as the Wombat turned into the rest area and I flopped inside. Sitting in my pink cotton dressing-gown and, resting my feet in a bowl of saline water, I brushed my hair, cleaned my face with cotton padding taken from a sanitary towel, and covered my sunburnt skin in moisturisers. No matter how long the day, I must keep up appearances. That day had begun on the road at 5.30 a.m. and had stepped off the road at 12.30 a.m. It was an hour shorter than average.

Day 80

The sun began to lick the moisture on my skin. Dazed but still determined, I stared at the horizons and knew I could do nothing but walk to them, one after another as though infinity were beckoning me to try and reach its end. The kilometres were slow in passing, not because my pace had changed, but because my mind thought only of getting to the Wombat, getting to shade. But why, I asked, do I want to get there and drink water which tastes like the desert dirt? Out here at least I am getting to my destination; in there I only suffer. Road Devils by the dozen brought their gifts to bait me. There seemed a time during that quarter when I became trapped in a double mirror of reflection where I continued to walk, but got no closer to my destination. I thought about Sisyphus and his bloody rock.

My eyes could not pick out individual trees from the green blur which bordered the road, nor could they see the stones or the leaves on the verge. I vaguely remember a police car stopping and hearing David's reassuring voice. I didn't participate; the only words in my head which were strong and clear were 'Keep Steady'.

The Wombat pulled away, a sign the end was near. I saw its shape pull up a kilometre ahead and then disappear into the dark green wall. 'Keep Steady.' The horizon was drawing me onwards and I gave myself to it. The tell-tale burps began. I must hold it in, there would be rest somewhere in the green. The blue and white shape I wanted broke through the haze and I slid open the door.

In my hurry to give my wounded feet a soothing soak, I ripped off the plasters too quickly and with them came a length of skin. I stared at the blood in the murky salt water. I looked up from my diary a few times to see glass shatter and hear the shouts of David's vented frustration as he hurled stones at a line of old beer bottles.

I slept and woke with the sun heading fast towards the west. It was time to re-dress the wounds, eat and push on.

'Will you be with me?'

'I will.'

Gently David urged me to complete the day. I was glad of his words because they gave me the chance to reject the temptation to sleep. My body was showing early signs of exhaustion but Norseman was sixteen and a half kilometres away and I wanted to get closer to it. I had something to push for and I would not let my body defeat me.

Weak and seemingly aimless, I left the warmth of the Wombat and dragged my body out along the road. I sought distractions in daydreams but they too were blurred.

'Fee?'

Minutes passed.

'You say something?'

'You OK?'

'Mmm.'

'I just realised I left the water jug back at the last break. I need to go get it.'

'Go.'

'Will you be all right?'

'I will. You'll be back in twenty-five minutes?'

'Yes. Is that OK?'

'Mmm.'

Alone in the dark night, walking over ground that David had not yet travelled, I was pioneering. My thoughts reached out to Care Australia and some of the handicapped children who would never know what it was like to walk on air, and to erupt with joy at endless freedom. I could push on, test my limits, fight with exhaustion because there was a goal, a relief. I had a taste of their pain but only for eighty days, not for the whole of my life. Though I could not spare the body fluids, I let myself cry for them in that dark night and wondered if it was only for them.

David came back and I was glad of the disruption. Now that he was there I only had another half an hour to go. Yet somehow I could not find the energy to walk more than fifteen minutes. I dearly wanted to flop my body over the ledge of David's window and let my legs plunge on alone. But that was not walking, that was being aided and the walk would be futile – every clenched fist and morsel of determination would be rendered useless if I made one slip.

I could go no further. David was some way ahead looking for a place to pull off the road. Some impulse made him turn back and stop the Wombat about two hundred yards in front of me.

Stretching for a few moments outside the Wombat, I calmed myself. No longer did I expect any words of praise, from David or from myself. This was my fight. Again I changed into my dressing-gown, pulled the comb through my hair and put the things away that I had used. Keeping my nest clean, keeping my head above water.

Day 81

'I'm going ahead to get some stuff. I'll wait for you in Norseman.' I knew he couldn't resist the temptation of civilisation. I, though, would bide my time. I was in no hurry to leave the outback and I wanted to savour my last few moments alone with it. The inspection border for South and Western Australia appeared in the distance. As I approached the barrier the road split in two – the first division I had seen for many weeks. Things would be different now.

I felt dirty and small coming out of the bush into the midst of a busy town, anonymous and unnoticed and I looked through windows with the wide-eyed innocence of a Tarzan child. The experience of being alone for so long at the eye of a perfectly circular skyline made everything in this gold-mining town seem threateningly close. I felt invaded and wanted to push away the buildings to a far horizon and look at them from a distance, pick up that patchwork of scrubby gardens and shake all the people off it. My senses were so sharp from the subtleties of the desert, that I could smell every skid of dog shit, every puff of pollution, even the cardboard boxes outside a general store. I looked ahead at the road. It was no longer *my* road; people lived beside it, did their business on it, littered it, crowded it, and split and tortured it with their heavy trucks. Nobody healed the road. Nobody seemed to love the road.

On a slant, almost in the ditch, was the Wombat.

'Fee, d'you see what I see?'

'Not yet. Let me see it first.'

I knew there would be a surprise on the road but I couldn't yet focus on it. But there, a few hundred paces ahead, a bank of trees crossed the horizon and no road continued through them. It was a T-junction. I was about to make the first turning since Port Augusta, leaving the bitter-sweet desert for a road that would lead me to Coolgardie where I would turn left for the final stretch to Perth. Reaching the signposts, I was torn between an engulfing sense of loss and a welling up of raw excitement. Perth was possible now that the desert was gone.

A mere 723 kilometres! It actually seemed worth celebrating.

Walking northward with the sun to my right, I passed the dilapidated buildings and mountains of dirt which were all that remained of the gold mining industry. Inside those immense tailings was an estimated $13 million worth of gold. But the inhabitants of this town were not busy digging it out, economics kept gold beyond their reach. This was the land of other people and their pollution. I suffered a feeling of anticlimax; Norseman had been a long sought after goal but nothing had changed for the better. David served up a meal of baked beans on burnt toast and handed me a cup of black tea.

'Milk?'

'We've run out.'

Norseman was the first town we had come to for 1,662 kilometres and there was no milk for my tea.

'Why didn't you get any in Norseman?' I mourned, staring at my cup.

'It was 7 a.m. The shops were shut.'

'But you waited there for me for two hours, they would have opened by then.'

He didn't answer, the atmosphere was tense. My obvious despair at having no milk for my tea was petty but how could I explain how badly I needed the small rewards of each break and how strategically important Norseman was as a milestone towards my destination?

Irascible, I slammed the cup down on the counter and left the Wombat without saying anything. I wanted to block out everything; it was a major crisis. I flung myself back into my daydreams as a defence against all that I had built Norseman up to be and all that it was not.

The walk was no longer composed of dark and light, hell and heaven, tarmac or Wombat. There was just grey. I no longer walked west and yet that was where I was supposed to be going, but there was no road there. I had to divert. Utter confusion. I didn't know any more what made me happy – getting to the Wombat to drink black tea and eat burnt toast, or getting out to the freedom of the road where there were many more cars and the noise was incessant. No silence, no place for solitude. I didn't want to be anywhere. I didn't even want to be in Perth because I had no energy to deal with the questions afterwards. In some way I had left civilisation behind to avoid the questions it prodded me with and yet there was an understanding that once I reached civilisation again I would find the answers there.

Rain fell heavily, stinging and soaking through my singlet, lashing against my face and dripping along the ridge of my sunglasses to dribble down my cheeks. My clothes clung to my body and were cold; at every step my shoes soaked up the water and rubbed. David was ahead, it may not have been raining over him.

The Wombat was parked on the far side of the salt-flat, and when I reached it I quietly stretched my calves and thigh muscles, giving them time to relax. Suddenly the Wombat's horn pierced the air; jumping wildly I let out an involuntary scream. Damn him, can't he remember where the horn is after all these months? And then I began to laugh, a nervous, convulsive laughter directed at myself, mocking the futility of my anger. Straightening, I howled. And David laughed, but while his giggles and tears only hummed around the Wombat, mine were echoing deep within, shaking me.

We sat in an airconditioned café and ate two plates of salad with fresh vegetables and drank gallons of clean cold water.

'Hey, Fee?'

'Mmmm?'

'D'you know where this water comes from?'

'No. Where?'

'This water is piped from Perth!'

Back at the starting place David invented a way to lessen the problem of heel rubbing. I put on a pair of the thinnest socks I had so that the pressure across the width of my toes would be eased while he cut three inches off the toes of the thickest socks. I slipped the tubes over my feet and adjusted them so that the edge wouldn't cause a pressure ridge. My shoes felt wonderful, there was less rubbing and the extra cushioning under my heels could prevent another bout of shin splints. I knew if they developed, it would be the end of the walk. I could not limp again for the last 720 kilometres, and the pain in my hips and knees indicated my body would not withstand it either.

'What were you dreaming about last night?'

'Don't remember.'

'You were dreaming about walking.'

'Oh?'

'Your legs were thrashing down on the bed like a march and you were breathing heavily.'

'Did I make it to Perth?'

233

I hoped there would be a chiropractor in Kalgoorlie, a short drive to the north; I needed my back to be manipulated and my buttocks massaged for they were stiffening at the end of every break. Also the joints at the base of both big toes were out of line and needed a thorough working. I wished David would do it but he drew the line at massaging or manipulating my feet.

Day 82

The dawn brought humidity and trapped the air between the high gum trees. The heavy dampness penetrated my clothing and tickled my armpits with runnels of sweat. I breathed harder to fill my lungs, and looked around happily; the lightheadedness was exhilarating. The desert had become transformed into a lush paradise where the singing of birds echoed around and light took on new dimensions of colour.

I watched David pass and, left behind at my own pace, I wondered if he could have done it. He had shown patience and stamina, he probably would have done it faster and without complaining. But he didn't know that I was content when alone and never complained to myself. A truckie back in Balladonia had told us he often passed me on the road and I always seemed caught up in a daydream with a broad grin across my face.

A vehicle parked on the verge ahead detached itself from the blur of the green: a road maintenance truck. The two workers were sitting in the cab having a break. Seemingly worried by my approach, they opened the door and fumbled with a tape measure.

'Working hard?' I called.

'Aw yeah. Why ya walkin'?'

'I left the inspection van down the road so I could sneak up on you.'

I passed them with a wink and called back with new swing in my step, 'keep up the good work.'

They lifted their mugs in a toast to the joke.

The bitumen bubbled in small glistening beads and sucked at my soles as I moved northwards. David and I made silly observations and competed with one-liners.

'Tell me a joke.'

'You've heard them all.'

'If you tell me one from the beginning, I won't remember it.'

'OK then, which ones haven't you heard?'

And we were off again, wiping away the tears.

'Hey, Fee, look! A dead emu.' He pointed to the other side of the road. It looked like a roo to me until I saw its head and a few inches of neck a full foot away from the body. It reminded me of an Aboriginal recipe for cooking emu. They roast it in an underground earthen oven with its head protruding and when steam comes out of its beak it is presumed to be done. There was no steam, I checked, and unfortunately no Aborigines either.

A strip of material from the bottom of one of my singlets was always kept on the side view mirror and I fiddled with it while I walked, twisting it around my fingers, flipping it, stretching it and tying it round and round the mirror. When I tried to disentangle it, David would watch my attempts then reach forward and with a few simple moves detach the material from the mirror, soak it in the water jug and hand it to me saying, 'I think you'd better cool off.'

Squeezing the material held under my chin, I would relish the cold trickles of water which seeped under my clothes. I was no longer shy of walking in a wet singlet.

'Suncream?'

'Please.'

He reached for the tube and I turned with my back to him, holding up the pony-tail of hair, keeping steady. It was not hard for me to apply the cream myself to shoulders and neck, but I liked David to do it. Sometimes his fingers were slightly more gentle than usual and I liked that too; our lives were so empty of touching. There were times when David would kneel in front of me at the break and my foot would rest on his thigh as he dressed it, turning my feet firmly to emphasise that the touches were not caresses.

The heat was tugging at both of us, extracting a mild state of delirium which gulps of water seemed not to abate. Clambering inside the van I cooled off with water and watched David make the tea. He looked decidedly rough and edible, just as I preferred men; let them smell a little and lose their glossy sheen and the city boy becomes the man. We sipped the tea and then tumbled into bed among the new pile of dirty washing which had begun to ferment in a heap.

We slept fitfully for a while and were woken suddenly by the horrendous sound of ripping sailcloth followed by a boom like a quarry blast. We sat up, safe from the pounding rain that hammered around, and watched the storm. I wondered how the Cocklebiddy divers would fare with the increase of water in the caves.

David opened the door. The smell of wet earth made me want to tear off my clothes and run out to roll in it.

'Grub?'

'Avocados on toast?' I beamed.

'We've had that every break since Norseman.'

'I don't care, I've missed them.'

The third quarter was a glorious stroll, feet confident, body focused just below the belly button, hips swaying, legs powerful, feeling as though they still had much latent energy.

David pulled into the truck stop at Widgiemooltha, and called Jan, the PR girl at Scholl to give her our estimated time of arrival in Perth. Scholl's financial sponsorship had helped put my dream into action, but it was their products which enabled me to reach my destination. Blisters are unavoidable in bad shoes on such long journeys, but if I hadn't had their products to ease the pain, I wouldn't even have made it to Melbourne. Scholl are supporting part of the Trans-Africa Walk and I hope to continue representing them until I finish my walk around the world.

I shyly pushed through the drinkers at the bar and used the lavatory. The truckies knew who I was and wished me well; many of them had passed me numerous times, one apologised for giving me a scare a few days back by hooting as he approached from behind. He even went so far as to offer me a beer. I would have liked to stay, but the darkening road tugged me back. I thanked him, and the others, asking them to perhaps dim their lights when they passed us at night. They laughed as I left, a kind of laughter I was beginning to understand.

This day my quarters were good: 16.5, 16.5, 16.5, 16.5 kilometres. The Road Gods were pleased.

Day 83

It was 36°C in the shade at 8.30 a.m. I stopped after only ten kilometres in the first quarter, with that terrifying feeling of overheating. I drank water, ate a pear and tried to walk again but after a few minutes I couldn't take any more of the heavy humidity and had to resign myself to waiting until cloud cover formed and cooled the day.

We found a convenient parking place under the shade of a solitary gum near a tumbledown wooden shack. After an hour or so a battered ute pulled up and out rolled a hardy Australian local who was a great advertisement for the use of sunscreens – his face was covered with skin cancer.

'You 'right?'

'We're just waiting for the clouds to form.'

'Aw yeah, they'll be along in an hour or two. How ya feet doin'?'

'Much better, thank you.'

He stayed with us for quite a while, telling us elaborate stories about the area's history. According to local legend, a previous owner of the shack was now awaiting trial for loading his car with explosives and driving into town. He parked in a shopping mall and told everyone he'd ignite the dynamite if his wife didn't come out and return home with him. The police eventually made him surrender and found a sawn off shotgun in the car with which he intended to shoot his wife and then himself.

'It's the gold, see, makes Bru's do strange things.'

He went on to tell us of another resident of the shack, a seventy-five-year-old gold prospector who was deaf as a post and should be stood upwind of. He was a bit of a gypsy and was often seen camping in the bush or sleeping in abandoned cars with his Gin (slang for an Aborigine lady). The story goes that as a young man he was caught messing around with the 'wrong woman' in an Aborigine tribe. The elders administered their traditional punishment by putting his 'ol' fella' on the hot coals until satisfactory damage was done. I could see David wincing at this and sympathised at the thought of *my* father being roasted. It wasn't until the storyteller mentioned that the Aboriginal woman *surprisingly* remained loyal to the man, that I realised the 'ol' fella' was a euphemism.

Slowly, the clouds gathered and the man bade us good luck and drove away. I was restless, and desperate not to fall behind schedule, knowing I would not be able to make up for lost time. But out in the full blast of the sun with humidity like a pressure-cooker, I was sure I couldn't keep up the pace. My breath came in gasps and when the world began spinning I couldn't judge where to lay my feet. I called out to David to find a place in the shade. I had only walked two kilometres. An hour went by and I tried again but still the pressure reduced me to an infuriated, sodden heap on the sofa for another two hours.

Lightning was my cue to get back on the road and within a few minutes the rain fell in torrents. The world looked relieved and the land was full of fresh colour, as though painted by the falling rain.

'Smell that!'

'What?'

'Cinnamon. And eucalyptus.'

'Can't smell a thing. You're just delirious.'

'Surely you can smell melting crayon?'

'No.'

'That's dead animal.'

The form of die back peculiar to the west is caused by cinnamon fungus which attacks the roots of the trees. Delirious my foot!

Lightning burst through the opaque amber of clouds across the setting sun. I found myself walking backwards to watch the best of the storm behind us.

The third quarter was violent with cosmic activity. The heavens swirled above us, bursting with white light, holding the world for a split second as though electrocuting it. Thunder ripped through the skies exposing a flash of lightning that made even the blackest of clouds grotesquely opaque. The air was so full of electricity that it sapped my energy and forced me to stop after only thirty-four kilometres. The day was a write-off.

Day 84

I stepped out into a grey, overcast morning and began walking. Hearing laughter coming from the Wombat, I turned to be part of it. David was standing outside looking at me.

'Hey, Fee!'

'Yeah?'

'You're walking the wrong way.'

'No I'm not. Perth is this way.'

'I parked on the right hard shoulder last night.'

'You sure?'

'Trust me.'

And there it was, the sign for Coolgardie. I touched it with a kiss on my fingers and kicked two stones over the boundary in gratitude to the Road Gods for my safe deliverance. Then I turned left at the second T-junction in months and walked towards Perth through the pouring rain.

Two blond, bespectacled German boys were standing with their thumbs out on the opposite side of the road.

'Where are you going?'

'Sydney,' they chorused.

'I hope you get a lift.'

David saw them later, buying bus tickets at the depot.

As Europeans they couldn't possibly comprehend the sheer vastness of Australia. It spans two times changes, four climates and takes five days of hard driving to traverse. It should be measured with its own unit of distance for kilometres simply aren't far enough, they dissolve into its deserts where everything takes on a new dimension of insignificance. Nothing of man looks big out there and what little of him there is lies scattered around the edges. Australia 'feels' like a continent.

The main road of the town was wide, bordered by pavements where nobody walked. The Wombat was parked next to an open-air museum so I eyed the exhibits and sheltered from the rain. The theme was the Gold Rush, or rather things that nobody wanted after the Gold Rush.

The museum, though, was not the centre of my attention. There was a flood going on outside and within half an hour the road had become a river, daring to push over the pavement edge in foaming waves. The water passed the Wombat like a tide of minestrone soup, carrying with it all the litter, twigs and small stones which had lined the verge.

'Hmm. I think I'll sit this one out,' I said aloud even though David was not there. He was stuck on the other side of the road under the veranda of the Town Hall.

Eventually the downpour subsided and David splashed across the road.

'Yuck!' He barged into the Wombat and sat down, filthy and soaking, on the sofa. 'That was *some* rain.'

I wondered if it was raining over Cocklebiddy. Somehow I couldn't get those divers out of my mind when I thought of rain.

'There's been quite a lot of interest about us, Fee.'

'Oh?'

'We've gone missing.'

'We have?'

'I called a guy called Bob MacDonald at the Perth *Daily News*. Apparently Trudy, the Hyatt PR girl, doesn't know where we are. Nobody knew, not even the police so she put out a press release asking anyone who'd seen us to call her.'

'How stupid. Did you call the Hyatt?'

'Yeah, she wasn't in. But, Fee,' turning to grin at me, 'there was a message for you from your parents.' Silence. Did I want to hear this? 'D'you want to know what they said?'

I stared out of the window at the grey swirling mess of Coolgardie, with a sulky feeling around my mouth.

'What did it say?'

'It was your father who spoke to the girl, he chatted with her for quite a while . . .'

'Odd that my father would waste time on a long distance call.'

'The message was something like "Congratulations, we're very proud of you, and we love you." '

Perhaps I was being unfair but I felt they could hardly say anything else.

'Did your mother call?' I asked him.

'No, oddly enough she didn't.'

I did feel a certain sense of pride that at last my parents had called and his had not, because in each previous Hyatt stop there were always messages from David's mother, never from mine. I hadn't been in contact with my parents because I hated my father's questions – they made me feel incompetent and criticised. I told him after the American walk that I didn't want his advice on anything – the time for that was past, he no longer had my respect. I had been rejected by him too often and I wouldn't let him be part of my successes. But I had missed my mother. I knew she would have 'felt' my journey with me for she was a very intuitive woman, and maybe that link between us had been responsible not only for drawing me west when I wanted to give up, but also for holding us together during those terrible silent years on that windy Scottish hill.

The world was wet; cars drove very slowly down the street pushing up great arcs of pinkish spray while the drivers peered through compressed leaves and other debris jamming their windscreen wipers. Small children dug handfuls of mud and threw them, played Pooh sticks with gum leaves, and waded around in the roadside fjords. They looked up at me and because there were no other grown-ups on the street I stuck out my tongue, pretending not to be one. They stuck out theirs and danced a little jig, showing off.

The radio was on, crackling with the storm.

'. . . divers on a record-breaking subterranean cave dive near Cocklebiddy in Western Australia have been trapped in the caves by boulders, dislodged by unprecedented rains, which have blocked the entrance shaft. Communication with the divers has not been affected. Reports suggest they have plentiful supplies of food and oxygen to last until rescuers can . . .'

How could these caves have remained the same for millions of years and only now collapse in the one month the divers were there? Could this have happened because I kept thinking about it?

'Oh God.'

'They'll be OK, Fee. They'll be rescued.'

'Yes.' I steadied myself. 'It was a well planned expedition, they'll get out all right.'

The night trembled on as my thoughts leapt from reality to premonition.

Inwardly, I began to slide. How hollow my father's words seemed to me. But had they come too late? At that moment those divers meant far more to me than anything he could have said.

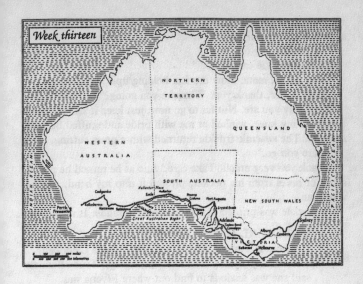

Day 85

A Day of Rest.

In Coolgardie I waited for the water to reheat in the showers after a wobble of women from a Deluxe long distance bus had used it all on their sweaty bodies.

As I tidied the Wombat, drivers stood and smoked, kicked their tyres and kicked the clay. One of them came towards me, an anaemic looking being in a denim jacket with sawn off sleeves.

'G'day!'

'Hullo!'

'So you've been found.'

'I was never lost.'

'Yeah I know, I passed yous yesterday. You seen what they're saying 'bout ya in Perth?'

'No, we haven't heard the full story yet.'

'Right, well, I kept the article for yous, in case I seen ya.'

He turned to his truck and called back with a grin, 'Not goin' anywhere, are yous?'

'No, it's my day off.'

Another truckie came up.

'Good on ya, mate. How the feet holding up?'

'Much better, thank you. Where're you going?'

'Same way you are. Not far to go now, just keep it steady.' And he patted my knee, winked at me with pride and scuffed back to the café. The anaemic truckie returned with a press cutting.

'There you go.'

'Thank you very much. Take care.' And as he turned he pulled a roll of notes from his pocket, pressed it into my hand, and he was gone.

The article was printed in *The Western Australian*. It read:

WALK GIRL HASN'T SHOWN UP

Where is Trans-Australia walk girl Ffyona Campbell?

Yesterday Hyatt public relations manager Trudy Bennett said she was anxious to find out where Ffyona was.

'We are extremely concerned as she was meant to ring every week to let us know her whereabouts (*I was?*) – but she hasn't,' she said.

Ms Bennett said the communication breakdown would have a dramatic effect on Ffyona's fundraising (*Oh really?*) which so far totalled only $1000. (*It has?*)

David came in from the shower.

'I think you'd better get on the phone to Trudy.'

We decided to drive into Kalgoorlie to spend our last full day of rest looking at the gold mines. We would make our calls from there since it was only 8 a.m. and too early, we thought, for venom.

A few kilometres east of Coolgardie we approached a car parked on the verge with the bonnet raised.

'Let's see if they need any help; people are always stopping for me.' We pulled over and David got out. He returned a few minutes later for the bottle of water, there was none in their radiator and the car had overheated.

We continued on our way but just as we reached the edge of

town, the couple who had broken down caught up with us and invited us to go home and have coffee with them. We were in no hurry to get anywhere so we accepted.

They were Greek, full of laughter and offering tiny glasses of Ouzo as if it were water. The woman was large, but hadn't always been, so she said. In her youth she'd had long hair and she waved her arms around her head and body to imitate the glory of it. 'But now I am getting old and my husband not like woman with long hair at my age. How old you do think I am?' She looked sixty, so I said forty.

'No, no.' She giggled. 'I am fifty-five next month!'

'But you look so young.'

'I don't smoke, I don't eat chocolate, I don't drink . . .' accepting another glass of Ouzo. 'And I believe in Jesus Christ our Lord,' crossing herself. 'But my husband he smoke, he drink, he eat chocolate, and he don't believe in Jesus and look at him!' He looked a good ten years younger.

We let her air her views a little more and then, with a sudden exaggerated glance at the time, we thanked them profusely and said we must be on our way. As we left, the woman bent and picked a pale, cream-coloured rose from the garden. It was the only one there.

'For yous.' And she tucked it into the buttonhole of my shirt. 'May you have as much happiness in your marriage as I haf in thirty yis.'

'Thank you, it's very beautiful. When I get married I hope I will be as happy as you.' She looked at David with mild disapproval.

'There is something between you, no?'

'We're just buddies,' David said to her and then, 'Eh, Fee?' And he ruffled my hair as though I were a small child.

'Yes, we're just . . . Thank you for everything, I hope your car doesn't give you any more problems. Take care.'

We bought piles of fresh vegetables, fruit and grapefruit juice. David looked at the bags of food and said, 'We don't need this you know. You can get to Perth on what we have.' The only way I was going to get to Perth was if I kept healthy. Although there were only ten days still to go, I wanted to make damn sure I had the proper nourishment to keep me going. And if we ran out of money, I'd beg.

We were hungry and not wishing to cook a meal on the day of rest, we pulled into a Big Rooster fast food restaurant where caricatures of chickens invited you in to eat them. The manager greeted us warmly.

'G'day! You've been found!'

'Hullo! We were never lost actually. The papers have a habit of sensationalising everything.'

'They've been running it on the radio for a while too.' I think he sensed that I had lost the habit of chat for he didn't push me on the subject. Instead he spread his hands and said, with a grin. 'What'll you have?' We ordered lots of white-fleshed chicken and corn on the cob, beautifully golden with melted butter. David pulled out his wallet but the manager waved his arm.

'You're doing something for the kids, this is my contribution.'

We scoffed the food like starving dingoes. When the final scraps had been tipped out of the bag and fingers licked and licked again, we talked of the impending calls to Bob MacDonald and Trudy Bennet.

'You've got to be really careful with what you say to the press from now on.' I knew it all anyway, but he liked to tell me. 'You've got to be positive, and don't say anything against Trudy when you talk to Bob. He sounds like a nice guy, but just don't go on about the blisters and the heat.' This would have stung if I had cared.

We said our goodbyes to the Big Rooster manager and drove to a telephone box. David phoned Bob while I waited outside, kicking stones. His interview was long, and there seemed little more I could add, but I needed to give Bob a few quotes. David handed me the receiver and mouthed 'be positive'. I breathed deeply and forced a smile.

'Hullo, Bob!'

'Hullo, Ffyona!'

'You know I really shouldn't be talking to you.' David winced. 'Oh?'

'You being a MacDonald and I a Campbell.' It was a good start to a positive interview. I asked him if there was any news on the Cocklebiddy cave divers.

'Yes, you'll be pleased to hear they were all rescued, safe and well, last night around 7 p.m.'

Afterwards David explained what he knew about the incident with Trudy. Apparently she had sent out the press release and once Bob received it he called her to tell her I was in Norseman. However, *The Western Australian* had already taken up the story and printed it.

Having fed the launderette machines, David took up his book and I went out to the Wombat to make us a cup of tea. When I returned, there were two men in the launderette. One was a rather attractive Aborigine and the other a hippy with a scraggly beard. They had got hold of my diary and were using it to cut cocaine.

Had I contested their casual assumption that drug taking would be met with no objection, I think my diary may have been taken hostage! So I ignored their habit and greeted them warmly, not wishing to rock the boat. The men's haunting cackles echoed uncomfortably around the launderette as they told us of the killings. It seemed in the gold field murder was frequent and life sentences were rarely heard of. I had a fairly uneasy feeling that they were telling us this for some particular reason. But with noses full of coke they ambled off in the direction of the Town Hall where a group of children were playing 'Good King Wenceslas' on wooden recorders.

In the last seven years I had only spent one Christmas with my family. Bursting out of home at sixteen, I swore I would never return until all our problems were resolved. After my walk across America, I tested the water by returning at the festive season but what I saw made me bolt away even further and with more conviction. But having spent seven years walking away, I was about to meet the halfway point in my walk around the world and begin the journey home. I now knew that I would never find what I was really looking for unless I looked beyond my search for revenge. And I was beginning to realise that all of us, even our parents, walk with feet of clay.

Day 86

I stepped onto the yellow mallee-lined road and called to David, 'Hey, maybe we can meet again some time?'

'Sure.'

'What are you doing for lunch?'

'Nothing much.'

'I know a really good restaurant about sixteen and a half kilometres down the road; they serve fabulous avocados on toast – see you there?'

'You bet.'

Nothing hindered the steady flow of walking that morning, not even the two new blisters that lay deep in my heels. When the end of that quarter came, we decided to drive back to Coolgardie to check the post office for messages and to call Trudy at the Hyatt. While I slept, David ran errands and woke me two hours later to brief me on the state of play. Times had changed since our frozen silence before the desert; he was ready and eager now to share the results of his efforts.

The Western Australian still presumed we were lost. This, we thought, would be rather embarrassing since the first feature article on the walk was to appear in the Perth *Daily News* that afternoon. But Trudy had charmed David into believing all the trouble had been caused by a lack of communication, whatever that meant; I never really found out.

We pulled up at the starting place just as a car pulled up beside us. David looked out of the window.

'I bet that's Bob MacDonald.'

It was. He got out of the Wombat and greeted Bob, a tall middle-aged man with what looked like a fly on his lip. I too got out and greeted him with a warmth that was unusual for me when it came to the press. From Bob's expression it was obvious he wasn't a typical journalist; there was a certain paternal concern, a mature sympathy which our journey had been sorely lacking. However, bad experiences with the media had taught me a lesson; I would give him facts and only facts, making damn sure he didn't have a chance to twist the meaning of what I said.

Bob had a photographer with him and they drove ahead of me as I stepped out for the next quarter. I felt a squeeze of excitement; I felt healthy and clean, strong and tanned. But seeing the photographer constantly stop, shoot and drive ahead gave me a distorted sense of distance; I didn't feel as though I was getting anywhere. I had been used to picking out a static object on the verge and walking to it, and so felt very resentful of this creature that danced and drove away and talked and laughed before my eyes.

Bob directed the photographer and then motioned to me to take off my sunglasses. The sun was directly in front of me and I knew I would lose my balance if I walked without them. I shouted back at him that I didn't want to, but after months of solitude I misjudged the range of my voice and my tone sounded belligerent. I resented my disability for making me seem like a spoilt child.

They seemed so excited for me, David, Bob and the photographer but they didn't know that if I allowed myself to relax I would never be able to finish. There were still nine days of walking ahead of me – over a quarter of a million steps. I must relax a little to take in all the beauty of the land but never, never, forget I had so far to go.

Night fell and we waved goodbye to Bob and the photographer. David had not slept that day and a pounding headache forced him to drive ahead for an hour of sleep. With my torch to light the way I wandered through the night humming a little ditty and thinking about nothing in particular. It was these moments which I enjoyed most about walking and they only came when my body was not fighting the endurance but accepting it, moving west with the light of the Chariot high in the sky.

The pale glow of the Wombat shimmered in shadows ahead. I didn't want to wake David before I had finished stretching outside and so breathed gently and watched the ground for stones which would slip and make noise. A car pulled up and I felt a rush of anger that they would wake David with their shouts of 'You 'right?' but the voices never came, just a man getting out of the car, a tall man with a fly still on his lip. With my vision distorted by walking, I had failed to recognise the 'fly' to be a scab from a cut.

'Hullo! Stopping for a break?'

'Yes. David's had a headache and I don't want to wake him so we must be quiet.'

'How long will you be?'

'About an hour.'

'Great! Would you mind if we light a fire and get some shots of you relaxing?'

'I'll just wake David then, if you're going to stay a while.' The suggestion of a fire saved him from a petulant onslaught at intruding on such a sacred ritual as the third break. David was still asleep, lying on the bed. I sat on the edge beside him, lightly patting his leg until he woke and quietly explained what was going on outside. I insisted that he stay in bed – I could manage the food – but he assured me he was fine, pushed away the covers and turned on the light. The firewood outside was catching well, the two men were having great fun in building it and gathering sticks from the bush. With bread skewered on to green twigs, David and I squatted by the fire.

Bob asked questions but I was unable to look at him while I talked. His sympathetic probing made me shy; the gentleness was dangerous and I couldn't respond to it naturally. My voice sounded strange to me then, a kind of unfocused chatter that jumped from topic to topic with enthusiasm and then trailed away while I bowed my head and scuffed the dirt.

It was a strange gathering, staged to sell papers and to raise money for the charity – but would anybody understand enough to give? Bob would get people fired up about the walk; money would be raised, people would be excited, he said – he could do it. I said nothing; I couldn't deal with my failure as a fundraiser.

After much subtle persuasion on their part I allowed them to take photographs of David tending to my feet in the dancing glow of the firelight.

The photograph spread across the front page of the *Daily News* the following afternoon was almost biblical in its composition: a bearded man tending to the wounds of a young woman.

'How will you cope with saying goodbye to each other when all this is over?' He was a good journalist; he asked the most hurtful questions. The silence was louder and more real than anything I could say.

'Like I deal with everything else – as it happens.' As I lied the tears came. I must not think of 'then'. The walk was all that mattered now; what came after it would be dealt with by a different person, not me as I was that evening.

We waved them goodbye and set out again. In between the convoys of fairground juggernauts, the sky was alive with the Milky Way. The Chariot had made its turn to the north, signalling that the Road Gods were near me and smiling.

Day 87

Before the end of the first quarter, Bob and the photographer were back. In the blinding exposure of daylight, my stamina was laid bare to their questions and probing cameras. I ignored them, trying to focus on reaching the horizon, keeping my pace even, forgetting they were there.

When I arrived at the Wombat, David was angry.

'You didn't talk to them, did you?'

'No.' I was surprised at the attack. 'I was concentrating on walking.'

'I'm sick of your uncompromising attitude to the media. They've driven all the way out here from Perth, after being up all night developing film. And all you can do is be ungrateful. These are not normal press, they're decent people. They're not doing this for you, you know, they're doing it for the charity.'

'But Bob said he wanted to keep a low profile and simply observe us. It's difficult to concentrate when the very presence of media makes me think I've almost finished. But I've still got a long way to go and I'm getting tired.' I bit into a sandwich and changed the angle of the subject. 'They got lots of photographs last night. Why do they need more?'

'They need more for another article. It's not just a one-off; they're going to follow you into Perth.'

'They are *what*?'

'Oh God, I'm dreading the end,' David growled. 'There'll be

so many people there to greet you and all you'll do is be rude to them. I'm so sick of you.'

'How many times do I have to tell you? I don't like people judging me when I'm walking. At the end I won't be walking and I won't be rude.'

'You know something, Ffyona?' He moved his face closer to mine. 'I don't give a shit any more what you do.'

We ate in silence. I realised again the power the charity, my sponsors and the media had over me.

The nagging heat almost made me erupt with impatience when I had to stand around for the different lenses to be fitted, light meters to be read, angles to be calculated and photographs to be shot. But they left with our smiles and thanks. I wandered away from the Wombat and, bending down for tiny flowers of rich magenta and cobalt blue, I heard a voice. 'Hullo!' I jumped, almost dropping my flowers. It was only a frog which turned and hopped into the bush. He didn't want a conversation, he just wanted to say, 'Hullo.' I wished there were more like him.

Carrying my gifts back to the Wombat, I hid them behind my back pretending that David knew nothing of what I had done.

'I don't want them,' he said with amusement.

'Actually, they're not for you.' I twisted the side view mirror and put them in my hair. We smiled at each other. But after a time I could bear it no longer and, taking them from my hair, placed them on David's lap.

'They were really meant for you.'

This obvious attempt at reconciliation was met with only superficial forgiveness, just as a child who wants to be a friend must give his playmates sweets.

A road-train thundered past and pulled over in the distance. The sun sent the truck swimming before my eyes into a gleaming ship anchored in a bay.

I walked up beside the cab, ready to explain we had not broken down but the man met my look with a grin.

'How ya goin'?'

'I'm keeping steady.'

'Not far to go now.'

'No, only another eight days.'

'You know something?'

'What?'

'I travel this road every day of my life and I think you're crazy.'

'You do, eh?'

'I'm serious, I think you're touched.'

'I wonder myself, sometimes.'

'Well, good on ya, you've got balls, I'll give you that.'

'Thank you.'

'I'll be passing you again before you finish, I'll give you a wave.'

David caught up with me.

'He said I had balls, that was a compliment, right?'

'From a truckie? I should say so.'

I relaxed on the road in the third quarter, taking each step easily, but at one point when I asked David how far I had gone and heard it was only eight kilometres, I panicked. He talked again of the end, I switched off and heard only a phrase, '. . . huge comfy bed with clean sheets.' I turned my eyes to the road in the falling light and listened to Bruce Springsteen singing mournfully of heartache.

As we moved in and out of the shadows, David talked about himself for the very first time, perhaps feeling free to let go now that the end was close and the pressure of spending weeks together, cornered in that tiny van, was behind us. Though we still planned to stay together after the walk in a house on a beach in Queensland, I knew I had hurt him so much through my journey that we must go our separate ways. Those last few days with David were very precious for he still did not know that he, alone, had pulled me on to the end. Perhaps he never will, perhaps he doesn't care.

Day 88

The record now meant nothing to me; it was only a means of getting myself out of bed in the morning. However, what really inspired me was the need to get to Perth before the money ran out.

The sign for Ghooli appeared on the road. Someone had added an 's' at the end and I silently cursed them for the laughter which dislodged the infected blister. On the western side of the village the land changed from bush and emu-scrub-gum to dry golden fields of stubble.

David returned.

'Have you noticed the bales of hay all around? This is farm country now!'

'What did you say those lumps in the fields were?' He was humouring me.

'Well, if they're not hay they're straw. It doesn't make any difference, it's just a mark of civilisation to us.'

'D'you want to know what they are?' I peered out at the fields and nodded.

'They're sheep.' The snide lecturing tone of his voice from the days before the desert had gone. I relaxed.

We had long wanted to make our own version of an advertisement for Campbell's Chunky Beef Soup. With spirits high and the sunshine bright it seemed a good opportunity to get out the video camera and discuss directing tactics. We based the format on dog-food adverts.

Having taken a few introductory shots of the product, the camera turned on to me holding the can and salivating. 'Ooooh! It's chunky, it's meaty . . .'

Then David's turn, standing by the stove, gormless and nervous with his arms held stiffly at his sides, he acted so well the part of a dog breeder. But there we had a few problems, for David was so hilariously accurate with his dialogue and his posture that we dissolved many times into hysterics. Eventually, in tears, he said, 'I feed it to Ffyona, and all my champions, and I couldn't ask for anything bedda.'

The day grew hotter and the morning tailbreeze subsided to a stifling calm. David drove ahead again to make phone calls in the town called Southern Cross, while I amused myself by waging war on kilometre markers; they were hopelessly inaccurate. I spied a bashful foot-high post, lamely displaying some muddle of figures. 'So, you think you're a help, do you?' A click as I cocked back my thumb, careful two-finger aim at the marker and then a resounding

'Piaw!' Each marker received a fatal bullet and I walked only for them, to cock and shoot down another.

Day 89

I don't remember how I made it through the first and second quarters. I was aware that my mind had gone to sleep, leaving only the word 'Perth' imprinted on the brain.

The 'villages' we passed were no more than two signs 400 feet apart bearing the name of the place. A capsule of empty land. And as though to substantiate the impression that we had found a black hole in time, an old man with a grey beard hanging down to his navel rode past on a bicycle of pre-war design. Sieves and pans, swags, shovels and animalskin-clad water bottles swayed from the frame of his vehicle. He was heading out to look for gold, to make his fortune, a man of eighty.

We drove back to the truck stop of Carradin and crawled into bed. Together we lay in one pool of sweat, treasuring the fingers of shadow from the gum overhead. We could have fought over those shadows.

A knock on the Wombat door awoke us.

'Hullo in there?'

David's weary voice. 'Yeah?'

'Look, sorry to disturb you, but there's a woman here who's broken down and we thought you might know something about cars.'

He dragged himself from sleep without uttering a single sound of resistance. Silently, I saluted him.

In my dreams I willed the rain to come. The tiny prisms of water vapour collected in my head. More came to the party, bringing their friends and children, clinging together, binding their bodies to make a mass of water. After two hours of willing the water to gather, I woke to see the sky darkened by clouds. And secretly I believed I had done something to change it.

The woman in the truck stop thanked David again for his help and offered the meal of our choice, gratis.

'What can I get you folks?'

'All the vegetables you can fit on a plate!'

'And a bit of ham?'

'No thanks, just anything that grows in the ground except . . .' and we looked at each other and chorused, 'beetroot!'

Goldfish butted the ridges of plastic coral with inquisitive kisses, and flies crawled up posters of faraway pleasures: beaches, palm trees and even suntans. David read his book and I sat quietly, picking at the calloused skin. Toenails came away in my fingers. I filled an ashtray with the story of my journey.

David looked up. 'Fee?' he whispered.

'Mmm?'

'We're in a restaurant; you mustn't do that in here.'

'Do what?'

'Pick your feet.'

'Oh.'

The food arrived and we ate it quietly.

Climbing out to the starting place, the heavens erupted with rain. I embraced the clouds with open arms. 'You big black fluffy things!' The water party whirled around me. The galahs, those bald, pink-faced men in morning coats, chittered and dipped with their synchronised partners. Grasshoppers, the shape of leaves and the odour of gum, sprang up to join in as I passed. In front of me was the brilliant pink lip of the sun. We dreamt of the end.

Day 90

Merredin passed by in the first quarter, full of trees with big purple flowers. I walked faster than everyone who was going to work or going to school, which boosted my confidence tremendously.

For the first time I felt strong enough to play with a dream of Africa. It would be a journey of wanderings where the Ceremony of the Syringe would be replaced by the rituals of local people. There would be no speed records to break for none exist, no thundering road-trains or stumblings in the night, only dusty tracks made by many men's footprints with the sounds of the African song. Somewhere there would be a Land Rover with a different driver for every country and a documentary film crew who wouldn't ask inane questions, but simply observe me from a respectable distance. And I would walk for the joy of discovery, exploring the land instead of closing my eyes to it as I had often done in Australia.

The countryside was spread with a feast of harvested wheat and the bundles I saw were certainly not sheep or they would have run when I shouted at them. Because of a late start the sun was high over the eastern horizon and by the end of that quarter I was stiff. Getting sweaty and weary felt good, for some reason. Pushing on through heat and pounding sun was enjoyable and I liked the way my body now responded to it like a drug on a limited course.

A car pulled over ahead of us and two girls clambered out; shyly, we walked towards each other. They were barefoot, delicately stepping over the glass and small stones, I was limping and stumbling, careless of what I trod on.

'Are you Ffyona?'

'Yes. Hullo!'

'We thought we might have missed you, we've been looking out since yesterday.'

'Where've you come from?'

'Melbourne, we met a cyclist there who told us about you.'

'Pete, with a beard?'

'Yes!'

'Small place, big desert.'

'You're doing a great thing for underprivileged kids, isn't it?'

'Yes.'

'We adore kids. Hang on.' They tripped back to the car and I followed them. They opened the glove compartment, scrabbled in the side pockets, shook out clothes and presented me with a large handful of change.

'Here!'

'Oh, you *are* kind. Thank you very much, but will you have enough to get home?'

'Yeah, we're not far now.'

And we waved as they drove past.

It was so windy in the last quarter that I bent low, pushing hard against its fury, but miraculously I could hear the radio in the Wombat. My hearing had deteriorated, so David turned up the volume to full capacity which must have been uncomfortable for him. We listened to a drama from England called *The Fosdykes – A Story of Tripe*. It amused us. The lights of Kellerberrin drew closer as *The Fosdykes* ended and gave me another distraction, the growing shapes and shadows of the town. Bats flew around the street lamps where insects pounded out their futile battle and the air was full of beating wings and high pitched squeaks.

Day 91

The morning was growing old as we left Kellerberrin. The land and I wore the same colours in the brown of our skin and the bleached gold of our hair. Kicking stones, walking on the small patches of salt flats, I drifted idly until the three bowls of cereal I had eaten for breakfast began to demand an audience. I hadn't consumed so much milk for a long time and even though it contained very little fat, the globules seemed to be moving, very slowly, back up to my mouth.

David had been shopping in Kellerberrin and bought more dressings for my feet. The infected blister had reluctantly healed and left only a deep well of fluid which was painful. With a peculiar sense of pleasure I watched David push the needle through the callus. Oh! how I would miss this pain – the pain of pulling a pint from my feet every week.

The second quarter was hot. The bitumen squirmed under my shoes, and the flies grew more fearful that they would die unless they found the oasis which was my face. In the blazing heat I began to feel cramps gripping my intestines. I could not stand up straight as I walked.

Crawling on to the bed I curled into a ball and breathed heavily against the contractions. When the cramps wrung my guts, I held my breath, slowly breathing out as the pain eased before another bout. I was sweating heavily. Neither of us knew what it was; the milk? The avocados at the first break? Dehydration? Whatever it was, I still had five and a half hours of walking to do that day.

An hour later the Channel 7 television crew drew up. There is something about being ill which makes most of us want to curl up and hide and there is something about deserts which turns even the most passive endurer into a tyrant if someone enters their sanctuary. David, for once, understood this and made allowances for me in the face of the intruding media. He told them I was still sleeping and asked them to return in an hour. Both of us were finding it difficult to deal with the greater numbers of people.

After the relief of sleep came the gentle touch of his hand. 'Come on, my darling, you must wake up now.' With bleary eyes and aching body I heaved myself upright and heard the television crew setting out their equipment. Pulling off the filthy clothes I had walked in for days I took out the last of the clean singlets and shorts and sat on the edge of the bed, dizzy and weary. They filmed the Ceremony of the Syringe and David making pasta for lunch while chatting with me. During the interview I began to tell them how vital it was to have a competent support man, that I couldn't do it alone, and then David kicked me. I turned to him, hurt that he had stopped me from expressing my gratitude.

'They don't want to hear about me; you're the star.' His words stung and being called a 'star' made me cringe.

'Why shouldn't I thank you in this way?'

'You should express it in other ways.' This puzzled me then, but now, looking back on the journey, I can understand how hollow my words had sounded after the lambastings I submitted him to so often. To say sorry after an event is never enough – the hurt is done.

At last the Channel 7 helicopter landed in a field to collect its passenger and then was airborne again.

Alone I walked towards the shimmering horizons. Small gullies beneath the road were marked as creeks, the first I had seen for many weeks although there was little water in them, just an opaque and salty puddle. I kicked a few stones into it for the Road God of Thirst and they made such a lovely sound that I stopped to do it again several times and watched the beads of light dance as the gravel hit the surface. My footprints were the first to crack the salt flats for a long while and I left my mark, giving the pain in the hollows of my arches and the dents of my heels back to the land.

The moon was lying on her back, a sight I would miss in England. And who would the Chariot guide on their journey? Who would walk these roads by the light of the stars and breathe warmth into their steely sparkle? Who would tap a rhythm on the road so broken and uneven? Only when I knew the end was coming, could I understand the importance the stars had been as my guides, as my 'constants' in a land where I never spent longer than a stride in one place.

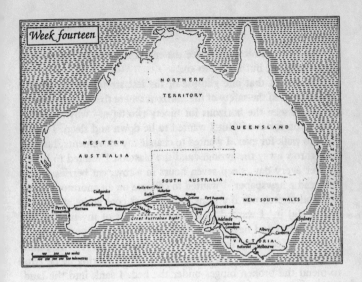

Day 92

Sheer terror of the end shook me as I walked. The whole journey
had consumed nearly two years of my life – planning, training,
searching hard for sponsors, building up overdrafts, losing friends
and the walking. All those days and nights of hell, the push and
the pain, the soul-searching doubts, all of that for one step in the
ocean to finish it all. Over and done with. Dead. Anticlimax.

A man leant out of a car and clapped. There was a fly on his
lip, a small one. As he stopped and got out his features were so
blurred, his speech so muffled and distant that I would never have
recognised him without the fly.

'Hullo! This is just a social call.'

Bob had spent many hours mapping out the route through Perth
into Fremantle; which streets were the best to take, organising
police escorts and taking photographs of the road junctions we
would meet so that we did not lose our way.

He was showing David the photographs of the end, and handed one to me.

'No! No! I don't want to see the end! I have to go. Thank you for helping us, but I have to go.'

Horrified at that one glimpse of the last stretch of the road, I turned back to the safety of the horizons where the road thundered on. I had seen the horizons for ninety-two days – why shouldn't they go on for ever? But I wanted to lie down and sleep, I didn't want to walk for ever. I wanted to change my movements, heal my feet, throw away the syringes and the plasters. I wanted to have a shower every day, sleep seven hours in a row, eat berries in bed and read a newspaper. I wanted to collapse on an enormous Hyatt bed and stretch out my arms into the soft cool white sheets and say, 'I did it.' I wanted to stand for the rest of my life ten feet from the end and never walk those last few steps into the sea.

At the Meckering truck stop I took out my duvet and pillow and slept on the ground, listening to David swearing as he tried to mend the broken hinges under the bed. I sank into the land, the land that had moulded me, fired me and glazed me. The land that somehow was healing me.

There were clean white showers at the truck stop. They were new; no mould between the tiles, no rust around the plughole. I stayed there, just standing under the spray of water, looking around at the whiteness.

My hair was so dry from the sun that when I towelled it, there was a rasping sound and the skin on my shoulders was so old under the deep brown that it felt like parchment. My eyes were bloodshot and the irises shone bright aquamarine. I brushed my teeth and stood there, looking in the mirror at the foam coming out of my mouth and took away the brush and growled at my reflection, spurting out the foam. The door opened, I spat out the paste and promptly finished cleaning my teeth. The girl who came in was very tanned with white-blonde streaks in her hair from the sun.

'Hullo,' I said shyly.

'You're the girl in the news, aren't you?'

'Yes I am. Would you like to wash your hands?'

'Yes,' she said and looked at her reflection in the mirror. We were alike, and smiled at each other in the glass.

'You can use my towel if you want – there isn't anything else.'

'Thank you. I couldn't have done it.'

'Maybe you could.'

'Not as well as you did.'

And we smiled at each other for a moment longer. The door opened and she left.

Christmas decorations fluttered in the airconditioning of the café as the white land outside melted and the sparrows flew among the palm fronds. Carols followed weather reports of 40°C heat on the radio behind the fruit bowl, and plum pudding was served with ice-cream.

A truckie in a purple-painted road-train slowed and called out my name, then thundered on as he honked out a tune that resounded down the white painted road. A woman leant out of her car and shouted, 'Keep going, Ffyona, you're doing a great job!'

And another slowed down to call out, 'Congratulations!'

I beamed at both of them and blushed a little, too.

As we sat down to eat at the break, a can of Coke fell off the shelf and as it hit the ground it exploded from the heat. The cans of tonic water Bob had brought us were too hot to hold and the margarine in the plastic tub had melted to a river of gold with small lumpy islands of fat floating on the surface.

The moon looked like a banana and there was the smell of honey in the air.

'I think the closest thing to us right now is a pot of blue gum honey.' And I imagined the delightful sweetness of it.

'Where d'you think it is?'

'Someone's standing on the edge of the next village holding a pot and waving it around.'

Of course the scents didn't come from anywhere. Just as a mirage may appear to someone who is driven by their sense of vision, so these smells were my 'mirage' at a time when my sense of smell had replaced sight as my primary gatherer of information.

'I can't smell it.'

The lights of Northam, the largest town before Perth, winked across a plain. It was the first mass of civilisation I had seen for over two months and the feeling, strangely enough, was one of comfort and relief, as though I had been lost and now was found. I bent to kiss the marker that read 'Perth 100 kilometres' and we drove up a track away from the road and parked on a hill where sheep bleated in the darkness. As I lay in the uneven bed, my spirit felt like the hinges that broke beneath us. I knew what was coming.

Day 93

Northam had little to do with civilisation; rather it was about cinderheaps beside rusting railway lines, children eating spilt ice-cream off the pavement and shops with shelves of expensive knick-knacks. Northam existed because of the Avon River which ran through its heart, but even that was polluted. Instead of being choosy about which stone I threw to the Road God of Thirst, I just picked up the nearest chunk of bitumen and lobbed it over the edge.

A campervan passed us very slowly. Out of it climbed Tweedle-dum and Tweedledee and stood there with cameras glued to me. David hissed that I should be nice as I passed them.

'Don't mind us,' they said cheerily.

The man ran along beside me, clicking away, focusing on my face. I knew I could outwalk his trot and I did so, leaving him behind, puffing and sweating but still clicking. My anger fuelled my strides, breathing in air that was heavy with a combination of evergreen sap, sandalwood essence and strong scented exhaust fumes.

The heat and the hills took away every thought I had left. I was vaguely aware that my body had settled into a quick, pushing pace that did not slow down as the ascents got steeper. My mind had relinquished its job to the reflex action of putting one foot in front of the other. Raw stamina had taken over in the 40°C heat. I did not know I was walking.

I arrived in Bakers Hill, described in the 1875–6 Tourist Guide as being a 'picturesque health-giving resort in the Darling Ranges with good kangaroo shooting when in season'. I gave up on sleeping when the temperature in the Wombat reached 42°C and joined David in the Bakers Hill Hotel where he sat talking to the proprietor. He and his wife had been expecting me and brought out ice cold Cokes. A two-inch wasp tapped against the window on the inside of the hotel. Oh, for England and simple bumble bees!

The proprietor was a portly man of good humour and twinkling eyes, his open-necked shirt bulged over a protruding beer belly. His wife had an efficient, patient tone about her, as though she had raised many children. She differed from her husband only in appearance; she was beautifully trim and she slipped around the tables and chairs with the poise of a Parisienne, leaving behind her a gentle scent of Chanel. She talked to me with down to earth concern and was glad to see I had not completely 'wasted away' as so many of the Comic Strip Gang seemed to have done.

We waved our goodbyes and headed back to the starting place, eager to cross the Darling Range and be done with the hills that lead down to Perth.

I left the hurt of my body to gaze at acres of grass-trees and young palms growing wild. The land became more hilly, the corners sharper, the trees thicker and closer to the narrowing road and the hard shoulder was a mess of small stones which slithered underfoot. I could get no grip on them for the heavy inclines and to walk alone on the bitumen would be suicide with the trucks thundering down the hills at an alarming speed.

David could not drive beside me for fear of cars smashing into the back of him, so we decided to finish that third quarter and then walk three quarters the next day. It would leave us just under two quarters for the final day since the day of rest had not been taken. I wanted the last day to be as normal as possible, to be a push rather than an amble; it would heighten the relief. Even though I could easily break the speed record by two days rather than one, I had to think of the charity and all the media that had been arranged for Wednesday. Re-organising them now could mean the loss of coverage, the loss of donations.

At 9.15 p.m. we pulled off the road down a track into the

forest. It was by far the earliest we had finished since the first week of the walk and neither of us knew what to do with the spare time before sleep took hold at around 1 a.m. This lack of forethought about how to 'fill the unforgiving minute with sixty seconds worth of distance run' was a punishing omission in preparations for the end. I simply presumed nothing would exist after reaching the Indian Ocean and if it did, I could deal with it as I had done with everything else over the last ninety-three days.

Day 94

The hard shoulder was nothing but gravel, inches thick, and it sucked down my footsteps, reducing my stride to a 'straight-skirt mince'. I walked on the bitumen when a break in the traffic allowed, but even at 5 a.m. lorries sent me leaping into the verge every few minutes.

I was covering very little distance and it grew hotter by the step. At one point I tore off my sunhat, stamped hard on it and beat my fists against a tree trunk. The frustration was too much to bear and I sobbed. I was so *close*, but the road was holding me back.

'Breathe deep, Ffyona, breathe deep.' Joshua appeared beside me, encouraging me. I took deep even breaths, trying to accept the handicaps even though my body longed to march up those hills. He held my hand.

The flies had become increasingly insistent with their assaults on my face for moisture and, as I breathed deeply against a hill, one of them shot up my nose. I didn't know whether it had come out or not, but there was something very deep in the nasal passage. I thought it must be a wing or a leg and blew my nose, induced sneezes and snorted to try and get it out. My eyes were streaming and my whole face felt as if it were humming from internal pressure but still nothing appeared.

My frustrations subsided as I rounded the side of a small traveller's café to see the Wombat parked there and David striding towards me. Joshua quietly released my hand.

Just as I was telling David I thought there might be a fly up my nose and just as he was beginning to think I was exaggerating, I was seized by a body shaking sneeze and out shot the fly. It lay quite dead in the palm of my hand, wrapped in a thick veil of mucus. I presented my evidence to David who was suitably impressed.

Beyond the treelined horizon, the road was transformed into a major two-lane highway on the outskirts of real 'civilisation'. A girl rushed out from a general store to quench my thirst with a carton of fruit juice and the cars passing me hooted constantly. Their friendly encouragement eased my fear of meeting the end.

I stopped a few times for a drink in the Wombat when David had found a place to cross the concrete road divider and pull over down a side street. But when he told me how little I had walked during the quarter I cried. Somehow I had the impression that when I came out of the bush into civilisation, I could run down the hill and into the sea. My experience of towns in Australia was that they took no more than an hour to walk through; I could not come to terms with the size of the city.

Pushing on, I felt nothing much but petulance. The noise was intolerable, the stench of burning rubber and the increased heat from traffic was suffocating. The white, clean-scrubbed, antiseptic halo of light I had imagined Perth to be, did not exist. The end was not salvation and it hit me hard. How I longed to remain in the bush, peaceful, clean and anonymous.

The Wombat had stopped up ahead with a television crew. My eyes were fixed on them just as a car careered off the road on to the shoulder, spinning back again in time to miss me, but showering me with an arc of gravel. Furious, I marched to the Wombat.

'Did you see that? That was inches, inches!'

I pushed on the roo bar and stretched my calves, then balanced on one leg to stretch my thighs. My buttocks had tightened because of those mincing steps up the hill.

David did the introductions and the usual questions were asked. The interview I gave was not very impressive, especially when they asked me to take off my hat and glasses revealing the sweaty mess I was in. I felt uncomfortable being filmed while looking so bad. It wasn't even attractive roughness, it was just unkempt, unhealthy filth.

Marching on in the bronchial morning, the road became a steep descent down to Perth. Pneumatic drills jarred my ears as I passed and the dry dust they kicked up stung my eyes. The sun streamed down on everything, casting the cars, the people, the hill and the road in putrid hues of stagnant ochre. When men tamper with yellow, they rape the spontaneity of it, leaving the colour of hope branded with jaundice. There was no peace to gather my thoughts, to cherish the last few beauties of Australia. They had already passed.

And there, around a corner, a sight which brought me to a stumbling standstill, beat in my heart and swelled a lump in my throat. This one sight I had dreamed of a thousand times, and there it was, waiting for me. Through the hazy crud of pollution, the thin grey lines of skyscrapers etched the only horizon. They were the lines of Perth.

There was no elation, no pain put into perspective by the sight of the end. I was numb. But I hadn't made it yet, there was still another quarter to walk and two more tomorrow. I clung to those quarters, desperate that they should reveal why I was there, why I was walking. At the beginning I thought I was walking to win my father's affection, his praise. But I was beyond that now. I hated this man who had the power to crush me by simply shaking his head, and I used this hatred to drive me through the desert – man can endure anything if only he has a reason. But I had no reason now; my hatred was exhausted. I just got up and walked on – I don't know why.

David had pulled the Wombat up a side street beside the first view of the city. But now there was no quiet place for us to move off the road, nowhere cool in the bush, away from the world, to sleep before the final quarter.

A lady in her garden called out to David when she recognised the Wombat and struck up a conversation. Upon hearing we were about to sleep in that tiny vehicle, she invited us into her house where airconditioning and ice awaited us. But I was shy; I always felt uncomfortable in other people's houses and I didn't have the energy to 'perform' for them, so I whispered to David that we mustn't stay long. Thinking I was being rude he spat back at me, 'Why?' It was more a statement of disappointment than an angry accusing question.

The woman's face was puffy and discoloured from nicotine, her hooded eyes were piercing but sad, and her middle-aged body, in need of exercise, hung down like the heavy fabric of a curtain; she didn't seem to move it – it moved itself. She brought glasses of water as we sat at a table spread with pieces of lace, ashtrays and a shy man reading his paper. The view of those pale grey shapes in the distance was framed by french windows, to which I glanced when the monosyllabic conversation became too uncomfortable. A small boy played with a truck on the floor, keeping himself away from the adults, but David bent to him and gently won his trust.

It was then I noticed the black band the woman wore on her arm. The boy wore one too. Life was going on while I walked and death too. Perhaps if I had had more interaction with people, my life would not have been so influenced and distorted by my own injuries. I regretted that I had retreated so far within myself. Thanking her, hugging her, we went back to the Wombat and the door shut on their world.

It would have been rude to sleep in front of her house so I walked on down the hill while David drove ahead to find a suitable place. I followed him into the general store where we hoped to find something to eat. There was only a salami sandwich and a greasy meat pie left curling in the hot cabinet.

We bought the food and returned to eat in the Wombat. It was parked in a narrow alleyway where flies swarmed over litter and dog excrement, scraps of decaying food were picked by crows more daring than those of the bush – scavengers with wounds from their civil wars. Perth, the city of my dreams.

David tried to convince me I didn't need to sleep. Damn you! Leave me alone! If I want to sleep I will. I pulled out the bed and lay down, struggling to escape to the reality of my daydreams. But I gave up, packed up and walked on.

Down the hill, David somehow got separated from me, caught up in the flow of cars, stopped at traffic lights; my support was a puppet to the public. An hour passed as I walked through the afternoon streets, not knowing if I was going in the right direction. I stopped many people to ask directions but they contradicted each other. I was lost, but it was not an adventurous feeling, nor the feeling of security I had in the bush.

As evening came, the sun's golden arms were hidden behind black buildings. In the night sky through the cloud of pollution the Chariot fought to stay bright but when I looked to him for guidance, he had distanced himself, he had left me too. Fluorescent daylight split the dark. The night was not allowed its peace.

Eventually David arrived with a pizza. He had been waiting for me with a group of children in a fast food store, but I must have passed by unnoticed on the other side of the road. An emptiness, a numbness was filling me, sullen, uncaring, blocking out the death of my walk. A slender black-haired woman rode by on a bicycle. David watched her closely as she passed. Turning back, he wiped his brow.

'Fuck, I need a cigarette.'

When he tried to film me eating the last supper, I wouldn't talk to him, just stared straight ahead when he pointed the camera at me. 'Don't get all emotional,' he said.

Another girl cycled up to me.

'Hi, Ffyona, I'm from a restaurant down at Fremantle. If you wear our T-shirt when you walk on the beach tomorrow we'll give your charity $300.'

'No. I'm sorry, my sponsors have that right.'

'$500.'

That was as much as we had raised throughout the entire journey.

'No, I'm sorry. But we'll put a small sticker on the van for $250.'

She agreed. I was rather pleased with that.

A huge sign towered over me – a sign saying 'Welcome to Perth'. Around it was a bed of flowers, still open in the night, showing their hearts of red and yellow. Feeling very small, I stepped carefully between the flowers to kiss the sign and to thank the Road Gods for my deliverance. I was to learn later that at that moment, on the other side of the world, my mother sat up in bed and said to my father, 'She's made it.'

Day 95

I scrambled to cover myself with the duvet as a car pulled up outside. David was already out of bed and slid back the door to greet the visitor. A woman with black hair and delicate Asian features looked into the Wombat and smiled at me, half naked, clutching the covers.

'Good morning!' she said.

'Hullo.'

'And you must be David?'

'Yeah. And a very good morning to you, Trudy.'

'We've organised a little lakeside breakfast for you both with the press and I've had printers on standby all night making the T-shirts.'

'Hang on, what T-shirts?'

'Trudy has very kindly printed them for the end.'

'I'll have to see them first. My sponsors have to be proportionately displayed.' The woman with the black hair went to her black BMW and brought them back. As I suspected, my sponsors were not displayed according to their participation. Adidas was printed at the top in black, Hyatt was beneath it in grey and then Scholl and James Capel beneath that, in smaller writing also in grey.

'This is not acceptable.'

'Ffyona, Trudy has been up all night making these.'

'I'm sorry, but . . .'

'I've had printers on standby all night . . .'

'Look, I'll tell you, Adidas put up less than a quarter, Hyatt put up no money, Scholl put up a third and James Capel put up the most, including additional money to save the walk.'

The woman with black hair took her head out of the Wombat, still laughing, while David reprimanded me.

'Don't fuck it up. We can't wear the Sport Aid '88 T-shirts now that they've gone bankrupt.' His venom was heightened in the presence of the woman with black hair. She put her head back in the Wombat.

'Why don't you wear it just for the breakfast? Bob MacDonald has promised us a front cover for this afternoon's paper.'

'I want to get dressed now. Can I have some privacy, please?'

'Sure!' giggled the woman with black hair as she and David closed the door on the outside.

We were driven in the black BMW to the lake. A park of short-cut grass stretched beside it, and over the water were the skyscrapers of Perth. Beside the lake, a tall man dressed in a white tuxedo stood by a table laid for two. He pulled out the chair for me, a white tablecloth fluttered in the breeze, white porcelain plates and silver glinted in the morning sun. David sat opposite me. The photographer was taking pictures, the others were standing behind him, watching us look aghast at the unexpected splendour. The photographer clicked the shot for the front page as we ate the delicate Hyatt pastries and drank fresh orange juice. I smiled at David.

'This isn't our honeymoon, Fee.'

I felt strong enough on that final morning to keep a smile fixed on my face. Time pressed, so we finished quickly, grabbing the remainder of the pastries and a few yoghurts.

Cars stuck in rush-hour traffic hooted their congratulations as I walked past them. People called out to me, waving, cheering and I called back to them, beaming and skipping.

A police car drew up beside me.

'Ffyona?'

'Hullo! How are you?'

'I'm very well thank you, and how are you?'

'Happy!'

'Where's the rest of your lot? I was given instructions to escort you through the city.'

'I don't need escorting just yet, but if you look out for David in the back-up van, he'll tell you what the form is. I don't know if the press are coming out on this stretch or not.'

'Right-o, see you later.'

Lilting along, up and over the small undulations bordered by clean, low buildings where people went to work, waving to them as they waved to me. It seemed the whole city was pushing me onwards. Wherever I turned my head, someone was calling my name, and I was alone, so very, very happy to be alone to savour the memories of the walk.

David pulled up for the break, the very last break. I could hardly bear to follow the usual routine of making tea, having a quick puff on a cigarette, before we were spotted. And all too soon, even before the bottom of the pot was reached, three television crews and two radio reporters were standing outside the Wombat, filming me, interviewing me. This time I didn't mind.

Out on the road again the two radio reporters trotted beside me, a miniature audio unit was strapped to my waist for one of the television crews, all of whom drove slowly ahead of me with the Wombat behind and the police car leading the procession. Cameras were everywhere, obscuring my view of the road.

'How are you feeling now?' they kept asking.

'I'm not there yet, I don't feel anything. I've still got a few more hours of walking. Ask me again when I've finished.'

A man standing beside the road taking photographs, suddenly rushed up to me and thrust a bulging wad of notes in my hand and then disappeared. An old lady handed out money, young boys in cars did the same. Laughter, horns, clapping and cheering filled the air as I walked on, talking to the reporters, keeping steady.

Soon the procession had whittled down to just the Wombat behind me and the police car ahead. I kept glancing back at David, and he hooted and waved back at me. And then there was something in the distance, just peeking out between the buildings, a small triangle of blue.

'Hey Fee!' I walked back beside him. 'What's that?'

'That's the ocean.'

Ahead I walked alone, clinging on to the last steps of my walk as the triangle of blue grew bigger. A cyclist rode beside me – a friend of Bob's. He told me he owned a pub down in Fremantle and had organised some champagne for the end. I wasn't listening to him – he was very kind – but I was listening to a ringing in my head, music, the music, sweet, sweet music that filled every single step. Holding in the memories of the walk, thinking back to times when I had hobbled, cried out, fought with sleep, fought with that burning hot wind, tripped, stumbled, vomited, crawled along that long, long road.

But all too soon, the triangle disappeared and so did the cyclist. Around a corner, following the lead of the police car, I came to a mall where the Mayor of Fremantle stood in his Chain of Honour with a Scottish Pipe Band playing. Beaming, surprised and delighted, I shook the Mayor's outstretched hand and accepted the shield of the city, suddenly aware of all the people cheering, clapping and shouting their pride. What a contrast to Los Angeles where there was no one to greet me, no one knew I was coming. The Mayor walked with me down the last street. At the end of it I could see a peach-coloured building with a dark archway running through it. The band marched behind us, photographers and cameramen running around, stooping, shooting, scurrying ahead. The music played and the Mayor kissed my cheek for the impatient little photographer who kept directing us. It didn't matter; I had said goodbye to the walk. I would give up these last few steps for the people who would make money for the charity.

Looking round for David, I saw him running up behind me waving a newspaper. The front cover bore my picture. He told me to slow down and looking back, the band were far behind, keeping in time to *their* music. The black archway grew ever larger. Beyond it was something that had drawn me for over eight and a half million steps.

Would the relief of the end equal the pain of those ninety-five days? Would I be engulfed by sobbing? Would I halt and be unable to set foot in the ocean? Would I embrace my back-up driver and tell him I loved him? If Perth had sprung out at me when I was in the bush, my face stained by tears and my feet by blood, then perhaps I would have reacted. But now I was numb. I could only think of one thing: gooseberry fool.

David and I and the cameramen walked into the archway. I whispered to him that I'd like to walk these last steps alone.

'It's OK,' he whispered. 'They're only here to help.'

I walked those last steps to the sea where a crowd was standing, shouting and cheering. As my feet touched the water I leapt in the air with a scream.

'I'VE MADE IT!'

Reaching down, I tore off my socks and shoes, calling out for David to do the same. Looking round I saw him trotting towards me. 'Ready? GO!' And together, sprinting as fast as we could, we ran out into the Indian Ocean and swam.

Floating for a while I looked back at the people standing there, waving to me from the beach, their voices lost over the gentle murmurs of the waves, and soon their forms melted into the white blur of the sand. I turned away from them, the ocean stretched out his arms to embrace me, nudging me with soft lapping kisses. I lifted my eyes and I looked to the far blue horizons, to Africa, committing myself with that long steady gaze to walk the length of it and, this time, I knew *why*.

Epilogue

David and I went our separate ways after we delivered the Wombat in Sydney. I set off in search of a bamboo hut on a Queensland beach in which to write and ended up in Bali for four months. David eventually returned to Hong Kong where he worked for a while as an estate agent. We began to correspond three months after the end of the walk, but the distance between us has grown and our differences were never resolved.

Back in London I established my own research company providing information to executive search firms in the financial markets. It has allowed me the time to find sponsorship for my next walk from Cape Town to Cairo and to train hard for a twelve-month journey. Though the physical injuries I suffered in Australia will never fully heal, my psychological problems are well on the mend.

After twenty-five years of moving around the country, my parents have returned to the town where they met and where I was born. The completion of this circle has given all of us, at last, a place where we belong and an answer to that other question, which we could never answer, 'Where do you come from?' I have been able to share with them the journey I made from angry young teenager to mature woman, and they, in turn, have acknowledged the things which drove me so far away for so long. If this book had told the full story of my childhood and the things which distorted it, old wounds would still fester and my walks would have been in vain. Now that my journey is done and I have found what I was looking for, I can walk away again to look out at the world, instead of stumbling blindly around it.

A Selected List of Non-Fiction Titles Available from Mandarin

☐	7493 0692 0	**A History of God**	Karen Armstrong £6.99
☐	7493 1028 6	**In the Psychiatrist's Chair**	Anthony Clare £5.99
☐	7493 0186 4	**The Sign and the Seal**	Graham Hancock £5.99
☐	7493 0497 9	**All Right OK You Win**	David Spanier £5.99
☐	7493 0887 7	**The British Constitution Now**	Ferdinand Mount £6.99
☐	7493 0618 1	**Justice Delayed**	David Cesarani £5.99
☐	7493 1031 6	**Catholics and Sex**	Saunders/Stanford £4.99
☐	7493 1491 5	**Erotic Life of the Married Woman**	Dalma Heyn £4.99
☐	7493 1412 5	**Sexual Arrangements**	Reibstein/Richards £4.99
☐	7493 1102 9	**Italian Neighbours**	Tim Parks £5.99
☐	7493 1254 8	**A Spell in Wild France**	Bill/Laurel Cooper £5.99
☐	7493 1328 5	**Among the Thugs**	Bill Buford £4.99
☐	7493 0961 X	**Stick it up Your Punter**	Chippendale & Horrib £4.99
☐	7493 0938 5	**The Courage to Heal**	Ellen Bass and Laura Davis £7.99
☐	7493 0637 8	**The Hollywood Story**	Joel Finler £9.99
☐	7493 1172 X	**You'll Never Eat Lunch in This Town Again**	Julia Phillips £5.99